A NEW CO
ENGL

A NEW
COMPREHENSIVE
ENGLISH COURSE

T. W. KNIGHT M.A. (Oxon.)

*formerly Lecturer at the City of Westminster College
and The Polytechnic, Regent Street, London*

HODDER AND STOUGHTON
LONDON SYDNEY AUCKLAND TORONTO

ISBN 0 340 12367 2

First published 1958
Second edition: fourteenth impression 1985
Copyright © 1960 T. W. Knight

Printed in Great Britain for Hodder & Stoughton
Educational, a division of Hodder & Stoughton Ltd,
Mill Road, Dunton Green, Sevenoaks, Kent by
Page Bros (Norwich) Ltd

PREFACE

THIS book is intended to provide a complete course for a variety of students preparing for preliminary examinations.

Though it has been written primarily for Day and Evening Classes in Technical and Further Education Colleges, it should prove equally suitable for use in Secondary Schools; it should also appeal to anyone who requires a practical and comprehensive guide to the understanding and writing of English for general purposes

The subject-matter has been divided into three sections:

(1) Words—with a separate chapter on each of the parts of speech, and chapters on spelling and vocabulary.

(2) The Sentence and the Paragraph; Correctness and Comprehension—a section which includes analysis, punctuation, syntax, figures of speech, etc.; and also précis, paraphrasing, and reported speech.

(3) Composition—with a separate chapter on each of the various types of composition.

The chapters need not, however, necessarily be studied in the order in which they are arranged. Many teachers will want their pupils to attempt the easier forms of composition at an early stage; those teachers who object to teaching formal grammar may prefer to omit such chapters as those on the parts of speech, or to use them solely for reference—though it is difficult to understand how students can be expected to avoid grammatical errors without some basic grammatical grounding, and a knowledge of the functions of the parts of speech is surely essential for the successful study of any foreign language.

The contents of this text-book provide either an intensive one-year course or a more leisurely two-year course, according to the number of lessons available weekly.

Finally, no work in English should be embarked upon without the help of a good dictionary, preferably one that gives the derivation and pronunciation of words in addition to their meanings.

Note: Considerations of space inevitably limit the number of exercises on Précis and Comprehension, but copies of past examination papers of the various examining boards can be obtained to supplement these.

T. W. K.

ACKNOWLEDGMENTS

FOR permission to use extracts from copyright works the author and publishers wish to thank the following:

Sir Harold Nicolson for a passage from his book *People and Things*; Messrs. William Collins Sons & Co. Ltd. for an extract from *Samuel Pepys, The Man in the Making* by Sir Arthur Bryant, and for a quotation from *Birds and Men* by E. M. Nicholson; Messrs. John Murray Ltd. for a passage from *The Thread of Gold* by A. C. Benson; the executors of the late H. G. Wells for an extract from *The History of Mr. Polly*; Mr. J. B. Priestley for a short quotation from his book *The Good Companions*; and the University of London for a number of questions taken from examination papers of the University.

CONTENTS

SECTION I

WORDS

9

SECTION II

THE SENTENCE AND THE PARAGRAPH: CORRECTNESS AND COMPREHENSION

SECTION III

COMPOSITION

CONTENTS

INTRODUCTION

THE ENGLISH LANGUAGE

THE language spoken by our first known ancestors, the Britons, was Celtic, which is still preserved in many words in Welsh, Gaelic, and Irish (i.e. in Wales, Scotland, and Ireland, to which countries the Celts moved in face of pressure from later invaders from Northern Europe).

The Roman occupation from A.D. 43 to 409 brought in Latin as the language of the upper and ruling classes, and even the peasants eventually began to speak a "vulgar" (or dialectal) form of Latin.

When the Romans finally left our shores, both Celtic and Latin were supplanted by a third language, English, which was evolved from dialects of the energetic tribes of the North Sea coast of Germany, who in the fifth and sixth centuries rapidly swept over most of England to settle here permanently.

The chief of these tribes were the Angles, Saxons, and Jutes, and the word "English" comes from the dialect spoken by the Angles. Our language belongs, therefore, to the Teutonic (or German) group of languages, whereas those languages based on Latin are called Romance languages, the chief of which are French, Italian, Portuguese, and Spanish.

Since the fifth century, the English language has been constantly developing, enriched by many borrowings traceable to the influence of later invaders, to foreign wars, and to contacts due to expanding trade with

Europe, and eventually with other more distant continents.

The invasions of the Danes in the ninth and tenth centuries; the Norman Conquest with its rich addition of Norman-French words (mostly Latin in origin) dealing with the Church and the Law; the long series of wars with France in the Middle Ages; the adoption of many Greek and Latin words fostered by the Renaissance* (or Rebirth of Learning) in the sixteenth century; borrowings through the contacts of war and peace from Spanish, Italian, and Dutch—these have given English the richest vocabulary of all modern languages.

England is rich, too, in dialects, of which we are secretly proud though we may publicly deplore their deviation from the standard form of English.

It is truly remarkable that the English language has spread from this small island to become by far the most important language in the world today, spoken as their mother tongue by at least one-sixth of its present inhabitants.

It is the task of each one of us to ensure that we maintain English as indisputably the greatest of all languages by setting ourselves the highest standards in speaking and in writing it—a task we should be proud to undertake.

* The Renaissance of learning in the sixteenth century was a revival in Western Europe of classical ideals in literature, art, and architecture, stimulated partly by the influx of scholars from Greece who sought refuge in Italy when Constantinople was captured by the Turks in 1453, and partly by the invention of printing.

SECTION I

WORDS

CHAPTER I

THE SENTENCE: PARTS OF SPEECH

To understand our own language, and to learn any other language, we must first study the construction of a sentence and examine its different component parts.

A Sentence is a group of words that makes complete sense (i.e. expresses a complete idea).

A sentence may be a *statement, question,* or *command,*

e.g. *Statement:* The postman brought the letter.
Question: Has the postman come yet?
Command: Bring me the letter.

We must next study the parts which individual words play in a sentence. There are eight *Parts of Speech,* each serving a different purpose: *Noun, Pronoun, Adjective, Verb, Adverb, Preposition, Conjunction, and Interjection.*

Definitions of the Parts of Speech:

Noun: A word used to name anything (i.e. person, animal, place, thing, quality, action, etc.).
(e.g. George, man, dog, London, town, book, courage, singing, etc.)   (Chapter II)

Pronoun: A word used instead of a Noun.
(e.g. I, you, he, she, it, this, who.)   (Chapter III)

Adjective: A word describing or qualifying a Noun or Pronoun.
(e.g. old, little, blue.)   (Chapter IV)

Verb: A word expressing an action or state.
(e.g. he writes, he is.)   (Chapter V)

17

Adverb: A word limiting or modifying a Verb, Adjective, Preposition, Conjunction, or another Adverb.
(e.g. quickly, often, very.) (Chapter vi)

Preposition: A word showing the relation between a Noun or Pronoun and some other word in a sentence.
(e.g. We are *near* the station, *in* the main street.)
(Chapter vii)

Conjunction: A word joining two words, phrases, or sentences.
(e.g. and, or, but.) (Chapter viii)

Interjection: A word "thrown into" a sentence to express some emotion—an exclamation that forms no part of the construction of the sentence.
(e.g. Oh! Ah! Hush!) (Chapter ix)

Each part of speech will be dealt with separately and more fully in subsequent chapters.

The following sentence indicates how each part of speech is used:

Oh,	*Interjection*, expressing an emotion (surprise).
the	*Adjectives*, here describing or qualifying the
old	noun "postman". "The" is generally given the additional title of *Definite Article*.
postman	*Noun*, here the name of a person.
very	*Adverb*, here limiting or modifying another adverb, "carelessly".
carelessly	*Adverb*, here modifying the verb "dropped".
dropped	*Verb*, here describing an action, making an assertion.
some	*Adjective*, here qualifying noun "letters".
most	*Adverb*, here modifying the adjective "important".
important	*Adjective*, here describing noun "letters".
letters	*Noun*, here the name of a thing or object.
and	*Conjunction*, here joining "letters" and "parcel".
a	*Adjective*, qualifying "parcel". "A" or "an"

is usually given the additional title of *Indefinite Article*.

parcel	*Noun*, here the name of a thing or object.
just	*Adverb*, here modifying the preposition "near".
near	*Preposition*, here showing relation between "parcel" and "you".
you	*Pronoun*, here used instead of noun "man" or "Smith", i.e. the person addressed by the speaker.

It is impossible to decide what part of speech a word is in a sentence until we have studied carefully what part it is playing in that particular sentence.

For example, to have a fixed idea that "only" is an adverb on all occasions because many adverbs end in "-ly" would be quite misleading in the sentence: "George was her only son." Here "only" obviously qualifies the noun "son"; it is the function of an adjective, and not that of an adverb, to do this: "only" is therefore an adjective in this case.

The classification of words and the study of their functions will be dealt with more fully in Chapter XI (parsing), but there is no reason why we should not practise some easy identification of parts of speech as soon as possible, before we discuss each part in greater detail.

Ability to identify the parts of speech is an absolute necessity when studying a foreign language, when we have to select the correct word to use from a dictionary. For one word without any alteration in spelling in English may be used as several parts of speech, each of which will be a different word in a foreign language.

e.g. I *cut* the grass. (Verb)
The *cut* is not serious. (Noun)
I have a *cut* finger. (Adjective)

As an additional aid, we must note the following points:
1. An *Adjective* can sometimes be used as a Noun.

e.g. The *good* are seldom rewarded.

19

2. A *Conjunction*, in addition to joining single words (e.g. "cats *and* dogs", "sooner *or* later"), may join:

  (*a*) *Phrases* (a phrase is a group of words that, having no complete verb, does not constitute a sentence).
      On a bus *or* in a car, . . .

  e.g. Searching carefully *and* looking everywhere, . . .

  (*b*) *Clauses* (a clause is a sentence which is part of a longer sentence).

  e.g. I shall go there *and* I shall complain.
     I shall go there *if* he does not reply.

    And notice that a conjunction may begin a sentence when the normal order is reversed for emphasis.

  e.g. *If* he does not reply, I shall go there.

3. *An Adverb* frequently begins a sentence when that sentence is a question:

  e.g. *How (When, Where, Why)* are you going?

In addition to limiting any part of speech except a noun or pronoun, these adverbs, and others like "since", "before", "as", "while", "after" sometimes act as Conjunctions.

  e.g. I shall go *when* he arrives.
    He saw me *before* I could escape.

4. A *Preposition* must not be confused with an adverb. A preposition always has its object noun or pronoun following it; an adverb merely limits the verb in these cases.

  e.g. I fall *down* the bank. (Preposition)
     I fall *down.*   (Adverb. No noun or pronoun following it and connected with it)

5. *Pronouns* sometimes come at the beginning of a sentence, the nouns they replace having not yet been mentioned, in questions.

  e.g. *Who* is there? *What* is that? *Which* do you prefer?

Do not confuse the pronoun "that" with "that" used simply as a conjunction, which has nothing to do with any nouns understood.

e.g. Here is the pen *that* I lost. (Pronoun = I lost *that*)
I think *that* he is very ill. (Conjunction)

6. *The Verb* will be dealt with fully in Chapter V, but at this stage it may be helpful to point out that a verb in a sentence can consist of more than one word.

e.g. I sing, I am singing, I have been singing.
I shall have been singing.

EXERCISES

A

Write down each word in the following sentence and state in separate columns (*a*) what part of speech it is, and (*b*) what it is doing:

"The new house that my friend George bought quite recently has a very large garden, and I often help him with it as I live near his road."

B

State the part of speech of the words italicised:

1. Have *you any* books?
2. I cannot walk *any farther*.
3. He has *two* stamps. Have you got *any*?
4. You must eat *or* you will be *ill*.
5. They spoke *to* me *when* I arrived.
6. I *am* sure it is *true*.
7. Go *round* the island.
8. *Henry* enjoys a *round* of golf.
9. *When* is he *due* to sail?
10. She is *happier since* he arrived.
11. He has been here *since Tuesday*.
12. We have *not* seen him *since*.
13. *This* is harder *than* I thought.
14. *Who* has done *so* well?
15. Our *needs need* satisfying.

C

Write sentences using the following words as the parts of speech indicated, giving a separate example for each use, stating in brackets the part of speech used.

1. any (adjective, pronoun).
2. back (verb, adverb).
3. bend (noun, verb).
4. before (adverb, conjunction).
5. can (verb, noun).
6. down (preposition, adverb).
7. enough (adjective, pronoun).
8. fine (verb, adjective).
9. for (preposition, conjunction).
10. half (adjective, noun).
11. less (adjective, pronoun).
12. more (pronoun, adverb).
13. near (verb, preposition).
14. only (adjective, adverb).
15. that (pronoun, adjective).
16. through (preposition, adverb).
17. well (adverb, noun).
18. what (interjection, pronoun).
19. which (pronoun, adjective).
20. yet (adverb, conjunction).

D

Compose sentences using each of the following words as *two* different parts of speech. Write a separate sentence for each use, stating the part of speech in each case:

after, bore, capital, far, forward,
late, plane, secret, then, when.

E

Compose sentences using the following parts of speech in the order indicated.

1. Definite Article, Adjective, Noun, Verb, Noun.
2. Noun, Conjunction, Noun, Adverb, Verb.
3. Pronoun, Verb, Adverb, Indefinite Article, Noun.
4. Adjective, Noun, Verb, Preposition, Pronoun.
5. Interjection, Verb, Preposition, Adjective, Noun.

F

Fill in suitable words where the parts of speech are indicated:

An Englishman (pronoun) was spending (indefinite article) holiday in Spain went (adjective) day (preposition) a restaurant (preposition) Madrid.

He (verb) to order (adjective) beef with mushrooms, but he (verb) not speak (noun). He took a (noun) of paper (preposition) (adjective) pocket, (conjunction) drew a cow and a mushroom. Then he (verb) the waiter and showed (pronoun) to (pronoun).

The waiter seemed to understand, and went (adverb). (Adverb) afterwards he returned, smiling, and (verb) the Englishman an umbrella (conjunction) a ticket for a bull-fight.

(Definite article) waiter could (adverb) understand why (definite article) Englishman was so (adjective).

The moral of (adjective) story is that (conjunction) you (verb) (preposition) **a** (adjective) country, (pronoun) should (verb) its language.

CHAPTER II

NOUNS

Definition: A Noun is a word that is used to name any person, animal, thing, idea, state, or quality.

e.g. George, man, dog, table, choice, poverty, kindness.

Kinds:

(1) *Common*, i.e. a name common to all of a numerous class of people, animals, or things.

e.g. man, dog, table, town.

(2) *Proper*, i.e. the special name of a particular person, place, or thing (hence the distinguishing capital letter).

e.g. George, London, *Pickwick Papers*, Piccadilly, Monday, the Emperor of Japan, H.M.S. *Victory*.

(3) *Collective*, i.e. names denoting a collection or group of people, animals, or things regarded as one.

e.g. crowd, team, fleet, herd.

(4) *Abstract*, i.e. the name of a quality, state, or action.

e.g. Kindness, captivity, flight.

Note: If a collective noun is considered as a single unit, the verb must be in the singular, but if it is considered as a number of individuals, a plural verb is required.

e.g. The committee is now meeting, *but* The committee are taking their seats on the platform.
(They cannot all sit on one seat, so are considered as a number of individuals.)

Gender:

Masculine (males), e.g. man, lion.
Feminine (females), e.g. woman, lioness.
Common (either masculine or feminine), e.g. child, animal.
Neuter (inanimate objects), e.g. pen, chair.

There are three main methods of forming the feminine of nouns:

1. By the use of endings (mostly "-ess"):

e.g. actor, actress; master, mistress; duke, duchess. hero, heroine; executor, executrix.

2. By changing the prefix (addition at the beginning of a word) or suffix (addition at the end of a word) of a compound noun (i.e. a noun made up of two or more parts).

e.g. *man*servant, *maid*servant; land*lord*, land*lady*; he-goat, she-goat; peacock, peahen.

3. By the use of a different word:

e.g. husband	wife	nephew	niece
earl	countess	fox	vixen
monk	nun	drake	duck
wizard	witch	uncle	aunt
bachelor	spinster	king	queen

Number: There are two numbers, Singular and Plural.

Methods of forming the plural:
1. Add "-s", e.g. book, books.
2. Add "-es".

(*a*) to nouns ending in a hissing sound (sibilant), or ending in "o".

e.g. box, boxes; tomato, tomatoes.
(but add "s" only to some foreign nouns, especially Italian musical terms: piano, pianos, solo, solos).

(*b*) To nouns ending in "y", after changing the "y" into "i".

e.g. sky, skies (but proper names keep the "y"—e.g. There were several Henrys; and nouns ending in "ey", "ay", "oy" add "s" as usual—e.g. key, keys).

(*c*) To most nouns ending in "f" or "fe", after changing "f" to "v", e.g. wolf, wolves (but "gulfs", "reefs", "safes").

Note: "hoofs" or "hooves" is permissible, but nouns ending in "-oof", "-ief" "-ff", and "-rf" are exceptions, e.g. roofs, chiefs, cliffs (but "scarves", "thieves").

3. Change of vowel to form plural, e.g. man, men.

4. A few nouns add "-en" or "-ren", e.g. oxen, children.

5. Words of foreign origin in many cases retain foreign plurals:

e.g. (Gk.) crisis, crises; phenomenon, phenomena.
(Latin) terminus, termini; datum, data; analysis, analyses.
[Latin and English forms: formula, formulae *or* formulas; fungus, fungi *or* funguses.]
(French) tableau, tableaux; bureau, bureaux.

6. A few nouns make no change for the plural:

e.g. deer, sheep, salmon, trout, species (but "fish" has plural "fish" or "fishes").

7. Some nouns have two different plurals, varying with their meaning.

e.g. genius geniuses (brilliant persons).
genii (magic spirits).

index	indexes (lists of contents).
	indices (in mathematics).
penny	pennies (coins).
	pence (value).
staff	staffs (body of officers, or of assistants).
	staves (sticks, supports, lines for music).
die	dies (embossing stamp for coins, etc.).
	dice (used in games).

8. Compound nouns form their plural according to the nature of their component parts (i.e. as suitable and sensible).

e.g. mothers-in-law.
  passers-by.
  lords-justices.

Most dictionaries indicate the correct plural form of nouns, or, at least, any irregular or alternative plurals.

Cases:

Case is the name given to the relation in which a noun stands to some other word in a sentence.

Subjective (or Nominative):

A noun is in the Nominative case when it is used as the subject of a verb, i.e. as the person or thing about whom or which something is said; or after the verb "to be".

e.g. The *bird* sings.
  It is a *blackbird*.

A noun is said to be used as a Nominative of Address (or Vocative) when the noun names a person or persons addressed.

e.g. *Charles*, you are late.
  My *boy*, you are wrong.

Objective:

(a) *Direct Object (or Accusative)*. A noun is in the accusative case when it is the direct object of a verb (i.e. an action); or when it is the object of a preposition.

e.g. I wrote a *letter* (obj. of verb "wrote").
   I write with a *pen* (obj. of preposition "with").

  (*b*) *Indirect Object* (*or Dative*). Some verbs take two objects, an indirect (for the person) and a direct (for the thing).

e.g. I give the *boy*   a *book*. (= to the boy)
         (indirect) (direct).

Note: If the preposition "to" is used, instead of being understood, "boy" will come last in the sentence.

e.g. I give a book to the boy.

Possessive (or Genitive):

A noun is in the possessive case when it indicates the possessor.

e.g. The boy's book; Mary's dress; the dog's tail.

The possessive case for persons and animals is formed by adding an *apostrophe* "*s*" to singular nouns (this is called the Saxon Genitive. In Old English the ending "es" was the sign of possession, and the apostrophe indicates that the "e" has now vanished), and to plural nouns that do not end in "s" in their plural form.

e.g. The man's hat; the men's hats.

Plural nouns forming their plural by adding "s" take the apostrophe after the "s".

e.g. The farmers' wives.

Compound nouns take the apostrophe after their final part.

e.g. My mother-in-law's cat.

This method of forming the possessive case is not usually used for things or abstract nouns (except in special phrases). For these a phrase is formed with the preposition "of".

e.g. The leg of the table; for the sake of peace.

An apostrophe is used with names of things or abstract nouns in expressions of space (a stone's throw); of time (a day's holiday); and of quantity (a shilling's worth); and in a few familiar phrases (for goodness' sake, for conscience' sake, for pity's sake, out of harm's way, at his wit's end, in his mind's eye, to his heart's content); and if an abstract noun is treated as a person.

e.g. Fortune's favourite.

Greek and Hebrew proper names ending in "es" take only the apostrophe (no "s").

e.g. Moses' words (Socrates', Sophocles', etc.); *but*
St. James's Park.

When in doubt about the correct possessive form of a proper noun, the best rule is to test by ear, and then to write it as pronounced. With group nouns (viz. names of firms, etc.) the apostrophe "s" is added to the last noun only, treating the whole as one noun.

e.g. Robinson & Weaver's Stores
William and Mary's reign.

In cases where the apostrophe would be awkward we may employ "of".

e.g. "The enemies of Louis XIV, the King of France."

Formation: Many nouns are formed by the addition of suffixes (a letter or syllable added to the end of a word):

(1) State, Quality, or Action: "-ness", "-ship", "-ing", "-hood", "-(a)tion", "-age", "-cy", "-ism", "-ice", "-ment", "-ance", "-ence", "-al", "-ry", "-dom".

e.g. friendliness, hardship, writing, manhood, consultation, bondage, accuracy, optimism, practice, banishment, conveyance, obedience, betrayal, archery, freedom.

(2) Agent, Origin, or Occupation: "-er", "-ar", "-or", "-ant", "-ent", "-ist", "-ic", "er", "-eer", "-ier", "-ian", "-man".

e.g. runner, actor, merchant, agent, artist, critic, Londoner, auctioneer, brigadier, Oxonian, musician, Chinaman.

(3) Smallness: "-en", "-et", "-ette", "-el", "-ling", "-ule", "-ock", etc.

e.g. maiden, casket, cigarette, morsel, duckling, capsule, hillock.

(4) Place: "-ry" factory, brewery, nursery.

(5) Compound Nouns are formed by joining two or more words.

e.g. (a) With hyphen:
        she-goat,
        son-in-law,
        will-o'-the-wisp (elusive person),
        humming-bird.

   (b) Without hyphen:
        pickpocket,   skyscraper,
        upstart,   madman,
        farewell,   outlook,
        taxpayer,   cowboy.

Note: Rules for the use of capital letters with nouns are given in Chapter XIII ("Punctuation").

Noun Equivalents: A phrase or a clause may do the work of a noun (see also Chapters XI and XII).

e.g. Phrases: *Climbing mountains* bores me.
             I like *to watch trains.*
     Clauses: *That he is ill* is true.
              I hear *what you say.*

Errors: For errors in the use of nouns, see Chapter XIV.

Note: For Nouns in Apposition, see page 151.

EXERCISES

A

Make a list of all the nouns in the following sentences, and state what kind each is, and its case:

1. Brown's dog carries parcels with great skill.
2. Waiter, bring my friend an egg, please.
3. There is always a crowd on the pier engaged in searching for amusement.

B

(i) Give the feminine of:
salesman, hero, lion, wolf, earl, marquis, lad, bachelor, horse, gander.

(ii) Give the masculine of:
niece, nun, duchess, testatrix, vixen, mistress, abbess, peahen, she-goat, countess.

C

(i) Give the plural of:

piano, spy, roof, sheep, ox, Henry, calf, goose, terminus, Miss Smith, passer-by, oasis, tableau, tomato, key, formula, chief, thief, crisis, gas, rhinoceros.

(ii) Give the singular of:
salmon, pence, indices, dormice, phenomena, data, termini, potatoes, species, MSS.

(iii) Give the possessive case of:
men, ladies, Moses, Venus, my friend Charles, son-in-law, actress, Smith and Brown, geese, chair.

D

Give the collective noun used to describe a group or collection of the following:

(e.g. a group of cows—a herd of cows)
bees, trees, fruit-trees, rooms, footballers, singers, guns, puppies, houses, sheep, soldiers, aeroplanes, whales, flowers, thieves, chickens, stars, fish, shots, dancers, actors, partridges, musicians, worshippers, listeners, watchers, wolves, cards, books, sailors, ships.

E

Form abstract nouns from the following words:

(e.g. child, childhood)

Nouns: dictator, captain, traitor, hero, coward, brother, slave, friend, judge, enemy.

Verbs: assume, occur, criticise, auction, continue, receive, banish, precede, stupefy, refuse.

Adjectives: moist, necessary, broad, moderate, majestic, wide, vain, simple, just, cheerful.

F

Give nouns opposite in meaning to the following:

happiness, optimism, luck, noise, descendant, miser, success, disappointment, wisdom, sickness.

G

Give a single noun for each of the following:

(e.g. a place where castings are made = foundry)

1. A place where furniture is stored.
2. A man who examines the books of a firm.
3. A picture before the title-page of a book.
4. A contrivance for keeping food cool.
5. A place where spirits are prepared.
6. A man in charge of a museum.
7. A list of items for consideration at a meeting.
8. A room where weapons are stored.
9. A machine for reproducing words spoken into it.
10. A legal officer appointed to find the cause of unusual deaths.

H

Fill in a suitable noun.

1. As fit as a . . .
2. As bold as . . .
3. As wise as an . . .
4. As quiet as a . . .
5. As heavy as . . .
6. As sly as a . . .
7. As cool as a . . .
8. As slow as a . . .
9. As clear as . . .
10. As old as . . .

I

Write sentences to show clearly the meaning and correct use of each of the following nouns:

(i) disposal, disposition; assent, ascent; interment, internment; principle, principal; observance, observation; warden, warder; council, counsel; yoke, yolk; meter, metre; break, brake;

(ii) allusion, illusion; boar, bore; canon, cannon; disease, decease; epithet, epitaph; glacier, glazier; guilt, gilt; peel, peal; receipt, recipe; suit, suite; rout, route; statute, stature; pale, pail; magnet, magnate; leak, leek.

J

Write down the phrases or clauses that are doing the work of a noun in the following sentences:

1. Do you know where he lives?
2. I enjoy playing golf.
3. He likes to run errands.
4. She knows how to drive.
5. What he earns nobody knows.

CHAPTER III

PRONOUNS

Definition: A Pronoun is a word that stands instead of, or takes the place of, a noun.

> e.g. George reads the book.
> *He* reads *it* (pronouns replacing nouns).

Kinds:

1. *Demonstrative:* e.g. this, that, the former, the latter.
2. *Distributive:* e.g. each, either, neither.
3. *Emphatic:* e.g. myself, ourselves, etc.
4. *Indefinite:* e.g. one, some, any, someone, anybody, etc.
5. *Interrogative:* e.g. who?, which?, what?
6. *Personal:* e.g. I, you, he, she, it, etc.
7. *Possessive:* e.g. mine, yours, his, etc.
8. *Reflexive:* e.g. myself, yourself, himself, etc.
9. *Relative:* e.g. who, which, that.

The above classification is given to assist in the study of other languages, in many of which these distinctions must be recognised.

Pronouns, taking as they do the place of a noun, naturally have the same cases as nouns. Notice that some pronouns still have the changes of spelling or of endings which marked the different cases in early English:

> e.g. *Personal*: Subj.: I, he, she, we, they.
> Obj.: me, him, her, us, them.
> Possessive: mine, his, hers, ours, theirs.

Relative: Subj.: who.
            Obj.: whom.
            Possessive: whose.

Notes:

1. *Demonstrative Pronouns* (= pointing out, indicating).
   (i) "The former" (first of two) and "the latter" (second of two) must not be used when speaking of more than two persons or things.
   (ii) "Such" is a demonstrative pronoun meaning "of that kind" in the following example:

e.g. *Such* is the demand for steel.

   (iii) "One" is a demonstrative pronoun in such examples as: "The one (ones) that I chose . . ."

2. *Distributive Pronouns.*
   (i) "Each" can be used for one of two, or of a greater number.

e.g. Each of the two brothers ⎱
    Each of the many runners ⎰ received a prize.

   (ii) "Each other" is used for one of two only: "one another" for one of more than two.

e.g. The two brothers often helped each other.
    Many spectators at the game fought one another.

   (iii) "Either" and "neither" can be used only for one or the other of two, and must always be followed by a verb in the singular.

e.g. Which of the two books do you require?
    Either is suitable.   A single thing.
    Neither is very interesting.   Considered separately.

   (iv) "None" (= not one, no one) should grammatically be followed by a verb in the singular, but usage now favours a verb in the plural, which is permissible, and in fact preferred.
   e.g. Of all the candidates, none have (or "has")

35

been successful. "Anybody" or "nobody", however, must always be followed by a verb in the singular, as must "one", "anyone", "everyone", "everybody", and "somebody".

e.g. Anybody is eligible.
Nobody is going there.

3. *Emphatic Pronouns.*

Do not confuse the emphatic pronouns with the reflexive pronouns, which have the same form.

e.g. I did it myself (emphatic), meaning "It was *I* who did it".
I hurt myself (reflexive object, the action happening to the doer).

Note: Write "oneself", and *not* "one's self".

4. *Indefinite Pronouns.*

(i) "One" and "they" are often used for "people" in a general sense, and are then indefinite pronouns.

e.g. One ought to obey the rules.
They say it is better to act cautiously.

("One" must not be followed by the adjective "his" or "their", but by "one's".

e.g. One should avoid expressing one's opinion unless one is an expert.

Once we are committed to the use of "one", a word to be avoided if possible on account of its monotony, we must be consistent in our use of pronouns and not indulge in such confusion as: "*One* can express an opinion if *he* likes, and *we* must not object to frankness.")

(ii) "All", "any", "another", "few", "many", "much", "some", "several", etc., are classified as indefinite when used as pronouns.

e.g. Many believe this. Few deny it.

5. *Interrogative Pronouns.*

(i) Notice that a question mark is not to be used to indicate a question in reported or indirect speech.

e.g. *Direct:* Who are you?
Reported—Indirect: I asked him who he was.

(ii) "Ever" can be added to the Interrogative Pronouns for emphasis.

e.g. Whoever (whatever) can that be?

6. *Personal Pronouns.*

(i) "Thou" (subject) and "thee" (object)—and the possessive form "thine"—are no longer used in modern English, "you" replacing them and serving for singular as well as for plural.

(ii) The plural "we" is used instead of the singular "I" in newspaper editorials, and in royal proclamations.

e.g. We feel it is time this law was altered.
We greet our loyal subjects.

(iii) "It" is used not only when referring to things, but also (*a*) Impersonally: e.g. It is raining (not referring to any previously mentioned thing). (*b*) As a provisional subject, the real subject coming later in the sentence.

e.g. It is sad to see him suffer (= To see him suffer is sad). In such cases "it" is an indefinite pronoun.

7. *Possessive Pronouns.*

(i) These are sometimes preceded by "of".

e.g. This book of yours.

(ii) For emphasis, "own" is added.

e.g. This car is his own.

(iii) Never be tempted to put an apostrophe before

the final "s" of "its", "hers", "ours", "yours", "theirs".

8. *Reflexive Pronouns.*

Reflexive pronouns are used with reflexive verbs to show that the action happens to or affects the doer.

e.g. He cut himself.

The difference between the reflexive and emphatic pronouns has already been shown.

9. *Relative Pronouns.*

People	*Animals and Things*
Subj.: who (that).	Subj.: which (that).
Obj.: whom (that).	Obj.: which (that).
Possessive: whose.	Possessive: of which, whose.

(i) Relative pronouns, unlike other pronouns, join sentences as well as standing instead of a noun.

The noun to which a relative pronoun refers or is "related" is called the antecedent of the relative pronoun.

e.g. This is the house that I have bought.

Here "that" is the relative pronoun, relating to its antecedent "house", and also joining the two sentences "This is the house" and "I have bought".

In the sentence "It is a fact that he is poor", the word "that" is a conjunction, not a relative pronoun; "fact" is not its antecedent.

Note: Sometimes the relative pronoun is omitted, but understood, in English.

e.g. This is the house I have bought.

(ii) "That" is used for persons or things, but only when introducing a defining clause, i.e. when the clause introduced selects clearly some par-

38

ticular person or thing, and so restricts choice. In defining or restrictive clauses there is no pause in the voice, and consequently there must not be a comma between "that" and its antecedent.

e.g. The man *that* I met at the station was my brother.
This is the house *that* Jack built.

(Both "that" clauses define clearly the selected "man" and "house" and are thus restrictive.)
but we write:

Mr. Smith, *whom* I knew well, waved to me.
The train, *which* was late, left at 7.30 p.m.

"Whom I knew well" clearly refers only to Mr. Smith, and as no other men are involved, there is no need for the use of the defining "that". "Which was late" might refer to many other trains. Both remarks are parenthetical statements or asides—additional remarks which are not particularly selective. As these remarks do not define, a comma separates the relative pronouns from their antecedents. If, however, we wrote "The train that was late" it would indicate that the only train that was late left at 7.30 p.m.

The use of "who" or "which" in a defining clause is not considered an error, but is optional.

(iii) "What" is a relative pronoun when it equals "that which" and is termed in such cases a compound relative pronoun.

e.g. What (= that which) he needs is experience.
I know what (= that which) you mean.

(iv) A relative pronoun is not necessarily in the same case as its antecedent or supposed antecedent. Its case depends on the part it is playing in its own clause.

39

e.g. The man, *whom* I had met often, was running towards the village. ("Man" is subject of "was running", but "whom" is object of "met" in its own clause.)

e.g. I saw the man who I thought was a spy. ("Man" is object of "saw" but "who" is subject of "was".)

(v) "Whose" may be used instead of "of which" when referring to animals and things.

e.g. The town, whose inhabitants were mainly factory workers, . . . (or "The town, the inhabitants of which were mainly factory workers, . . .).

(vi) "As" is a relative pronoun (= that) after "same" or "such" in such sentences as:

It is not the same one *as* (= that) I have chosen.
Such stuff *as* (= that) dreams are made of.

(vii) "But" is a relative pronoun in such sentences as:

e.g. There was not a man but (= who did not do) did his best.

(viii) Ambiguity (a double or confused meaning) must be avoided when using relative pronouns, which should be placed as near as possible to their antecedents.

e.g. The price of the ticket includes meals on the journey, which should be taken in advance.

Here "which" has been wrongly placed next to "meals on the journey", which obviously cannot be taken in advance. "Which" should come immediately after "ticket".

It has been said that "ambiguity is the soul of hilarity", and this is very often true.

(ix) Do not be confused about the case of a pronoun owing to the presence of a parenthetical clause (i.e. an aside, such as "I thought").

e.g. The man, who I thought was dying, made a rapid recovery (= who was dying, I thought). Do not write "whom" here, thinking it is the object of "I thought".

Who did you say was coming? ("Who" is correct, as "did you say" is an aside.)

"Whom" is correct in an accusative and infinitive construction, however:

e.g. The man, *whom* I thought *to be dead*, revived. ("Whom to be dead" = a phrase, object of verb "thought".)

(x) The antecedent is sometimes omitted, but understood.

e.g. Whoever (= every person who) disobeys me will be punished.

We know who (= the person who) did this.

Errors: For errors in the use of pronouns, see also Chapter XIV.

EXERCISES

A

Make a list of all pronouns in the order in which they occur in the following sentences, stating what kind and in what case each pronoun is:

1. These are the books that I borrowed.
2. Each of the men will be rewarded. Are any of them here?
3. The student whose pen is lost need not worry. Surely this is his?
4. Which of the three spoke? It is certain that someone did.
5. Peter has cut himself, but he can tie up his finger himself.
6. There were some who did not know what their orders were.

B

Correct the following sentences, explaining briefly what is wrong with the use of the pronouns in each. (See Chapter XIV.)

1. He is a footballer whom I think will play for England.
2. Between you and I, Henry has made a serious mistake.
3. The three brothers divided the money between each other.
4. This is the man which did it.
5. Who was this done by? At any rate, it wasn't him.
6. One ought to do as much as possible for one's self.

7. Let you and I do this alone.

8. This hat is not mine. Is it her's?

9. Here is a friend of mine, living near me, and who is an expert gardener.

10. This is one of the finest films that has ever been produced.

C

Join the following sentences by using a relative pronoun.

1. He had a daughter. Her name was Mary.

2. This is the house. George designed it.

3. Here is my friend Smith. You wished to meet him.

4. This is my favourite tree. It bears fine apples.

5. I am proud of my hens. Without them I should have no fresh eggs.

D

Compose sentences illustrating:

1. "Myself" used as a Reflexive Pronoun; as an Emphatic Pronoun.

2. "Whom" used as an Interrogative Pronoun; as a Relative Pronoun.

3. "What" used as a Relative Pronoun; as an Interrogative Pronoun.

4. "That" used as a Demonstrative Pronoun; as a Relative Pronoun.

5. "His" used as a Pronoun; as an Adjective.

CHAPTER IV

ADJECTIVES

Definition: An adjective is a word that describes or qualifies a noun or pronoun.

> e.g. (*a*) A *fine red* rose. *Lucky* you.
> (*b*) This book is *new*. She is *gay*.

When an adjective comes next to a noun or pronoun it describes (as in (*a*)), it is said to be used as an *epithet*; when it follows the verb, saying what the noun is stated to be (as in (*b*)), it is said to be used *predicatively*.

Kinds:

Demonstrative: this, that, these, those.
Distributive: each, every, either, neither.
Interrogative: which (book)?, what (boy)?
Numeral: one, two ⎫
Indefinite: all, many, several ⎬ (*Quantitative*)
Possessive: my, your, his, our.
Qualitative: (= showing what kind) large, blue, brave, English.

There is no necessity to memorise this classification, which is given only as a guide to the recognition of adjectives.

Notes:

(1) "The" is usually referred to as the Definite Article, as it indicates a special noun or nouns. "A" is called the Indefinite Article, as it does not specify any definite noun.

"Some" is sometimes referred to as the Partitive Article. It is used to indicate an indefinite quantity (e.g. I have some books) but is often omitted in English (e.g. I have books, pens, and paper). When emphasised, some = "only a little" (e.g. I have *some* bread).

(2) Write "a" before a consonant, before a vowel group having the sound long "u" as in "unique", and before "o" when it has the sound "w", and before "h" beginning a word whose first syllable is stressed.

e.g. a cat, a useful idea, a one-legged man, a hero.

Write "an" before a vowel (except above exceptions, before a silent "h", and before a word beginning with "h" when the first syllable is not stressed).

e.g. an apple, an (h)onest dealer, an historical play—*but* a history of England.

Comparison:

Positive	*Comparative*	*Superlative*
(Simplest form)	(Comparing two)	(Comparing three or more)

(*a*) One syllable and some two-syllable adjectives:

| big | bigg*er* | bigg*est* |
| happy | happ*ier* | happ*iest* |

(*b*) Most adjectives of two syllables, and all of more than two syllables:

| splendid | *more* splendid | *most* splendid |
| beautiful | *more* beautiful | *most* beautiful |

(*c*) Irregular:

good	better	best
bad (evil, ill)	worse	worst
little	lesser, less	least
much, many	more	most

late	$\begin{cases} \text{later} \\ \text{latter} \end{cases}$	$\begin{cases} \text{latest} \\ \text{last} \end{cases}$
fore	$\begin{cases} \text{further} \\ \text{former} \end{cases}$	$\begin{cases} \text{furthest} \\ \text{foremost, first} \end{cases}$
up	upper	uppermost
old	$\begin{cases} \text{older} \\ \text{elder} \end{cases}$	$\begin{cases} \text{oldest} \\ \text{eldest} \end{cases}$

Notes:

(1) "Elder, eldest" can be used only for persons, and are usually used only when comparing members of the same family or group: "older, oldest" are used for persons and things in other cases.

e.g. My elder brother. The oldest inhabitant or town.

(2) "Farther, farthest" refer to distance; "further" = additional.

e.g. The farthest hills. Some further facts.

(3) The adjective "unique" (= there is only *one* of its kind) cannot have a comparative or superlative form.

e.g. This specimen is unique (not "more" or "most unique").

(4) Use the Comparative correctly, i.e. when only two things are compared.

e.g. This is the better of the two books (not "best").

Conversely, use the Superlative for three or more things.

e.g. Which is the easiest language to learn, French, German, or Spanish? (not "easier").

(5) Do not say: "The three best (first, last, etc.) books", as only one idea can be superlative.
Correct to: "The best (first) three books."

(6) "Last" = final; "Latest" = most recent.

e.g. His last book was published after his death.
I enjoyed reading your latest book.

45

("Latter" = the second of two, contrasted with "former", and is usually used as a pronoun.)

Use of Adjectives:

(1) An adjective used as an epithet must accompany the noun or pronoun that it qualifies: a pronoun can stand alone and is always used in place of some noun.

e.g. I have not *much* bread (adjective).
I did not bring *much* (pronoun).

(2) An adjective can be used as a noun when the noun it qualifies is omitted but understood.

e.g. The brave (men) deserve the fair (women).

(3) "Very" is an emphasising adjective (and not an adverb) in such cases as "This is the *very* thing I want ("very" = "exact").

(4) Use "fewer" for mere number, and "less" for quantity and size.

e.g. Fewer people; less milk.

(5) Note the use of the singular in compound adjectives.

e.g. a six-*foot* wall. A ten-*acre* field.

Errors: For errors in the use of Adjectives see also Chapter XIV.

Formation: Many adjectives are formed by the addition of suffixes.

e.g. wood*en*, dai*ly*, lov*able*, edi*ble*, re*gal*, life*like*, gif*ted*, truth*ful*, Eng*lish*, hope*less*, tempor*ary*, kind*ly*, wool*ly*, fortun*ate*, act*ive*, redd*ish*, glor*ious*, home*less*, com*ic*, viol*ent*, child*ish*, etc.

The opposite or negative form of an adjective is formed by placing various prefixes (letter or syllable placed at the beginning of a word, changing its meaning) before the adjective.

e.g. worthy   *un*worthy
     experienced   *in*experienced
     legal   *il*legal
     movable   *im*movable
     probable   *im*probable
     reverent   *ir*reverent
     tasteful   *dis*tasteful

Sometimes a change of suffix has the same effect.

e.g. thought*ful*, thought*less*.

Nouns are sometimes used as adjectives:

e.g. a *theatre* queue; a *team* captain; a *market* stall.

Adjective Equivalents: A phrase or a clause may do the work of an adjective (see also Chapters XI and XII).

e.g. Phrases: This is a book *worth reading.*
              Here is a drink *to quench your thirst.*
     Clauses: The man *to whom you refer* is an artist.
              The house *that I bought* is too small.

Position of Adjectives: In many languages adjectives normally follow the noun when used as epithets, whereas in English they usually come before their noun.

In the following cases, however, adjectives used as epithets follow their nouns.

(*a*) In certain phrases influenced by French, in which language most adjectives follow the noun.

e.g. a court *martial*; a knight *errant;* an heir *apparent.*

(*b*) When a series of adjectives is used; in this case we can write either

the towering, dark, windswept hills
               or
the towering hills, *dark and windswept.*

(*c*) In adjectival phrases.
e.g. This is a fact *worthy* of note.

EXERCISES

A

Make a list of all adjectives in the following sentences, in the order in which they occur:

1. These Turkish cigarettes are really excellent. Try some of mine.

2. Have you any picture postcards? These are the only ones that I have now.

3. What book does your brother want? This is his, but either book will do.

4. We think that Smith, whom we elected our team captain, should show more leadership.

5. "Every man has two countries: France and his own" is a French saying.

B

Make a list of all the adjectives in the following paragraph, and say whether they are used as epithets or predicatively:

My friend arrived in a small red sports car, which was the latest model of its kind, and of which he was obviously very proud. "It's very fast", he said, delighted, as he got out, "and well sprung!"

C

Give adjectives opposite in meaning to each of the following:

permanent, legible, worthy, intelligent, united, reverent, extravagant, violent, rural, movable, thoughtful, experienced, probable, safe, insolent, tasteful, gentle, loyal, cheerful, physical.

D

Give adjectives corresponding to the following nouns:

child, essence, horizon, panic, lion, five, fashion, villain, persuasion, ass, theory, water, giant, wonder, elephant, monk, volcano, humour, science, affection, race, night, ancestor, instant, problem, trifle, Spain, Malta, Greece, George, Scotland.

E

Give the Comparative and Superlative of the following adjectives:
bad, mad, cheerful, happy, good (or little).

F

Give a single adjective to replace exactly the words in italics (e.g. These potatoes are *not fit to be eaten*—inedible):

1. This custom is *found in all parts of the world.*

2. His contribution was *made of his own free will.*
3. That machine is of a type *no longer in use.*
4. Waterloo was a victory *which will never be forgotten.*
5. This rag soaked in petrol is *liable to catch fire.*
6. Your problem is *one that cannot be solved.*
7. Henry is *unable to pay his debts.*
8. Swallows are birds *that fly from one country to another.*
9. Here is a plant *that comes up year after year.*
10. I require a residence *that will last me the rest of my life.*

G

State which adjectives are used incorrectly in the following sentences, and give the correct version, with reasons:

1. This is by far the better car of the three for sale.
2. There were less people at the meeting than I expected.
3. The three best players in the team are getting old.
4. I shall not allow any farther argument.
5. This stamp is most unique; it is worth a fortune.

H

Fill in a suitable adjective in the following comparisons:

1. As . . . as a mule.
2. As . . . as an ox.
3. As . . . as a monkey.
4. As . . . as a needle.
5. As . . . as a peacock.
6. As . . . as a bat.
7. As . . . as a pancake.
8. As . . . as an eel.
9. As . . . as a kitten.
10. As . . . as a lamb.

I

Write down the phrases and clauses that are doing the work of an adjective in the following sentences:

1. A cottage in the country is a pleasant retreat.
2. Here is the house that is to let.
3. We admired the tall girl with long fair hair.
4. The village in which I live is unspoilt.
5. He was wearing a suit of rough tweed.

49

CHAPTER V

VERBS

Definition: A Verb is a word that denotes an action or state. This action or state can be indicated in the form of a statement, a question, an order, or a wish:

e.g. (a) He *goes*. He *is going*.   Statement
     (b) *Are* you going?   Question
     (c) *Go* with him.   Order
     (d) If only I *were going* too.   Wish

Classification: Strong and Weak Verbs

Verbs are broadly classified as weak or strong verbs, according to the way in which they form their principal parts, i.e. their past tense and past participle.

Weak (or Regular) verbs are those that form their past tense and past participle by adding "-d", "-ed", or "-t" to the present tense, without any change of vowel, e.g.

Present	Past	Past Participle
I move	move*d*	(I have) move*d*
I walk	wal*ked*	(I have) wal*ked*
I learn	learn*t* or learn*ed*	(I have) learn*t* or learn*ed*
I send	sen*t*	(I have) sen*t*

Note: No addition, with "t" retained throughout, e.g.

I cut	cut	(I have) cut

Vowel shortening, e.g.

I breed	bred	(I have) bred

Strong (or Irregular) verbs mostly form their past tense and past participle by a vowel change, some adding "-n" or "-en" in past participle, e.g.

Present	*Past*	*Past Participle*
I see	I saw	(I have) see*n*
I swim	I swam	(I have) swum
I write	I wrote	(I have) writt*en*

Some are very irregular, being made up of parts of two or more *Defective* (or incomplete) verbs. These are called *Anomalous* verbs, e.g.

I am	I was	I have been
I go	I went	I have gone

There are many variations in weak and strong types, and complete classification would be lengthy and difficult. The principal parts of verbs are given in most dictionaries.

Note also that some verbs are defective, or incomplete —some parts having fallen out of use, and having been replaced by other verbs, e.g.

I can	I could	(I have been able)
I must	(I had to)	(I have had to)
I ought	(I should have)	(I should have)

Note the differences in meaning (and spelling) in the following verbs:

I bid, I bade, I have bidden—to invite or command.

I bid, I bid, I have bid—to make an offer at an auction sale or when playing cards.

I hang, I hanged, I have hanged—referring to death by hanging.

I hang, I hung, I have hung—referring to all other meanings of "to hang".

I lie, I lay, I have lain—to lie down (and this verb cannot be used with an object).

I lay, I laid, I have laid—to put down somewhere (with an object always required).

I lie, I lied, I have lied—to tell a lie.

Also: I bath the baby, but I bathe in the river or sea, or I bathe a wound.

Note the difference in spelling between the past participle of, and the adjectives formed from, the following verbs:

Verb	Past Participle	Adjective
to drink	I have *drunk*	a *drunken* brawl
to melt	I have *melted*	*molten* lead
to rot	I have *rotted*	*rotten* beams
to shave	I have *shaved*	clean-*shaven*
to shear	I have *sheared*	a *shorn* lamb
to shrink	I have *shrunk*	*shrunken* cheeks
to swell	I have *swelled*	a *swollen* ankle

Types of Action: Verbs are of three types, depending on the particular type of action they perform.

1. Transitive Verbs

A verb is called transitive if the action does not stop with the doer, but passes on to something else (the object of the action).

e.g. I kick the ball (ball = object).

Note: There are several types of object which a transitive verb can take, and this classification is given for reference purposes, and not to confuse students, who will find that it is quite sufficient except in special questions to state simply that some particular word is the object.

Types of Object with Transitive Verbs:

Direct: He teaches *French*.

Indirect: He teaches *the students* French.

(= *to* the students, the second and less direct of the two objects in the sentence.)

Retained: The direct object is retained as an object

when we turn the active verb in the first example into the passive.

The students are taught *French* by him.

Reflexive: He cut *himself*.

2. Intransitive Verbs

A verb is called intransitive if the action stops with the doer.

e.g. I fall.

It is impossible to add any object that will make further sense. If we add "a long way", these words are really doing the work of an adverb and form an adverbial phrase explaining how far, and this is termed an Adverbial Accusative but is not strictly an object. We can similarly "walk a mile", "live a long time", etc.

Impersonal verbs (i.e. those whose subject is the pronoun "it" used indefinitely) are all intransitive.

e.g. It is raining, it seems, etc.

Notes: (i) Many verbs can be used either transitively or intransitively, as required.

e.g. I am writing a book (transitive).
I often write (intransitive—no object expressed).

(ii) Intransitive verbs which make complete sense by themselves are called verbs of Complete Predication.

e.g. Swallows fly. Babies sleep. Ducks swim. Horses canter.

(iii) There are, however, two special types of object which even an intransitive verb can take.

(a) *Cognate Object*

This is an object already implied or inherent in the verb itself; it is not an "outside" object, and is the one and only word that each verb can possibly take.

e.g. He slept a sleep, ran a race, lived a life, died a death, laughed a laugh, sighed a sigh.

(*b*) *Causative Object*

Certain intransitive verbs when causing something to happen, become transitive and take a causative object, e.g.

Intransitive	*Causative*
The horse walks	I walk the horse round the ring. (= cause it to walk)
The milk boils	I boil the milk (= cause it to boil)

(iv) Certain intransitive verbs, particularly the verb "to be", and such verbs as "to become" and "to seem", require a word or group of words to make complete sense (i.e. to complete the predicate).

This addition is called the *Complement*, and intransitive verbs requiring it are called verbs of Incomplete Predication, e.g.

Subject	*Verb*	*Complement*
He	is	ill
He	became	king
He	seems	to be happy

(v) A complement must not be confused with an object.

A group of verbs called Factitive verbs (i.e. verbs of *making* such as "to make", "to elect"), which are transitive verbs requiring an object, also require the addition of a complement to make complete sense, and so to make a complete predicate. This is sometimes called a factitive object, e.g.

Subject	*Verb*	*Object*	*Complement*
They	made	him	leader
We	elected	her	queen

54

3. Auxiliary Verbs

The types of verbs we have discussed hitherto are verbs which can be used alone, without the help of another verb, and are called Principal verbs.

There is a group of very important verbs, however, which help to form the tenses of other verbs, and are therefore called Auxiliary (= helping) verbs.

These are the verbs "to be", and "to have", with the incomplete or defective verbs, "shall, will, may, do".

e.g. I *have* seen, I *am* going, I *shall* go, he *will* go.
So that I *may* see, *do* you see?

The auxiliary verbs "to be" and "to have" can be used alone, however, as principal verbs, as also can "shall", "will", "may", "do".

e.g. I am a man, I have a book, he shall speak (command).
I will go (determination), You may go (permission).
I do my duty.

Note: The defective or incomplete verbs "can", "must", and "ought" are *not* auxiliary verbs forming tenses, but principal verbs followed by an infinitive (the form of the verb which gives the verb its name, e.g. "to go"), the "to" of which has been omitted after "can" and "must".

e.g. I can go, I must go (= to go).
I ought to go.

Voice is a term to show whether the subject of a verb *does* the action or *suffers* the action.

There are, therefore, two voices: the Active Voice and the Passive Voice.

e.g. I push (Active).
I am pushed (Passive).

Person and Number: The form taken by the verb depends on the subject of that verb, i.e. on the Person (1st, 2nd, or 3rd) and on the Number (singular or plural).

	Singular	*Plural*	
1st Person	I	we	(Person speaking)
2nd Person	you	you	(Person spoken to)
3rd Person	he, she, it	they	(Person spoken of)

Note: "Thou" is no longer used for the 2nd person singular, but is, of course, used in most translations of the Bible, and sometimes in poetry.

The only inflection added (or addition made) in English is "-s" in the 3rd person singular of the present tense.

e.g. I give, we give, you give, he give*s*, they give.

A verb must agree with its subject in number and person. This is termed the concord of verb and subject.

e.g. He and I (= we) *go.*

(With "either" and "neither" avoid "Either he or I am right" and "Neither the boys nor the master was late" by "Either he is right or I am" and "The boys were not late, neither was the master".)

Mood is the name given to the form of a verb which shows the manner (i.e. mode) in which the action is represented.

There are four moods: Indicative, Imperative, Subjunctive, and Infinitive.

Tenses. The Tense of a verb shows the *time* of the action or state indicated—whether past, present, or future; it also shows the completeness or incompleteness of an action at the time indicated.

(It must be noted that the terms used to name tenses in some other European languages differ in some respects from our terms, the main difference being that these other European languages do not recognise or employ a separate *continuous* form for each tense as we do.)

The following tables, showing the moods and the tense

scheme of a verb in English, are included for the benefit of foreign students.

1. Indicative Mood

This mood is used for statements of fact (or suppositions regarded as facts) and for questions.

Verb: to move.

Present
- *Simple:* I move. (Passive: I am moved, being moved, etc.)
- *Continuous:* I am moving.
- *Perfect:* I have moved.
- *Perfect Continuous:* I have been moving.

Notes: (i) The two perfect tenses are called Present Perfect because although the actions were in the past, they are viewed from the present by the speaker or writer.

(ii) The Present Perfect ("I have moved") is used: (*a*) For an action just concluded (e.g. A short while ago I was reading, but now I have finished). (*b*) For a completed action at an indefinite time (e.g. I have read that book). (*c*) For an action in the past *continuing into the present* (e.g. I have studied languages for many years, and I am still studying them).

(iii) In English the Present Continuous, in addition to describing an action actually continuing (e.g. You see that I am moving), is often used to indicate an action that is going to take place in the *near* future (e.g. I am moving my furniture tomorrow).

Past
- *Simple:* I moved. (Passive: I was moved, was being moved, etc.)
- *Continuous:* I was moving.
- *Perfect:* I had moved.
- *Perfect Continuous:* I had been moving.

Notes: (i) The Simple Past ("I moved") is used *when a definite occasion in the past is indicated.*

e.g. I saw the Queen last Tuesday (definite).

57

(ii) The Past Continuous ("I was moving") is called the Imperfect in most European languages, and the Past Perfect ("I had moved") is called the Pluperfect.

Future
- *Simple:* I shall move. (Passive: I shall be moved, shall be being moved, etc.)
- *Continuous:* I shall be moving.
- *Perfect:* I shall have moved.
- *Perfect Continuous:* I shall have been moving.

Notes: English has two forms for the Future, as follows:

1. Idea of future time only.

2. Idea of determination, intention, promise, or willingness in 1st person. Intention, and sometimes a command by other persons (in 2nd, 3rd person).

I *shall move.*	I will move (determination or willingness).
You will.	You shall move ⎱ (intention or command
He will.	He shall move ⎰ *by other persons*).
We *shall.*	We will move (determination or willingness).
You will.	You shall move ⎱ (intention or command
They will.	They shall move ⎰ *by other persons*).

It will be seen that the two versions are exactly the reverse of each other, and that the 1st person singular and plural is the change to master.

e.g. Mere futurity.	I shall move soon.
Determination.	I will move (whatever you do).
Intention, promise, or willingness.	We will help you.
Intention or command *by other person.*	He shall have the book he wants. You shall move (or be prosecuted).

The standard and tragic example of confusion over "shall" and "will" is that of the drowning Frenchman who shouted: "I will drown. Nobody shall save me" —and, of course, he was drowned and nobody did save him.

Practice will help the student to master this point. The

only exception to this rule is when the determination is not in the mind of the speaker, but is stated to be in the mind of the person *spoken about*; e.g. "Poor old Jones, he will do (i.e. Jones is apparently determined to do) too much work in his garden and tire himself out."

Conditional
or
Future-in-the-Past
{
Simple: I should move. (Passive: I should be moved, I should be being moved, etc.)
You would move.
He would move, etc.
Continuous: I should be moving.
Perfect: I should have moved.
Perfect Continuous: I should have been moving.
}

(So called because this tense describes an action or state that was at some time in the past *regarded as future*.)

Note: The following scheme may help in dealing with the use of "would" and "should":

A

(i) Future in the Past.
(ii) Consequence after Condition.
(I said that)
I *should* move, you would move, he would move, we *should* move, you would move, they would move.

B

Conditional clauses after "if".
(If)
I should move, you should move, he should move, etc.

C

Duty.
I should move, you should move, he should move, etc.

D

Determination or Willingness.

I would move, you would move, he would move, etc.

e.g. A. (i) I said that I should move soon. (= Future in the Past.) (Direct speech: "I shall move soon" = Future.)

(ii) If he met her, he would recognise her. (Consequence after Condition.)

B. If they should move, let me know. (Or simply: "If they move, . . .)

C. I should really work harder.

D. He would climb the tree, regardless of danger. (Determination.)

He would willingly help you, I am sure. If you would help me, I would try to escape. (Willingness.)

And "would" is used for all persons for custom or habit.

e.g. He would often fish all day when he was a boy.

2. Imperative Mood

This mood is used to express orders, requests, or sometimes advice. It presents no difficulties, as it is formed from the 2nd person of the Present Tense:

e.g. Come here. Forgive me. Never despair.

Notes: (i) The only exception to the rule for the formation of the Imperative is the verb "to be", the imperative of which is "be".

e.g. Be careful.

(ii) For the 1st or 3rd person the verb "let" is used.

e.g. Let us run.

3. Subjunctive Mood

The Subjunctive, the mood of supposition, is now very little used. In form it is the same as the Present and Past Tense of the Indicative (except for the verb "to be", which

60

has Present Subjunctive "I be", etc., and Past Subjunctive "I were", etc.; and the fact that the ending "s" of the 3rd person singular of the Present Indicative of other verbs is dropped in the Present Subjunctive, e.g. "Thy kingdom *come*").

The Subjunctive expresses uncertainty, wish, or hope, whereas the Indicative expresses certainty or fact.

The following are the only types of sentence in which its use survives in English:

(a) *Expressing a Supposition not likely to be realised.*

e.g. If I *were* you, I should accept his offer.
Were he to win a fortune, he would be surprised.

(b) *Expressing a Wish.*

e.g. Long *live* the Queen (= may live).
I wish he *were* coming.
Far *be* it from me to complain (= may it be).

(c) *Conditions not fulfilled.*

e.g. *Had* you come earlier, you might have seen him.

(d) *Commands.*

e.g. The judge ordered that the fine *be* paid at once.

Note: 'May", "might", and "should" are used as subjunctive equivalents or substitutes in sentences where there is purpose or supposition.

e.g. I give (gave) you this advice so that you *may* (*might*) succeed.
If you *should* meet him, give him my message.

4. Infinitive Mood

As its title indicates, this is the non-finite part of the verb, and the terms "Finite" and "Non-Finite" must now be defined.

Finite Parts are those parts of a verb which have endings imposed upon them by a subject, and so are influenced by number and person (e.g. he sing*s*). The three moods we have just discussed—the Indicative, Imperative, and Subjunctive—comprise the finite parts of a verb.

Non-finite Parts of a verb are those parts which have no endings imposed on them by number or person, and these are the Infinitive, the Present Participle, the Gerund, and the Past Participle.

e.g. Infinitive Present: *to* move.
Infinitive Perfect: *to* have moved.
(Also Future: *to* be about to move; Passive: *to* be moved.)
Present Participle and Gerund: mov*ing*.
Past Participle: mov*ed*.

The Infinitive: The Infinitive is the title given to the name of a verb, e.g. "to move". "To" forms a whole idea with "move" and is not considered as a separate word. In some cases the "to" disappears but is understood. "To" is omitted after "shall", "will", "may", "can", "must", verbs of perception, and "make".

e.g. I can *go* (= am able to go).
I saw him *run* (= to run).

In addition to its use as part of a verb, an infinitive can be used as:

(*a*) *Noun.*

e.g. Subject: *To hesitate* is a mistake.
Object (of verb): He likes *to swim.* We saw him *climb.*
(of preposition): There is no solution except *to go.*
Complement: What I wish is *to succeed.*
Exclamatory: *To think* he is dead!

(*b*) *Adjective.*

e.g. (with noun) Here is a flat *to let* (= vacant).
(with pronoun) You want a tie for this suit? Here is one *to match* (= matching).

(*c*) *Adverb.*
(i) Modifying a verb.

e.g. He comes *to read* to me.

   (ii) Modifying an adjective.

e.g. This story is hard *to believe.*
(Answers question "In what way hard?")

The Present Participle, Gerund

These are the same in form, both ending in "-ing", but are different in function.

  (i) The **Present Participle** is used

    (*a*) To help to form the continuous tense of a verb.

e.g. He was singing.

    (*b*) As a verbal adjective (used as epithet).

e.g. a talking parrot.
a *sitting* hen.

    (*c*) As a verbal adjective used predicatively.

e.g. *Arriving* at the inn, the traveller entered, *being* tired.
(Actions actually taking place, hence the name *present* participle.)

Note: Sometimes a present participle is used in a phrase which has no connection with the real subject of the sentence, e.g. The evening being near, the traveller entered the inn. "The evening being near" has no connection with the traveller, but is equivalent to an adverbial phrase, not to an adjectival phrase, here.

This type of phrase is called an Absolute construction.

  (ii) The **Gerund** (or **Verbal Noun**) is used partly as a noun and partly as a verb.

  e.g. (Subject) *Running* is exhausting.
     (Object) I like *singing.*
            I like *singing* hymns.
     (Complement) My hobby is *collecting* stamps.

Notes: (i) Some grammarians called "singing" in the first example a verbal-noun, as it is doing the work of a noun only, and "singing" in the second example a gerund, because it is followed by its object "hymns" and is therefore more clearly doing the work of a verb. These separate titles are used merely to distinguish the two functions, and it is simpler and quite correct to use the term Gerund in all cases.

The main problem for most students is to distinguish between a present participle and a gerund. For a present participle say, "Is this an action actually going on at the moment in question?" For a gerund say, "Is this equivalent to the idea of an action that is not necessarily actually going on at the moment in question?"

> e.g. *Singing*, the man entered the inn.
> (= Present Participle, "singing" actually taking place as he entered. The words "who was singing" can be substituted.)
>
> I am fond of *singing*.
> (= Gerund, "singing" being here "the idea of singing" and not necessarily actually taking place at time of statement.)

(ii) When gerunds are used alone, without an object, they are really nothing more than abstract nouns.

> e.g. You must study *reading*, *writing*, and arithmetic.

(iii) As a gerund is used as a noun we must remember to write: I regret his going (not "him"). I dislike Henry's playing with George (not "Henry").

As a gerund is a form of a noun, it is often preceded by an adjective ("his going") or a preposition ("on arriving", "by moving"), which helps to identify it.

The Past Participle: This usually ends in "-(e)d", "-(e)n", or "-t".

It has three uses, similar to those of the Present Participle.

(i) To help to form perfect tenses.

e.g. I have mov*ed*, tak*en*, cu*t*, etc.

(ii) As an adjective (used as epithet).

e.g. The *promised* land.

His *chosen* career.

(iii) As an adjective used predicatively.

e.g. The thief, *seized* with fear, fled (= who was seized).

Formation of Verbs: Notice the use of the suffixes "-ate", "-en", "-fy", "-ise" (or "-ize"), "-ish", to form verbs from nouns.

e.g. regul*ate*, streng*th*en, terri*fy*, critic*ise*, fin*ish*.

Errors: For errors in the use of Verbs see Chapter XIV.

EXERCISES

A

Give the past tense, and past participle, of each of the following verbs:

to bear, to choose, to cling, to drink, to fly, to lie (position), to lie (tell a lie), to lay, to eat, to ride, to shrink, to spring, to sting, to tear, to weave.

B

Write three sentences for each of the following verbs, (1) using the verb transitively, (2) using the verb intransitively, (3) using the verb in the passive:

bend, catch, fly, grow, wear.

C

State which verbs are used as auxiliary and which as principal verbs in the following:

1. I am glad to say he is going away.

2. Have you read the news? No. Have you a newspaper?

3. I have to go now, but I hope we may meet next week.

4. He shall apologise. I shall tell him to do so.

5. I did this sort of work for several years, but I did not find it interesting.

D

State the mood, voice, and tense of each verb in the following:

1. When the lecturer had finished, the class went home.

2. We were walking along the avenue when we were stopped by a policeman.

3. If I were you, I should not sign the document.

4. He said he would go, if possible.

5. Tell me if I have been deceived.

6. Smith ought to have told us the truth.

7. I am going to visit the Roman temple that has been discovered.

8. You can go now your work is finished.

9. It had been raining for hours, and I was wet through.

10. He is claiming to have been an army officer.

11. Did you hear him say he would come with us?

12. I do not think he will have been here a month by next Tuesday.

E

Make a list of (*a*) present participles, (*b*) gerunds, (*c*) past participles, and (*d*) infinitives in the following sentences, stating in the case of participles which are used as epithets:

1. We can see he is enjoying his swimming.

2. Opening the door, the warder was surprised to find the condemned man singing.

3. I must finish writing this chapter, as it ought to have been completed yesterday.

4. Playing games is good exercise, but I prefer reading.

5. The closed shutters showed that it would be useless to try knocking at the door.

6. Riding lessons may be booked at these stables.

7. The chosen candidates were summoned to be interviewed.

F

State what is wrong with the verbs in the following sentences, giving reasons for your answers. (See Chapter XIV.)

1. The number of people who have been invited are very small.

2. He will be the first scientist to have received this award.

3. Shall you lend me your umbrella? I will be most grateful.

4. Matthews is one of the greatest footballers that has ever lived.

5. I shall go if he would come with me.

6. We do not like him neglecting his work.

7. Cycling through the park, a stag attacked us.

8. The runner was so exhausted that he laid down on the grass.

9. I used to often frequent that restaurant.

10. He hoped that his painting would be hanged in the exhibition.

G

Form verbs from the following nouns:
description, abstinence, compulsion, loss, satisfaction, black, start, monopoly, abolition, adhesion.

H

Fill in the blanks in the following sentences with "shall", "will", "should", or "would" to complete the correct version (sense).

1. . . . you close the door, please.

2. . . . I help you with your Latin? . . . your teacher mind if I do?

3. If you . . . see him, tell him I . . . like to meet him.

4. We . . . fall if nobody . . . throw us a rope.

5. He said he . . . come if the rain stopped.

6. I . . . lend the money with pleasure, but I think you . . . ask the bank first.

7. My wife and I . . . be so pleased if you . . . come to dinner.

I

State whether the infinitive in the following sentences is used as a noun, adjective, or adverb.

1. All we can do is to await further instructions.

2. Here is a film to see at all costs.

3. To lose hope would be a foolish thing.

4. These diamonds are very difficult to cut.

5. This student hopes to take the examination in June.

6. I have set you this work to punish you.

J

Fill in a suitable verb to indicate the sound made by each of the following:

1. Burning sticks . . .
2. A cow . . .
3. An elephant . . .
4. A fox . . .
5. A hound . . .
6. A snake . . .
7. A beaten dog . . .
8. A monkey or a jay . . .
9. A loose board . . .
10. A hyena . . .
11. A sparrow . . .
12. A donkey . . .
13. Distant thunder . . .
14. A spinning top . . .

K

Write sentences to illustrate the correct use of each of the following verbs, showing clearly how each pair differ in meaning:

precede, proceed; effect, affect; allude, elude; prescribe, proscribe; emigrate, immigrate; lose, loose; deprecate, depreciate; omit, emit; jib, gibe; request, require.

L

State whether the words in italics are complements or objects, stating in the case of objects what grammatical type they are:

1. This man seems to be their *leader*.
2. Mr. Johnson taught the *students* Latin.
3. The students were taught *Latin by him*.
4. He unfortunately cut *himself* while shaving.
5. The committee elected him *chairman*.

CHAPTER VI

ADVERBS

Definition: An Adverb is a word that limits or modifies the meaning of any part of speech, except a noun or pronoun.

> e.g. I *rarely* go (limiting verb).
> I am *very* tired (limiting adjective "tired").
> I live *quite* near him (limiting preposition "near").
> I walk *rather* slowly (limiting adverb "slowly").
> I shall go *simply* because I wish to (limiting conjunction "because").

An adverb can also modify a whole sentence, in which case the adverb comes first in the sentence.

> e.g. *Unfortunately* the money was not paid.

Note: In many cases the adverb helps to form a verb, and forms one idea with it, being thus really inseparable from it.

> e.g. I speak up. I shout out.

Kinds: It is best to divide adverbs into three groups: (*a*) Simple, (*b*) Interrogative, and (*c*) Conjunctive.

> (*a*) *Simple.*
>> 1. *Time:* now, soon, yesterday, etc.
>> 2. *Place:* here, inside, below, etc.
>> 3. *Manner:* quickly, badly, well, etc.
>> 4. *Degree or Extent:* very, quite, too, etc.
>> 5. *Number:* once, firstly, again, etc.
>> 6. *Certainty or Uncertainty:* certainly, perhaps, not, etc.

7. *Reason or Consequence:* therefore, so, consequently, etc.

Note: "There" is not an adverb of place but only an introductory word in such sentences as:

"*There* are some chairs here."

(*b*) *Interrogative.*

How? When? Where? Why? (Whence? Wherefore? Whither?). These are used for asking questions and occasionally for exclamations.

e.g. *Why* did you ring?   *When* do you go?
How are you?
(Exclamation: *How* good of you!
          What a pity it is!)

(*c*) *Conjunctive* (or Connecting).

The adverbs "how", "when", "where" ("whence" = "from where"; "whither" = "to where"), "why" can be used as conjunctions, and are then called conjunctive adverbs.

e.g. *He* showed me *where* he lived.
Tell me *why* you have come.

Note: In the sentence "The house *where* he lived" the word "where" = "in which" and is doing the work of a relative pronoun relating to "house", so "where" can here be called a relative adverb. Similarly, in "The day *when* he came", "when" = "on which" *but* in "Tell me where you went", the word "where" has not the meaning of "in which" and has no relation to "me".

Formation: Though many adverbs are formed by adding "-ly" to an adjective (e.g. wrong, wrong*ly*), some adverbs have the same forms as the adjective: e.g. I run *fast* (advb.); I am a *fast* runner (adj.).

A few adverbs have both the form identical with the adjective, and the form with "-ly" added to the adjective, and in these cases there is often a difference of meaning.

e.g. I arrived *late* (= at a late hour, or late for appointment).

I arrived *lately* (= recently).

Some adverbs are formed from nouns, with the aid of prefixes or suffixes.

e.g. *back*wards, *a*shore, side*ways*, week*ly*.

Comparison:

		Comparative	*Superlative*
(*a*) Adverbs of one syllable (and also "early") add "-er", "-est":	fast	fast*er*	fast*est*
(*b*) Adverbs of more than one syllable add "more", "most":	rapidly	*more* rapidly	*most* rapidly
(*c*) Irregular comparisons:			
	well	*better*	*best*
	badly	*worse*	*worst*
	little	*less*	*least*
	much	*more*	*most*
	late	*later*	*latest, last*
	forth	*further*	*furthest*

Note: "The" is really an adverb in the comparison: *the* sooner *the* better (the = by so much).

Position: The position of an adverb is very important, and can make a great difference to the meaning of a sentence.

e.g. *Foolishly*, I spoke to her (= unwisely).

I spoke *foolishly* to her (= in a foolish manner).

I *only* sleep in class (= do not listen or work).

I sleep *only* in class (= in class, but not in other places).

Rule: An adverb must, as a general rule, be placed next to the word it limits; it is usually placed just before this word except when the adverb limits a verb, in which

71

case it can come after the verb, if there is no danger of the adverb appearing to limit a word which follows.

> e.g. I sing *only* popular songs (limiting adj. "popular").
> I sang *only* yesterday (limiting advb. "yesterday").
> I whistle *frequently* but do not sing ⎫ (limiting verb
> I *only* whistle tunes; I cannot sing ⎭   "whistle").
>   (*not* I whistle *only* tunes).

Use: (1) An adverb should never be confused with an adjective, as the latter describes a noun or pronoun, which are the only parts of speech an adverb can never limit.

> e.g. I like to drive *fast*[1] in a *fast*[2] car.
>   ([1] advb. limiting verb "drive"; [2] adj. describing noun "car").
>   His *only* son, George, sang ("only" describes noun "son", so "only" must be an adjective here).
>   George *only* sang, and did not play the piano ("only" limits verb "sang". It is an adverb here).

(2) The difference between an adverb and a preposition is that the latter is always followed by, or governs, a noun or pronoun, thus completing a phrase.

> e.g. I fall *down* ("down" is here an adverb limiting verb "fall").
>   I fall *down* the steps ("down" is here a preposition showing relation between "I" or "fall" and "steps").

Errors: For errors in the use of adverbs, see Chapter XIV.

Adverb Equivalents: A phrase or a clause may do the work of an adverb (see also Chapters XI and XII).

> e.g. Phrases: He came *as quickly as possible, at full speed, by car.*
>   Clauses: I fell *when I was running, because I slipped.*

EXERCISES

A

Give adverbs corresponding to the following words:

day, angry, side, pride, heat, back, shore, sides, marvel, drift.

B

State which words are adverbs in the following sentences, and which word each limits.

1. He was hard hit.
2. I shall not sign.
3. Have they come yet?
4. Too many cooks are helping.
5. There are some pens here.
6. How are you feeling?
7. He tried to speak again.
8. I like French best.
9. She is so lovely.
10. Tomorrow it will be hot.

C

Write two sentences for each of the following words, using each as an adjective in the first and as an adverb in the second.

early, hard, last, much, only, wide, direct, enough, high, straight, late, further, ill, more, best.

D

In the following questions state whether the word in italics is an adverb, adjective, preposition, or conjunctive adverb.

1. Finally I went *inside*.
2. *Inside* the house I found a dog.
3. You are a *better* player.
4. I sing *better* than you.
5. That is where I went *wrong*.
6. That is a *wrong* use of a word.
7. He went a few days *after* to Paris.
8. He went *after* a few days.
9. *When* will you arrive.
10. *When* he arrives I shall leave.

E

Explain the difference in meaning in the following sentences:

1. (*a*) This lawn wants mowing badly.
   (*b*) This lawn badly wants mowing.
2. (*a*) My only pencil is lost.
   (*b*) Only my pencil is lost.
3. (*a*) He stopped short.
   (*b*) He will stop shortly.

4. (a) Happily, I found him alive.
   (b) I found him living happily in London.
5. (a) The burglar was hard pressed by his pursuers.
   (b) He pressed hard on the lever.
6. (a) Once I went to the cinema every week.
   (b) I went to the cinema once every week.

F

Write down the phrases or clauses that are doing the work of an adverb in the following sentences:

1. Please answer without delay.
2. I shall go if you give me permission.
3. In a few minutes the clock will strike.
4. He looked as white as a sheet.
5. We were treated with great kindness.

74

CHAPTER VII

PREPOSITIONS

Definition: A Preposition shows the relation between a noun or a pronoun and some other word in a sentence.

e.g. a gift *from* Mary
     from her ⎬ (noun and noun or pronoun).

   good *at* chess
        at it ⎬ (adj. and noun or pronoun).

   work *for* fun
        for me ⎬ (verb and noun or pronoun).

   energetically *for* his age ⎬ (adverb and noun or
                 for him ⎬ pronoun).

Types: The word "preposition" means "placed before". A large number of prepositions indicate position or direction.

e.g. on, in, above, under, to, from, towards.

Some prepositions consist of two prepositions, often combined in one word.

e.g. into, throughout, upon; on to, from behind.

Others are prepositional phrases.

e.g. on top of, by means of.

Some participles have prepositional force when they have no idea of actual action and are impersonal.

e.g. considering, regarding.
   Considering the weather, he ran well. (= in view of; "he" was not actually considering the weather.)
   Regarding this . . . (= in connection with.)

Prepositions help to make adjectival and adverbial phrases:

e.g. The house *near the corner* (adj.).
He ran *in front of the bus* (advb.).

"To" is used as a preposition to complete the infinitive of a verb.

e.g. I hope *to go*.

Case: A preposition is said to govern the noun or pronoun with which it is connected, and it requires this noun or pronoun to be in the objective case.

e.g. Between *him* and *me*.

Mistakes are easily made when the pronoun comes first in the sentence in questions, with the preposition placed at the end of the sentence.

e.g. *Who* were you speaking to? ("Who" should be "whom".)

Position: If possible, it is preferable to avoid ending sentences with a preposition, especially in writing. This is a question of style, however, and in speaking we naturally say in questions "What are you talking about?" and not "About what are you talking?"

Notes: (1) The preposition "to" is omitted in English before the indirect object, when this precedes the direct object.

e.g. I give (to) him a book.

(2) The words "a" and "o" are disguised prepositions in such expressions as:

sixpence a pound (= per).
nine o'clock (= of).

(3) Distinguishing between a preposition and an adverb. A preposition, unlike an adverb, is always followed by, or governs, a noun or pronoun, thus completing a phrase.

e.g. I fall *down* (adverb—modifying verb "fall").
I fall *down the ladder* (phrase, "down" showing relation

between "I" or "fall" and "ladder", and so acting as preposition).

(4) We must learn the correct preposition to use after certain nouns, adjectives, and verbs.

e.g. Noun: He was a contemporary *of* someone.
Adjective: He was contemporary *with* someone.
Verb: I congratulate him *on* winning.

In the case of verbs, we must also carefully distinguish between:

(i) Verb + preposition + noun.

e.g. I call *to* a friend.
(Shows relation between "I" and "friend".)

(ii) Verb + adverb + noun.

e.g. I call *in* the child (= I call the child in).
("In" does not show relation between "I" and "child", but is an adverb here, as the rearranged sentence shows.)

(iii) Verb + prepositional suffix. The preposition has lost its original force and function, and has become part of the verb, giving it a new meaning.

e.g. I call *on* the new doctor (= I visit him).
(No idea of "on" in adverbial or prepositional sense.)

There are numerous instances in English of prepositions used as suffixes to give the stem-verb different meanings.

e.g. I look up a word (no idea of "up").
I run in a new engine (no idea of "in").
I bring round an unconscious man (= I restore to consciousness).
I bring about a reconciliation (= I effect or negotiate).

Notice, too, the considerable difference in meaning between the following examples in the second of which "over" is a prefix to the verb.

e.g. I look *over* your work.
I *over*look your work.
(Similarly, "I take over his work, but overtake his car".)

77

In the case of nouns and adjectives, the choice of preposition often varies according to the meaning:

e.g. *Noun:* I have the key *of* the house.
I have the key *to* the problem.
Adj.: I am vexed *at* this happening (thing).
I am vexed *with* you (person).

A dictionary—and practice—will solve the problem of the correct preposition to use. Prefixes such as "e, ex," (out of, from), "con, com" (with), and "in, em, en" (in, into, on) give valuable clues.

In the case of some words, either of two prepositions is permissible, both being considered correct and conveying the same meaning.

e.g. aversion, averse *to* (or *from*) doing homework.

(5) Distinguishing between a preposition and a conjunction.

If there is ever difficulty in making this distinction, remember that a conjunction, unlike a preposition, does not govern a noun or pronoun in the objective case, but acts as a link only.

e.g. He ran *after* me (preposition + object "me").
He ran away *after* I turned round (conjunction linking two clauses).

"Without" can never be used as a conjunction.

e.g. He went *without* me (preposition).
He will not go *without* you come (wrong. Use conjunction "unless").

(6) The word "but" is an excellent illustration of a word used as preposition, adverb, and conjunction.

e.g. All *but* him were first (prep. but = except).
There is *but* one solution (advb. but = only).
It was clever, *but* (it was) dangerous (conj.).

Errors: For errors in the use of prepositions, see Chapter XIV.

EXERCISES

A

In the following sentences state which words are prepositions, and which words they govern as objects.

1. He lives near Bristol.
2. The man to whom I spoke.
3. In singing the head is raised.
4. All but Smith were invited.
5. We shall call after tea.

6. Between meals they rest.
7. Which of us is guilty?
8. He is free from danger.
9. I work till midnight.
10. What are you looking for?

B

State whether the words in italics are prepositions, adverbs, or conjunctions, and give reasons.

1. I have *but* one pen.
2. All *but* this were lost.
3. He is stupid *but* he is honest.
4. Will you do this *for* me?
5. Whom are you thinking *of*?

6. He *only* lent me this.
7. I wished to go, *only* I could not.
8. You were standing too *near*.
9. I work *after* tea.
10. *After* he has gone I am lonely.

C

Correct the following sentences, giving reasons for alterations. (See also Chapter XIV.)

1. I shall not go without you come too.
2. There was a wall between each garden.
3. He is paying no attention to you and I.
4. Divide this among the two boys.
5. She does not play the piano like George does.
6. Who are you referring to?

D

Write sentences with a suitable noun object of the preposition, to show clearly the different meanings of the following verbs when followed by the prepositions indicated.

1. to account for, to.
2. to break through, off.
3. to buy off, up.
4. to charge for, with.
5. to excuse for, from.

6. deal in, with.
7. inquire after, into.
8. live for, on.
9. succeed in, to.
10. take after, over.

79

E

Fill in the correct preposition.

1. to answer — a crime.
2. to border — the absurd.
3. to break — relations.
4. to confer — problems.
5. to encroach — property.
6. to live — one's means.
7. to preside — a meeting.
8. to reflect — a problem.
9. to trade — textiles.
10. averse — doing homework.
11. conspicuous — bravery.
12. different — others.
13. insensible — pain.
14. remote — towns.
15. an authority — painting.
16. a contemporary — Nelson.
17. a key — the problem.
18. a parody — a poem.
19. a reflection — his character.
20. an antipathy — Smith.
21. conversant — French.
22. prejudiced — amateurs.
23. incensed — such conduct.
24. acquiesce — this plan.
25. confident — success.

CHAPTER VIII

CONJUNCTIONS AND INTERJECTIONS

CONJUNCTIONS

Definition: A Conjunction is a word used to join words, phrases, or sentences:

> e.g. cats *and* dogs: in the day-time *and* at night;
> I saw him *and* I spoke to him.

Kinds: Conjunctions are divided into two kinds:

    A. Co-ordinating (= joining parts of equal value).
    B. Subordinating (= joining a dependent clause to a principal or main clause).

Types of A. Co-ordinating conjunctions are of four types:

1. *Adding*: and, both.

e.g. He is intelligent *and* energetic.

2. *Alternative* (i.e. giving a choice):
otherwise, or, either . . . or, neither . . . nor.

e.g. He is *either* a scoundrel *or* a fool.

3. *Contrasting* (i.e. setting one idea against another):
but, yet, nevertheless.

e.g. He is poor *but* he is honest.

4. *Proving* (i.e. giving reasons or consequences):
therefore, then, for, so.

e.g. It is late, *therefore* we must go.

Notes: (i) Note the correlating pairs which must

always go together in Alternative Conjunctions; i.e. either . . . or; neither . . . nor; not only . . . but also.

e.g. He is *neither* honest *nor* poor

and these pairs must always precede words that are the same part of speech.

e.g. He is either *lazy* or *stupid* ("lazy" and "stupid" are both adjectives).

(ii) Note the use of "not", "or", and "nor" in the following sentence:

I will not write *or*[1] call, *nor*[2] will I apologise.

    1. One idea *added* to another.
    2. One idea *alternating* with another.

Types of B. Subordinating Conjunctions join a dependent or subordinate clause (a sentence which is part of a longer sentence, and which would not make complete sense alone) to the main or principal clause.

e.g. I shall start (Main Clause) *when* he arrives. (Subordinate Clause.)

These are of three types:

1. Those introducing clauses doing the work of an *Adverb* (i.e. modifying or limiting the meaning of a verb, adjective, or adverb).

e.g. as, when, before, after, where, though, because, so that, if, etc.
I shall go *before* he arrives.
He will write *if* he can.
Look *where* you are going.
We like him *because* he is kind.

For details of the nine types of Adverbial Clause, see Chapter XII.

2. Those introducing clauses doing the work of a *Noun* (acting as subject, object, or complement of a verb).

(i) "that" e.g. I think *that* he is ill (= "an idea", object of "think").

"That" is often omitted in English.

e.g. I think he is ill.

(ii) The adverbs "how", "when", "why", "where" can be used as conjunctions (as we have seen above), and are then called conjunctive adverbs. They introduce clauses doing the work of a noun in the following examples:

e.g. I wonder how he did this (= object of "wonder").
Why he did this is inexplicable (= subject of "is").

3. Those introducing clauses doing the work of an *Adjective* (i.e. describing a noun).

e.g. "when", "where", "as".
This is the house *where* I live ("where I live tells us which "house" here).
That is the day *when* we arrive.
This is the same book *as* you have bought.

Notes: (i) The pronouns "who, which, that" are called relative pronouns rather than conjunctions, though they join clauses and do the work of conjunctions and introduce adjectival clauses.

(ii) The word "as" when preceded by "such" or "as" is used as a pronoun and a conjunction simultaneously, and is called a conjunctive pronoun or relative pronoun:

e.g. He is not such a fool *as* he looks (= as that he looks).

(iii) "Whilst" is another and less usual form of "while". Similarly, "though" or "although", "until" or "till", may be used. "Until" is preferable when starting a sentence.

Errors: For errors in the use of Conjunctions, see Chapter XIV.

INTERJECTIONS

An interjection is a word used to express some emotion or to call the attention of some person. An interjection plays no part in the grammatical construction of a sentence. Interjections can be either exclamatory sounds (e.g. "Oh!", "Ah!", "Hi!"), or various parts of speech used as exclamations (e.g. "Nonsense!", "What!", "Splendid!", "Well!", "Hark!"). An interjection = a word or words "thrown into" a sentence, and interjections can occur in various positions.

> e.g. *Ugh!* This tastes horrible. You've tried it, *eh?*
> *Hullo!* Is anyone in? *Dear me,* the house is empty.
> It is, *alas,* too late.

Notes: (i) Exclamations such as "Help!", "Listen!", "Look!", etc., are commands—complete sentences (so *not* interjections), with subject understood, i.e. (You) listen!

(ii) Other parts of speech are also often really complete sentences, with certain words understood, used exclamatorily.

> e.g. How sad! = How sad it is!

(iii) "Yes" and "No" are termed particles, and are equivalent to affirmative or negative sentences.

> e.g. Yes = I accept your statement, or request.

EXERCISES

A

CONJUNCTIONS

(*a*) Insert suitable conjunctions, and state whether they are co-ordinating or subordinating:

1. I have — paper and pencil.
2. He has neither skill — courage.
3. They will fail — hard they try.
4. He will escape — you stop him.
5. She is slow — she always succeeds.
6. I held the rope — I should fall.
7. Your house is as old — mine (is).
8. We shall pay you — you sign this.
9. She will not wait — the rain stops.
10. He must — apologise or go.
11. Why don't you do — I am doing?
12. We wonder — he shouted.

13. You will fail — you are lazy.
14. I think — you are unwise.
15. He showed us — he did it.

(b) State which words are conjunctions in the following passage:

"As soon as I saw him, I knew that he was an escaped convict. He had neither hat nor coat, and was shivering, though he tried not to show it. I did not know what to do, but if he escaped before I telephoned the police it would be I who was to blame. I wished to avoid a struggle, for I was smaller than he was, so I pretended not to notice him."

(c) State whether the subordinate clauses in the following sentences are doing the work of a noun, adjective, or adverb:

1. That he is ill is evident.
2. That is the office where he works.
3. Tell me what he says.
4. If she does not want to go, I shall start without her.
5. I wonder if she will arrive.
6. Here is the house that I designed.
7. Do you think that this house is attractive.
8. He is happy although he is poor.
9. You should look where you are going.
10. I do not know where we are going.

B

INTERJECTIONS

Write down one suitable interjection for each of the following:

Alarm, surprise, pain, warning, annoyance, approval, amusement, joy, disgust, sorrow.

CHAPTER IX

VOCABULARY

The vocabulary of the English language is a very extensive one; our language is as rich in words as our history is in incidents.

The two main sources of our language are, as we have already seen, firstly Anglo-Saxon (or Old English), the language brought by those bold invaders from northern Europe who gave us our basic language (words dealing mainly with the simple life of the home, the field, and also with fighting); secondly, Latin and Greek, which came into our language mainly at the time of the Renaissance in the sixteenth century, when classical scholars brought us books, art, philosophy, and the first developments of science and medicine, with a wealth of new words.

No living language stands still, and words have been and are still constantly being added by borrowings from other languages—centuries of foreign wars, of exploration, and of trading have brought us a rich harvest of these—or by the composition of entirely new words to express some fresh development or invention. Thus we have such borrowings as "banana" and "cigar" from the Spanish; "fiancé" and "attaché" from the French; "piano" and "crescendo" from Italian; "coffee" and "cotton" from Arabic; "bazaar" and "caravan" from Persian; and "cocoa" and "chocolate" from Mexican, to illustrate the importance and variety of these additions.

The constant development of new ideas and inventions

has made necessary also the introduction of new words by composition (i.e. by joining a prefix or suffix, or even a complete word, to another word, the basic or root word) to form a compound word. Examples of this during the last century of astonishing invention and of scientific and medical research are "submarine" (Latin "sub" = *under*, and "mare" = *sea*), "aerodrome" (Greek "aer" = *air*, "dromos" = *a course*), and "television" (Greek "tele" = *afar*, and Latin "videre" = *to see*), and simpler words such as "fountain-pen" and "wireless". Other words called for by modern inventions or developments have been borrowed from other languages, such as "camouflage" and "queue" from the French; others have been taken from our own language and given a new meaning, such as "tank" for the armoured vehicle, or based even in this modern form on Latin, as in the case of "radio" (Latin "radius" = *a ray*).

If we wish to understand the meanings of difficult words and to increase our individual vocabulary, we must have available a good dictionary. It is worth the extra expense to have a dictionary which gives not only the meanings of words but also their pronunciation and derivation (i.e. source from which they come)—and it will be an added advantage if the dictionary also gives derivatives (i.e. words formed from the original words), phrases, and expressions in which the words are employed, and synonyms (i.e. words of very similar meaning).

Most of our prefixes and suffixes come from Early English, Latin, and Greek.

The following lists will be found helpful:

Prefixes (additions to the beginning of words):

Early English

a (= on)	aboard, afloat.
be (= by)	beset, bemoan, beside.
for (negation)	forgo, forget.
(intensive)	forlorn.

87

fore (= before)	foresee, foretell.
mis (= wrong)	mistake, misspelling.
un (= not)	unprotected, unwilling.
with (= against)	withstand.

Latin

a, ab (= from)	avert, abstain.
a, ad (= to)	affix, admit.
ante (= before)	anteroom.
bene (= well)	benefactor, beneficent.
bi, bis (= two, twice)	bicycle, biscuit.
co, con (= together)	co-operate, concur.
contra (= against)	contradict.
demi (= half)	demigod.
ex (= out of)	extract.
in (= in)	inject, immigrate.
in (= not)	ineligible, impossible.
inter (= between)	international, intervention.
multi (= many)	multicoloured.
male (= badly)	malefactor, malnutrition.
non (= not)	nonsense.
post (= after)	postpone, postscript.
pre (= before)	precede.
re (= again)	renew, replace.
re (= back)	retire, retract.
semi (= half)	semicircle.
sub (= under)	submarine.
super (= above)	superimpose, supervise.
trans (= across)	transport, transpose.
ultra (= beyond)	ultramarine.
vice (= instead of)	viceroy, vice-consul.

Also note numbers, e.g.

unus (= one)	unilateral.
duo (= two)	dual, duplicate.
tres (= three)	tripod, triangle.
quattuor (= four)	quadrangle, quartet.
quinque (= five)	quintuplets.

sex (= six)	sextet.
octo (= eight)	octet.
decem (= ten)	decade, decimate.

Greek

anti (= against)	antipathy.
arch (= chief)	archbishop.
auto (= self)	automatic.
dia (= through)	diameter.
epi (= upon)	epitaph.
ge (= earth)	geology, geography.
hyper (= over, too)	hypercritical.
homo (= same)	homogeneous.
mono (= single)	monoplane.
pan (= all)	panorama.
peri (= around)	perimeter.
phil (= loving)	philanthropy.
poly (= many)	polytechnic.
syn (= with)	synchronise.
tele (= at a distance)	telephone.

Suffixes (additions to the end of words) are chiefly used to form verbs, adjectives, and nouns from a root or basic word, and their use has already been shown in the chapters on those parts of speech.

Latin and Greek Roots

There are certain Latin and Greek words which form the root or basis of so many words in English that they should be learnt. The following list gives some of the most important of these:

Latin	*English Derivatives*
annus (year)	annual, biannual, perennial.
caput (head)	capital, caption.
civis (citizen)	city, citizen, civic.
colere (cultivate)	cultivate, culture.
dicere (to say)	diction, contradict.

ducere (to lead)	conduct, conducive.
facere (to do, make)	factory, manufacture.
flectere (to bend)	inflection, reflect.
jungere (to join)	junction, conjunction.
legis (of the law)	legal, legislature.
magnus (great)	magnify, magnitude.
manus (hand)	manuscript, manual.
mittere (to send)	missile, mission, emit.
spectare (to gaze)	spectator, spectacle.
spirare (to breathe)	inspire, perspire, aspire.
terra (earth)	terrestrial, territory, Mediterranean.

Greek

aster (star)	asterisk, astronomer.
chronos (time)	chronometer, chronic.
gramma (letter)	telegram, gramophone.
grapho (I write)	telegraph, geography.
hudor (water)	hydraulic, hydroplane.
logos (word)	logic, mythology.
metron (measure)	geometry, meter.
mikros (small)	microscope.
pathos (feeling)	pathetic, sympathy.
phone (voice)	telephone, microphone.
sophos (wise)	philosophy, sophisticated.
therme (heat)	thermometer.

Words Derived from Proper Names

Many words owe their origin to the names of people and places, but are not themselves written with an initial capital letter, e.g.

sandwich—the Earl of Sandwich "invented" sandwiches in the eighteenth century so that he should not have to leave the gaming-tables for meals.

vandal—the Vandals laid waste Rome and much of Europe in the fifth century.

silhouette—Silhouette, a French barber, cut "silhouettes" of his clients from paper.

boycott—to refuse social or commercial relations with someone, as the Irish did in the case of a Captain Boycott.

quixotic—doing noble deeds impulsively, from the character Don Quixote in Cervantes' book of that name.

port—wine from Oporto (Portugal).

calico—material, originally from Calicut (India).

Months and days have retained the capital letter, e.g.

July, August—months named after Roman Emperors Julius and Augustus.

January—from Janus, mythical god who faced two ways, backward to the old year, forward to the new year.

Thursday—day of Thor, god of thunder.

Other words used as similes or comparisons, retain their initial capital letter, and indicate a person possessing the qualities of the original character, e.g.

Biblical: a Solomon (wise man), a Samson (strong man).

Mythical: a Hercules (strength, courage), a Venus (beauty).

Most dictionaries will give the origin of these interesting words.

Phrases borrowed from foreign languages without alteration

There are many Latin phrases which we use because they express some idea with admirable brevity.

e.g. "vice versa" (the relationship being reversed: the other way round).

"ad nauseam" (to a degree that causes disgust).

"post mortem" (examination of dead body to ascertain cause of death).

There are also many French expressions which we employ for the same reason.

e.g. "carte blanche" (authorisation to do whatever one wishes).

"tête-à-tête" (intimate conversation between two persons).

Foreign phrases should not be employed if a word or phrase exists already in English which can express the idea equally effectively.

Most dictionaries include a list of frequently employed foreign phrases and classical quotations, with their meanings.

Words that have changed their original meaning

Many words in every language, and particularly in English, have a very different meaning from that which they had originally. "Prevent" originally meant "to come before" (as it did in its Latin form "praevenire") as exemplified in the Prayer Book ("Prevent us, O Lord, in all our doings"). Now it is used only in the sense of "to stop or avoid".

Sir Christopher Wren, in the reign of James II, writing of his architectural masterpiece, St. Paul's Cathedral, used "amusing" for "amazing", "awful" for "awe-inspiring", and "artificial" for "artistic"—all used perfectly correctly at that time.

Some words have degenerated in meaning, such as "crafty" which used to mean "skilful" but now is used only in a derogatory sense for "deceitful". "Shrewd", on the other hand, which once meant "mischievous", is now used for "wise" or "clever", but it is also used for "effective" in the phrase "he dealt him a shrewd blow".

Americans ("divided from the English by a common language as well as by a vast ocean") have naturally tended to coin many new words and to give different meanings to many English words (as well as to employ different methods of spelling English words in many cases). The word "pants", meaning in England an undergarment worn by the male sex, becomes "trousers" in America, and "suspenders" which keep up Englishmen's socks (and Englishwomen's stockings) become "braces" in America and suspend the American's "pants"; and "petrol" becomes "gasoline" or more simply "gas". Equally surprisingly, candidates in America "fill out" forms (i.e. documents) and "run" for office (i.e. Government appointments), while Englishmen still "fill in" official forms and "stand" for office.

Figurative meanings (when an implied comparison is made by the use of a word in other than its literal or usual meaning) have given numerous additional meanings to many words. For example, the word "head", in addition to its anatomical meaning, can mean "chief" in the case of the head of a house, or school, or business, and is also used for the top of a mast or the upper end of a lake.

Similarly, many verbs are used figuratively, for though we "run a race" we also "run a risk" and "run through a book", not to mention "run over a pedestrian", "run into trouble" and "run up a bill". Engines also "run", and we "run them in" when they are new.

Slang or Colloquialisms (= words used in everyday conversation that are not literary)

The above terms are used to describe words and phrases that are frequently employed to give force to the daily casual conversation of most individuals, but which are not recognised or permitted in correct literary usage.

> e.g. "dud" (useless or faulty).
> "fed up", "browned off" (very depressed).
> "to kick the bucket", "peg out" (to die).

Some slang expressions are merely convenient abbreviations, such as "pub" for "public-house" (= "an inn", for foreigners' guidance), and "exam" for "examination". Others are merely cases of using a word in its wrong context or as an exaggeration, as in speaking of "a divine dance" or "a revolting meal". Many have a quality of humour, apart from their force and brevity. To call "handcuffs" "bracelets", or "mad" "cuckoo" is a humorous softening of the hard truth, and such metaphorical phrases as "a big noise" (an important person) or "a live wire" (an energetic person) are admittedly most colourful and effective.

93

Slang expressions are found in many walks of life, but especially in the armed forces and in school life. Most trades and professions have their own particular colloquialisms or jargon.

Dialect Words or Provincialisms

There are many words that are not slang, but are used only in the everyday speech of certain regions and are not permissible in correct literary usage.

The foreign visitor will find a vast difference in dialect in the different parts of our small island, the greatest variation being between the West Country dialects and the North Country dialects, many of which are unintelligible to an Englishman who is unfamiliar with them.

In the West "ourn" for ours", "childer" for "children", "varmint" for "vermin", are common examples; in the North "laking" for "playing" and "gradely" for "excellent"; in Scotland "bairns" for "children" and "to greet" for "to weep" are common examples.

Archaisms or Obsolete Words (i.e. words no longer in current use)

Just as words are always being added to a language, and other words are changing their original meaning, there are some words which have vanished from present-day English because a more suitable or modern word has supplanted them.

e.g. yclept (named, called).
prithee (I pray thee = please).
anon (later).
twain (two).

To read Chaucer's "Canterbury Tales" in its original form we should now require a special dictionary of Early English, and Shakespeare's plays are full of words the Elizabethans knew, but which are no longer in current use.

Synonyms (= the same name) are words that have a similar or almost similar meaning. There is, strictly speaking, a slight shade of difference between most synonyms, as, for example, between "tired" and "exhausted", the latter indicating a more advanced degree of tiredness. A person can have a "look of despair" without throwing a despairing "glance". If a person has an "inquiring" mind, he is praised, but if he is "inquisitive" he is liable to be unpopular. We say these words are not exactly "synonymous".

Examples:

Nouns: anger, rage, fury, alarm, fear, fright, terror.
Adjectives: famous, celebrated, noted, renowned.
Verbs: retort, reply, answer, respond, ask, beg, entreat, request, implore.
Adverbs: quickly, rapidly, hastily, speedily.

Antonyms are words opposite in meaning.

e.g. *Noun:* doctor, patient.
 Adjective: active, passive.
 Verb: create, destroy.
 Adverb: quickly, slowly.

Homonyms are words that have the same spelling and sound but are not connected in meaning or use.

e.g. canon (a rank in the Church).
 canon (a rule or law).
 bill (an account).
 bill (beak of a bird).
 down (small feathers).
 down (hill).
 down (direction).
 down (to knock down).

Similarly: arm, hide, bank, blow, stage, hand, fair, mine, etc.

Homophones are words that have the same sound but are different in spelling and meaning.

e.g. a *pair* of gloves.
　I ate a *pear*.
　I *pare* my nails.

Similarly: rain, reign, rein.
　　　　　current, currant.
　　　　　beech, beach.
　　　　　peel, peal.
　　　　　pier, peer.
　　　　　vane, vein, vain, etc.

Homographs are words that have the same spelling, but differ in their meaning and pronunciation, as they are derived from different words.

e.g. lead (noun), a metal.
　lead (verb), to conduct.

Similarly: row, tear, etc.

Choice of Words

An excellent principle to adopt is the rule that on no occasion should a long word be used merely for the sake of length, when a shorter word is available that expresses the same idea.

We should not write "I intend to undertake a peregrination of limited duration in the metropolis" for "I am going for a short walk in the city", or "a terminological inexactitude" for "a lie" (unless, of course, we wish to employ such lengthy circumlocutions as a form of humour).

Words Frequently Confused

There is a number of words in English which are neither homonyms nor homophones, but which are sufficiently similar in sound for their meanings to be confused.

e.g. affect, effect; luxurious, luxuriant; precede, proceed; eminent, imminent; etc.

In all cases when we are called upon to write sentences to show clearly the difference in meaning between two words that are very easily confused, it is essential to add an extra phrase or clause after the selected word has been introduced to show clearly that we understand its meaning. For example, if we are asked to show the difference between "illegible" and "eligible", the mere statement "His writing was illegible" conveys no definition of "illegible" at all, as it could equally well mean "excellent", "small", "neat", etc., to the uninitiated. If, however, we write a sentence with an explanatory clause such as: "His writing was illegible, as the letters were badly formed, and obscured by numerous blots", the meaning of "illegible" is quite clear.

Similarly, in the sentence "He obtained the post for which he was eligible" the word "eligible" might mean "recommended", "interviewed", or "competing", etc., whereas if we write "He was eligible for the post of lecturer, as he had the necessary qualifications and experience", the meaning of "eligible" (= suitably qualified) is no longer uncertain.

Words used too frequently and too carelessly

There is far too great a tendency to be lazy and to overwork adjectives such as "nice", "good", "lovely", "awful"; the verbs "have" and "get", and the adverbs "awfully", "terribly", and phrases such as "a lot of", "kind of", "a sort of", when more suitable words exist to give greater accuracy and variety.

Do not write:

"I got up early, and got my own breakfast. As it was a nice day, I got out my bicycle to go for a nice ride into the country, where I had a lovely time enjoying the lovely scenery."

It is less vague and less monotonous to write:

"I got up early, and prepared my own breakfast. As it

was a fine day, I took out my bicycle and went for a pleasant ride into the country, where I spent an enjoyable time admiring the beautiful scenery."

Dictionary Definitions

An excellent way of improving our knowledge of the real meaning of words, of widening our vocabulary, and of learning to express ourselves clearly and concisely is to practise giving a dictionary definition of words. These can be checked afterwards with the definitions given in a good dictionary.

In defining any word, we must remember three basic rules: (1) To be accurate, (2) to be as brief as possible, and (3) to avoid using long or obscure words that really require further explanation and definition themselves.

It is an excellent plan to study the definitions of a few common words in a dictionary before attempting any definitions by ourselves.

For example, it is obviously insufficient to define a zebra as a "quadruped with alternate black and pale stripes", as this description would be equally applicable to a tiger, to some domestic cats, and to various other quadrupeds. It is similarly inaccurate to say that a table is "a piece of furniture with a square flat top supported by four legs", as many tables are not square, but round or oval, and the number of legs can be anything from one (in the case of a pedestal table) to a dozen or more. A table can also be a set of facts and figures arranged in columns. If, however, we define a zebra as "a striped horse-like quadruped", we have achieved an accurate and helpful answer to an inquirer.

The importance of accuracy and the avoidance of jumping to hasty conclusions cannot, therefore, be too strongly stressed, especially when we are confronted with Smith minor's most unfortunate description of a vixen as "a vicar's wife", and of an epistle as "the wife of an apostle", or his confused though colourful definition of a cuckoo as "a bird which lays other birds' eggs i.1 its own nest".

If a word has more than one meaning, number these (1), (2), etc., and in the case of a word used in an unusual way in some special figurative phrase, quote the phrase.

Phrases: We have in English a great many "stock phrases" based on contrast or similarity, on repetition, and on rhyme or alliteration, all of which emphasise some idea.

e.g. *Contrast:* It was a question of sink or swim.
Similarity: He was well and truly beaten.
He has a free and easy manner.
Repetition: They raced neck and neck.
Rhyme: I will succeed by hook or by crook.
He was fairly and squarely beaten.
Alliteration: He struggled with might and main to escape.

EXERCISES

A

Give a "dictionary" definition of the following:

Nouns: saucer, cork, mallet, needle, glacier, barrister, diary, dormouse, taxi, mortgage.

Adjectives: brusque, tepid, abnormal, formal, rustic, nocturnal, septic, pneumatic, transparent, aural.

Verbs: decimate, surmise, precede, expunge, supersede, rectify, petrify, pacify, facilitate, redress.

B

Write sentences to show clearly the difference between the following pairs of words

Adjectives	*Adjectives*
callow, callous.	official, officious.
fatal, fateful.	eminent, imminent.
continuous, continual.	honourable, honorary.
credible, creditable.	ingenious, ingenuous.

Adjectives

incredible, incredulous.
luxurious, luxuriant.
masterly, masterful.
negligent, negligible.
necessary, necessitous.
rural, rustic.
sceptical, septic.
superfluous, superficial.
hypocritical, hypercritical.
urban, urbane.
social, sociable.
exhaustive, exhausting.
practical, practicable.
popular, populous.
unapproachable, irreproachable.
insoluble, insolvent.
judicious, judicial.
imaginative, imaginary.
momentary, momentous.
explicit, implicit.
forceful, forcible.
notable, notorious.
economic, economical.

Verbs

lose, loose.
adopt, adapt.
accede, exceed.

Verbs

accept, except.
defer, differ.
collaborate, corroborate.
deprecate, depreciate.
deduce, deduct.
precede, proceed.
insulate, isolate.

Nouns

allusion, illusion.
cemetery, symmetry.
descent, dissent.
stimulus, stimulant.
disposition, disposal.
genius, genus.
receipt, recipe.
precedent, precedence.
elegy, eulogy.
timidity, temerity.
warder, warden.
emigrant, immigrant.
bravery, bravado.

Various Parts of Speech

affect, effect.
elicit, illicit.
principal, principle.
stationary, stationery.
confidant, confident.

C

Give one synonym for each of the following words:

shorten, permanent, hateful, uncertain, endure, blame, calm, unite, courteous, retire, examine, result, alarm, praise, confess, error, alter, completely, reply, conquer.

D

Replace the phrases or clauses in italics by a single word, making any necessary changes in sentence construction.

(a) Write down a *word similar in meaning to this word*.
(b) The arrangements I have made are *only for the time being*.

(c) This animal *can live both on land and in water.*

(d) I am sure she *has no right to the title she uses.*

(e) The price of tea *goes up and down from day to day.*

(f) The country is at present in a state *where there is no law or order.*

(g) The patient is now *recovering his health* at the seaside.

(h) *A disease which spread rapidly* broke out in the village.

(i) The farmer's fields were *entirely covered by the floods.*

(j) He is fortunate, for he *can use either hand equally well.*

(k) I am suffering from *loss of feeling* in my left leg.

(l) The general has just published *the story of his own life.*

(m) This plant is *one which comes up year after year.*

(n) That house is in such a state that it is *not fit to live in.*

(o) She *spoke almost the whole time* during the conversation.

Explain, by giving brief definitions, the difference between the following homophones:

curb, kerb; assent, ascent; beach, beech; bridal, bridle; serial, cereal; colonel, kernel; cord, chord; current, currant; councillor, counsellor; hoard, horde; muscle, mussel; cue, queue; reign, rain; sow, sew; vane, vein; yoke, yolk; story, storey; complement, compliment; sight, site; peer, pier.

E

Give an antonym (word opposite in meaning) for each of the following:

Nouns: failure, coward, poverty, chaos, surplus, fault, ascent, sense, stupidity, sympathy.

Verbs: attract, suppress, praise, inspire, construct, help, embark, magnify, clarify, accelerate.

Adjectives: literal, benevolent, optimistic, luxuriant, noble, enormous, logical, temporary, senile, final.

F

Write separate sentences to show clearly two different meanings of each of the following words:

down, bear, bill, seal, blow, stage, arm, bank, sole, pier, mean, toast, tear, toll, fair, mine, row, lead, right, fine.

G

Replace the words in italics by more suitable words:

(a) There is an *awful lot* of coffee grown in Brazil.

(*b*) I think the hat she has bought is *ghastly*.

(*c*) That was a *pretty good* rose you exhibited.

(*d*) We must try *to get hold of* a ticket.

(*e*) My aunt gave us a *lovely* meal, and took us to a *nice* film.

H

Give the equivalent in English of the following words or phrases borrowed from other languages:

sang-froid, siesta, début, sub rosa, cul-de-sac, sine qua non, pianissimo, entre nous, ipso facto, prima facie, coup de grâce, viva voce, esprit de corps, prima donna, bona fides, modus operandi, vice versa, soirée, hors de combat, au fait, faux pas, ad nauseam, fait accompli, locum tenens, post mortem.

I

Select the correct word from the words in brackets:

(*a*) The conditions under which he worked were (intolerant, intolerable).

(*b*) His story "Journey to the Moon" was a fine piece of (imaginary, imaginative) writing.

(*c*) The flower show was a (biennial, biannual) event, taking place in May and August.

(*d*) He repeated the prayers in a (reverent, reverend) voice.

(*e*) The manager was pompous, and treated me in a most (imperial, imperious) manner.

(*f*) The general wore all his medals, as it was a (ceremonious, ceremonial) occasion.

(*g*) We are afraid of hurting his feelings, as he is very (sensitive, sensible).

(*h*) I cannot find my lost relative, though I have made (exhausting, exhaustive) inquiries.

J

Divide the following words up into their separate parts, and explain the meaning of each part:

gramophone, hinterland, agriculture, philosopher, autobiography, biscuit, Mediterranean, sympathy, antarctic, preview, proceed, impecunious, withstand, immigrant, perimeter, heterogeneous, perennial, subscription, telephone, peninsula, posthumous, polytechnic, malefactor, synchronise, atheist, asterisk, forgo, thermometer, hypersensitive, multilateral.

K

Use the following words in pairs of sentences, to show that they can differ in meaning:

discover, invent; inquiring, inquisitive; irregular, abnormal; odd, strange; capacity, ability; group, gang; calamity, misfortune; illiterate, ignorant; neglect, negligence; house, dwelling; cruelty, ferocity; courage, audacity; stoop, cringe; think, ponder; value, appraise; renew, revive; vigorous, violent; observe, notice; contrary, opposite; senseless, stupid.

L

Explain briefly the meaning of the following:

a bottleneck, a blueprint, a green belt, an omnibus edition, a service flat, face value, a red herring, a blank cheque, a moral victory, Dutch courage.

M

Find suitable adjectives to replace the following phrases:

(a) living in or connected with water;
(b) above the speed of sound;
(c) able to speak two languages fluently;
(d) slow to relinquish a hold or purpose;
(e) relating to events of the present time;
(f) taking place during the night;
(g) full of gaiety and life;
(h) displaying or showing off anything unduly;
(i) dating from the time of a person's birth;
(j) showing patches of different colours.

N

Find suitable verbs to replace the following phrases:

(a) to spend the winter in sleep;
(b) to prove or test the truth of some fact;
(c) to make more beautiful or handsome;
(d) to throw overboard to lighten a boat;
(e) to draft or lay down a law;

(*f*) to settle a quarrel between two parties;

(*g*) to recover from illness or exhaustion;

(*h*) to speak or write in praise of somebody;

(*i*) to move or appear like waves;

(*j*) to increase the speed of some event or machine.

O

The following proper nouns have given us adjectives spelt with a small initial letter. Use each in a sentence to illustrate its meaning:

McAdam, Satan, Meander, Pasteur, Mercury, Hercules, Gargantua, Quixote, Mars, Stentor.

P

Find a single noun to replace each of the following phrases:

(*a*) The practice of talking about oneself.

(*b*) A man who thinks of the welfare of his fellow-men.

(*c*) A person who studies insects scientifically.

(*d*) A person who wishes to destroy all law and order.

(*e*) A person who gives false evidence in a legal case.

(*f*) A person who has attained the age of 100.

(*g*) The product of two metals fused together.

(*h*) An animal or plant living in or on another.

(*i*) A person who takes a dismal view of everything.

(*j*) A many-sided geometrical figure.

Q

Write sentences to illustrate clearly the correct use of each of the following words:

Nouns	*Verbs*	*Adverbs*
migration	resuscitate	evasively
hypocrisy	co-ordinate	implicitly
sinecure	obliterate	superficially
intuition	perpetuate	ceremoniously
anthology	supersede	quixotically
environment	instigate	involuntarily
probation	ostracise	automatically
criterion	assimilate	precipitously
dilemma	prohibit	obtrusively
obsession	irrigate	irrevocably

Adjectives	*Adjectives*
hydraulic	gregarious
meticulous	phlegmatic
exorbitant	subversive
cosmopolitan	omnivorous
precocious	fundamental
synthetic	garrulous
thermostatic	obsolete
posthumous	derelict
ephemeral	deleterious
plausible	lucrative

CHAPTER X

SPELLING

Statisticians compute that misspellings account for one-fifth of all errors committed in examinations, so the subject of spelling is certainly worth a chapter to itself.

There are teachers, and they are numerous and despairing, who say that it is impossible to teach spelling. It seems worthwhile, however, to make a list of the few definite and helpful rules that can be applied to English spelling; it is also valuable to make a list of some words in everyday use which are frequently misspelt.

The whole trouble with English spelling is, of course, that we do not in so many cases spell words phonetically (i.e. by sound), as such overworked examples as "though", "through", "thorough", and "cough" illustrate. The foreigner studying English pronunciation who, after a day spent in mastering such problems, excusably abandoned all hope and shot himself on being confronted by the statement "Noel Coward's 'Cavalcade'—pronounced success" in neon lights above a theatre, has every Englishman's sympathy. It is too late now to make our spelling more logical and more phonetic, especially as so many words with the same sound show their different meanings by their spelling, such as "beach" and "beech", "cord" and "chord", etc. Even if at some future date Parliament, with the aid of television and radio, were to attempt a reformation, "I luv u" is unlikely to take the place of "I love you" in prose or poetry.

The fact is that, apart from a few helpful rules, spelling

can largely be mastered (*a*) by writing out daily a few words commonly misspelt, and (*b*) by a process of visual concentration, an effort to remember a pictorial image of a word so that any misspelling of that word offends the eye. A knowledge of the derivation of any word is also, obviously, most helpful.

Accents: There are no written accents in English as there are in French and many other languages.

A hyphen is used to combine two words closely connected which it is desired to pronounce as one word without a separating pause, e.g. ex-president, mother-in-law, public-spirited.

A diæresis (¨) is placed over the second of two consecutive vowels when it is desired to show that they must each be pronounced separately, e.g. "coöperation" (or "co-operation").

In such borrowings from the French as "café", the accent is retained even when the word is not written with inverted commas or printed in italics to show it is a foreign word, e.g. They went into a café. Similarly "clientèle", "fête".

Definitions

A syllable is any part of a word which has a distinct sound of its own.

e.g. syl-la-ble.

The vowels are "a, e, i, o, u".

("y" is sometimes used as a vowel, taking the place of "i", e.g. sky. "w" is a vowel in such combinations as "-ew", "-ow".)

(Vowels denote a simple sound of the voice that can be produced without the help of a consonant.)

A diphthong is the union of two vowel sounds in a single compound sound.

e.g. *oil, out, please.*

A *consonant* is a letter that can be sounded only with the aid of a vowel (viz. b, c, d, f, g, h, j, k, l, m, n, p, q, r, s, t, v, w, x, y, z).

A *prefix* is a syllable or syllables added at the beginning of a word.

e.g. *mis*spelling, *un*wind.

A *suffix* is a syllable or syllables added at the end of a word.

e.g. need*less*, excite*ment*.

(The word to which a prefix or suffix is added is called the "root".)

A *ligature* (joining of two vowels: i.e. Cæsar) is no longer necessary in English, e.g. manoeuvre. In "mediaeval" and "encyclopaedia" the "a" may now be omitted.

Stress: Although there is no written accent in English, there is often a very definite accent or stress on one particular syllable in the pronunciation of words of more than one syllable. This is marked at the end of the stressed syllable (e.g. hyp'ocrite, indefat'igable) in most dictionaries.

In some pairs of two-syllable words the stress on the first syllable indicates a noun or adjective; on the second or last syllable, a verb, e.g.

Noun or Adjective	*Verb*
ab'sent	absent'
ab'stract	abstract'
ac'cent	accent'
con'duct	conduct'
com'pound	compound'
con'tract	contract'
con'verse	converse'
de'sert	desert'
es'say	essay'
fre'quent	frequent'
in'crease	increase'

Noun or Adjective	*Verb*
per'fect	perfect'
pre'sent	present'
pro'gress	progress'
reb'el	rebel'
trans'fer	transfer'

Spelling Hints

1. *Prefixes*

   (*a*) A double "n" occurs when "un-, in-" are added to words already beginning with "n".

e.g. unnecessary, innumerable.

   (*b*) A double consonant is required when "il-, im-, ir-", precede words beginning with "l, m, r" respectively.

e.g. illegal, irreparable, immovable.

   (*c*) A double "s" is required when "dis-, mis-" precede words beginning with "s".

e.g. dissatisfied, misspelling.

2. *Suffixes*

   (*a*) Words of *one* syllable ending in a single consonant following a *single* vowel double the final consonant before a suffix, i.e. before "-ed, -en, -er, -ing, -y".

e.g. run: runner, running.
   mad: madder, madden.
   tar: tarred, tarring, tarry.

   (*b*) Words of more than one syllable also double the last consonant if it follows a single vowel and the final syllable is stressed or accented.

e.g. begin': beginner, beginning.
   refer': referring, referred.

   but there is no doubling when the final consonant follows *two* consecutive vowels (e.g. proceed, proceeding), or when the stress is *not* on the last syllable (e.g. ben'efit: benefited).

(*c*) Final "l" after a single vowel is always doubled wherever the stress falls.

e.g. la'bel: labelled.
   control': controlling.

(*d*) In the case of words ending in "s", doubling is optional.

e.g. bias: biased *or* biassed.
   focus: focused, focusing.
      or focussed, focussing.

(*e*) A double "l" occurs when adjectives ending in "l" add "-ly" to form an adverb.

e.g. joyful: joyfully.

In other cases, when adding "-ly", words that end in "e" following a single consonant retain the "e".

e.g. lone: lonely

But words ending in "e" following two consonants drop the "e".

e.g. probable: probably.

(*f*) Words ending in "e" keep the "e" before a suffix beginning with a consonant but drop the "e" before a suffix beginning with a vowel.

e.g. excite: excitement.
but love: loving.
   smoke: smoky.
   move: movable.

Exceptions: After "c" and "g" the "e" must be retained to make the consonant have a soft sound.

e.g. notice: noticeable.
   manage: manageable.

Note also

    like: likeable, rateable, saleable.

The "e" is also retained in "dyeing" and "singeing" to distinguish these words from "dying" and "singing".

Note: In the case of the suffix "ment", either "judgment" or "judgement" may be written. Similarly, "abridg(e)ment" and "acknowledg(e)ment". The "e" is dropped in "argue; argument".

(g) Final "y" after a consonant in words of more than one syllable changes into "i" before a suffix.

e.g. lady: ladies.   beauty: beautiful.
    fury: furious.   busy: business.
    apply: applied.   funny: funnier.

and this change also applies to most words of one syllable with final "y".

e.g. sky: skies.
but shy: shyer.
    sly: slyer.
but "y" is retained when preceded by a vowel.
e.g. key: keys; gay: gayer (*but* "gaily, daily"), and before suffixes "-ing", "-ish".
e.g. dry: drying; baby: babyish.

(h) When the suffix "-ness" is added to an adjective which ends in "n", there will be a double "n" in the noun formed.

e.g. keen: keenness.

Remember that adjectives ending in "y" change to "i" before "-ness".

e.g. manly: manliness.
    happy: happiness.

(i) Note the change of spelling in the following:

    picnic: picnicking

humour: humorous
pronounce: pronunciation
proceed: procedure

3. *Miscellaneous*

(*a*) In words having the sound "ee", place "i" *before* "e", except after "*c*".

e.g. thief, believe, niece.
but receive, deceit.

> *Exceptions:* Counterfeit, seize, weir, weird.
> When the sound is *not* "ee", we write "ei".

e.g. reign, sovereign.

(*b*) Notice that "c" indicates the noun and "s" the verb in cases such as the following:

e.g.

Noun	*Verb*
advice	advise
practice	practise
prophecy	prophesy

Also note: "Wise counsel", "I counsel"—but "the County Council".

(*c*) Many nouns end in "-us", whereas adjectives end in "-ous".

e.g. *Nouns:* Census, fungus, genius.
    Adjectives: Marvellous, ingenious, spacious.

(*d*) In a number of verbs of three or more syllables the final syllable can be spelt either "-ise" or "-ize". The form 'ise' is preferable.

e.g. organise *or* organize.
    realise *or* realize.

> Note: Always "s" in "advertise".

(*e*) Note carefully:

    (i) "already", but "all right".
       "upon"
       "into" } but preferably "on to".
       "until", but "till".

"skill"
"full" } but "skilful".

"each other", not "eachother".

Do not confuse "it's" (= it is) and "its" (possessive).

(ii) A knowledge of the meaning of prefixes will help in such cases as:

*ante*room (room *before* the main room).

*anti*dote (remedy *against* poison or disease).

(iii) It will also be found helpful to learn in pairs words that have some similarity, but differ in spelling and meaning.

e.g. affect   (= to influence or concern).
  effect   (= result (noun), to accomplish (verb)).
  complement (= full number, completing some number or thing required).
  compliment (= expression of praise).
  currant   (= fruit).
  current   (= movement of water, occurring at present time).
  principal   (= chief (noun or adj.)).
  principle   (= idea, rule, system).
  stationary (= motionless).
  stationery (= writing material).
  lose   (= to mislay (verb)).
  loose   (= to free (verb), not tight (adj.)).

and also words that, deceptively, rhyme but are spelt differently.

e.g. siege, s*ei*ze.
  harass, embarrass.

(iv) It is unfortunately impossible to formulate rules for choosing the correct suffix in the following cases, experience and practice being the surest guide.

-ant } extravagant, combatant.
-ent } prominent, recipient.

(Similarly "-ance" and "-ence".)

-ary ⎱ contemporary, complimentary.
-ory ⎰ advisory, compulsory.

-able ⎱ capable, portable.
-ible ⎰ credible, responsible.

-ence ⎱ absence, pretence.
-ense ⎰ expense, intense.

-ar ⎱
-er ⎬ burglar, beggar.
-or ⎰ barrister, designer.
      doctor, survivor.

-eer ⎱ engineer, profiteer.
-ier ⎰ cashier, brigadier.

-el ⎱ tunnel.
-le ⎰ vehicle.

("-al" is sign of an adjective, e.g. comical.)

In the case of prefixes (see Chapter IX), which are often complete words in themselves, a knowledge of their meaning is often very helpful.

e.g. "aqua" (water) helps to spell "aqueduct", "aquarium" as distinct from "ac-" (to) in "acquisition", "acquiesce", etc.

EXERCISES

A

Make a list of the 10 words in the following list which are misspelt:

neccessary, aquarium, sergent, niece, accomodation, skillful, gauge, referred, comparitive, woolen, quarrel, proceedure, commitee, monastery, noticable, miniature, benefitted, technical, calendar.

B

Give a short definition of each of the following pairs of words, to show clearly the difference in meaning between them:

assent	bridal	cord	corps	current
ascent	bridle	chord	corpse	currant
desert	glacier	gilt	human	leak
dessert	glazier	guilt	humane	leek

| loth | magnet | peel | peer | yoke |
| loathe | magnate | peal | pier | yolk |

C

(a) Add "-ly" to the following, after any necessary alterations, to form adverbs:

occasional, fortune, skill, necessary, contempt.

(b) Add "-ed" to the following:

benefit, occur, conceal, label, focus.

D

Fill in the blank spaces with

(a) "ie" or "ei":
rec . . pt, s . . ze, s . . ve, l . . sure, bel . . ve.

(b) "-able" or "-ible":
respons . . . ., incred . . . ., advis . . . ., sens . . . .,
indispens . . . .

(c) "-ant" or "-ent":
promin . . ., depend . . ., (person), defend . . .,
correspond . . ., superintend . . .

(d) "-ar", "-er", or "-or":
collect . ., begg . ., advis . ., indicat . ., govern . .

E

Rewrite the following extract, correcting all misspellings (12):

The two cyclists did not see each other untill it was too late to avoid an accident. George put on his breaks, and skillfully avoided a head-on colision, but Anne's bicycle hit his rear wheel, and he proceded to crash into a lamp-post.

"I'm alright," he said, picking himself up immediatly.

"It was my fault," admitted Anne. "There's no arguement about it."

"No neccessity to apologise," George assured her. "The only damage is to my tire."

Anne, embarassed, recieved this information with relief.

F

(a) Write down any five words ending in "-ous", and five words ending in "-us".

(*b*) Write down any five words ending in "-ence" and five words ending in "-ense".

(*c*) Write down any five words ending in "-al", and five words ending in "-le".

(*d*) Write down any five words ending in "-ary", and five words ending in "-ory".

G

Correct the spelling of the following:

umberella, potatoe, woolen, picknick, humourous, pavillion, medecine, managable, emmigrate, paralised, comparitive, aereoplane, procede, litterature, buisness, preceed, calender, minature, mischievious, benificial.

LIST OF WORDS FREQUENTLY MISSPELT

accommodation
achieve
acquaintance
acquiesce
acquit
aerial
aeroplane
allege
already
anonymous
antidote
aquarium
architect
arctic
argument
ascent
automatic
autumn
auxiliary
awkward

bachelor
battalion
beginning
benefited

bicycle
boar (animal)
bough (branch)
Britain
Briton
buoy
business

calendar
cannon (gun)
canon (priest)
canvas (painting)
canvass (to recruit support for)
carriage
casualty
cauliflower
ceiling
cellar
cereal (food)
changeable
chaos
cheque
chord
chronicle

circuit
colonel
committee
comparative
compliment (praise)
connection *or* connexion
council (meeting)
counsel (advice)
cue (billiards, theatre)
currant (fruit)
current (stream)
cypher

dairy
deceased (dead)
dependant (noun)
dependent (adj.)
derelict
descendant
development
diary
dilapidated
diphthong
disciple
dyeing

ecstasy
effervesce
embarrass
encyclopedia
exaggerate
exorbitant

February
feign
foresee
forfeit
freight
fulfil

gait (walk)

gaol (prison)
gauge
gnaw
goal
government
guarantee
guard
guild
guillotine

handkerchief
harass
hoard (store)
horde (crowd)
humorous

immigrant
indictment
irascible
isosceles
isthmus

jeopardy
judg(e)ment

kaleidoscope
keenness
knead (press)
knowledge

laboratory
labyrinth
leisure
leper
lieutenant
lightning
liqueur
liquor
literature
loathe (dislike)
loth (unwilling)

machinery
manageable
manoeuvre
mechanical
medicine
medieval
Mediterranean
melancholy
miniature
miscellaneous
mischievous
mourn
muscle
mussel (shell-fish)

necessary
negligible
neigh
nephew
niece
nuisance

occurrence
omitted

palate (of mouth)
palette (for paints)
pantechnicon
paraffin
parallel
paralysis
parliament
pavilion
peal (of bells)
peel (skin)
permanent
permissible
petrol
physics
picnic
picnicking

piece
plaice (fish)
pneumatic
poplar (tree)
precede
prejudice
principal (chief)
principle (rule)
privilege
procedure
proceed
pronunciation
psychology

quarrel
quay
queue

raspberry
raucous
receive
reconnoitre
referring
Reverend (title)
reverent (with respect)
rhapsody
rhyme
rhythm
roe (of fish)

saleable
secretary
seize
separate
sergeant
silhouette
simultaneous
singeing
skilful
sleigh
solemn

stationary (not moving)
stationery (paper)
strait (narrow)
supersede
syllable
synchronise

technical
theatre
thyme (plant)
tortoise
tunnel
tyre

umbrella
unnecessary
until
vaccinate
variegated
vehicle

vengeance
victuals (food)

wag(g)on
Wednesday
weird
whimsical
whirring
woollen

xylophone

yacht
yoke (harness)
yolk (of egg)

zealous
zoological
zoology

SECTION II

THE SENTENCE AND THE PARAGRAPH:
CORRECTNESS AND COMPREHENSION

CHAPTER XI

DETAILED ANALYSIS OF A SIMPLE SENTENCE AND PARSING

Analysis is the process of closely examining something in order to split it up into its component parts. The opposite process, building up, is called *Synthesis* (e.g. synthetic rubber is built up from various materials or ingredients to have the qualities and appearance of natural or real rubber), which is dealt with in Chapter X.

Parsing is the description in terms of grammar of individual words.

This detailed study of the grammatical function of words in a sentence is of great value for two reasons: (1) It is essential in helping us to explain grammatical errors in faulty sentences, and (2) it will help us later when we deal with clause analysis, because noun, adjectival, and adverbial clauses then replace nouns, adjectives, and adverbs, whose function we shall have learnt to recognise.

ANALYSIS

I. **Detailed Analysis of a Simple Sentence**

Before attempting detailed analysis we must first clearly define the difference between a phrase and a sentence, and then examine the construction of a simple sentence.

A **Sentence** must have a subject (stated or understood) and one finite verb (i.e. a verb limited in number and person by a subject, with which it agrees). It need not necessarily contain an object or a complement, e.g. fish swim.

A **Phrase** differs from a Sentence by reason of the fact that it is a group of words that does not contain a finite or complete verb, and so it does not make complete sense, i.e. it does not express a complete idea.

> e.g. On arriving at the lake, to speak fluently, in a very short time, at an early date, to and fro.

Phrases, as will be shown, can do the work of nouns, adjectives, and adverbs.

A **Simple Sentence** consists of a **Subject**, a word or words denoting the person or thing of whom or which something is said (sometimes not spoken or written, but understood), and of a **Predicate**, a word or words expressing something about the subject ("predicare" = to express) in either a statement, a question, a command, or an exclamation.

Here are some examples of this simplest form of sentence analysis:

SUBJECT	PREDICATE
Statement	
Mary	sings.
The old lady	is reading a book.
Mary and John	are reading books and magazines.
(Double subject)	
Question	
Who	killed the dog?
You	are there? (= Are you there?)
Command	
(You)	give me that! (= Give me that!)
(You)	do not touch it! (= Don't touch it!)
Exclamation	
I	am how tired (= How tired I am!)
You	gave me what a surprise! (= What a surprise you gave me!)

We must now prepare for a more detailed analysis by defining the various component parts of a simple sentence.

A **Subject** has already been defined.

A **Verb** is a word that denotes an action or state. In sentence analysis we must always start by finding the finite verb, which is limited in number and person by its subject.

e.g. (Action) The men *run.*
(State) I *am* ill.

An **Object** is the sufferer of an action.

e.g. George kicked $\begin{cases} \text{the } dog. \\ \text{the } dog \text{ and the } cat \text{ (double object).} \end{cases}$

Some verbs take a direct object *and* an indirect object.

e.g. He gave the boy (him) books.   (=to the boy, to him.)

Such verbs as "give", "show", "tell", "ask", and "bring" frequently have indirect objects.

Subject: He.
Verb: gave.
Object: books.
Indirect Object: the boy, him.

Retained Object: A verb that in the active voice takes a direct and an indirect object still takes or retains its original object when it is used in the passive voice.

e.g. *Active:* I teach him (indirect) *Latin* (direct).
Passive: He is taught *Latin* by me.

In the sentence "Latin is taught *him* by me", there is a retained indirect object, but this is a rare and ugly construction.

A **Complement** is the term applied to the word or words which complete the sense of a sentence after a verb of incomplete predication (i.e. a verb that needs some additional words to complete the sense).

(i) The chief of these is the verb "to be", which, with

the verbs "to seem", "to become", and "to appear" can never take an object.

(ii) Factitive or "making" verbs (such as the verbs "to make", "to elect", "to proclaim") require a complement as well as an object, as do a few other verbs.

e.g. (i) He is the *leader*. He is *sad*.
He became *manager*.
He seems *to be running*.
(ii) They made him *king*.*
(iii) I saw them *go*.

The words in italics are the complements.

* Some grammarians say factitive verbs take a double object and call "king" one of these.

Enlargement of Subject or Object: Both the Subject and the Object may in some sentences have enlargements.

e.g. A narrow road led there:
Subject: road.
Enlargement: (Any word describing the Subject) a narrow.

Also there can be more than one subject or object in a sentence.

e.g. My *uncle* and *aunt* (Subjects) keep a *cat* and a *dog* (Objects).

The Extension of the Verb: The Verb may have an extension in some sentences.

e.g. He climbed slowly and painfully.
Verb: climbed.
Extension: (Any words telling more about the verb, e.g. how? when? where?) slowly and painfully.

We are now ready to analyse a simple sentence, and this analysis may be set out in the following ways: (1) Line by line. (2) In columns. (3) Graphically.

e.g. (*a*) *Sentence:* This small river now cuts in two the straggling village.

(Remember to find *first* the finite verb, then the subject.)

(1) *Subject:* river.
Enlargement of Subject: this small.
Verb: cuts.
Extension of Verb: now, in two.
Object: village.
Enlargement of Object: the straggling.

(2)

Subject		Predicate			
Subject	Enlarge-ment of Subject	Verb	Extension of Verb	Object	Enlarge-ment of Object
river	this small,	cuts	now, in two	village	the straggling

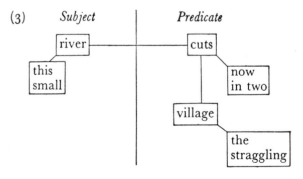

(3) *Subject* | *Predicate*

The second method is probably the clearest and most satisfactory, and the following hints may help those who find detailed analysis confusing:

Subject		Predicate				
Subject	Enlarge-ment of subject	Verb	Extension of verb	Object	Enlarge-ment of object	Comple-ment
The per-son or thing named	Any words describing the subject	The action of the sub-ject or its state of being	Any words telling more about the verb (How? When? Where?)	The thing affected by the action (Who? What?)	Any words describing the object (What sort of person or thing?)	Word or words com-pleting the sense, es-pecially after verb "to be"
Noun, Noun-Phrase, or Pronoun	Adjective or Adjectival Phrase	Verb	Adverb or Adverbial Phrase	Noun, Noun-Phrase, or Pronoun	Adjective or Adjectival Phrase	See above

Examples:

1. My black cat sometimes catches wild birds in the garden.
2. Books describing foreign countries are usually very interesting.
3. On seeing the joke, he laughed heartily.
4. They have elected him mayor.
5. John and Mary gave me presents.
6. I was given presents by John and Mary.

Subject		Predicate				
Subject	Enlarge-ment of subject	Verb	Extension of verb	Object	Enlarge-ment of object	Comple-ment
1. Cat	my black	catches	some-times, in the garden	birds	wild	—
2. Books	describing foreign countries	are	usually	—	—	very interesting
3. He	—	laughed	heartily, on seeing the joke	—	—	—
4. They	—	have elected	—	him	—	mayor
5. John and Mary	—	gave	—	1. presents (Direct) 2. me (Indirect)	—	—
6. I	—	was given	by John and Mary	presents	—	—

Notes: 1. Find first of all the finite verb, then the subject (which may not be written, but understood, as in orders: e.g. (You) come here). There need not necessarily be an object; and complements are rare, except after the verb "to be".

Ask yourself what part each remaining word is playing in the sentence, and do not make wild and illogical decisions. For example, an adjective cannot be an extension of a verb, and the verb "to be" can never take an object; and do not put any and every word about which you are doubtful in the complement.

2. Notice that verbs do not necessarily consist of one word.

e.g. He *is eating, has eaten, will eat* his lunch.

But beware of verbs like "can" and "must" (and "shall" or "will" when they express determination) which are not auxiliary, but principal verbs.

e.g. I can sing = *Subject* I *Verb* can *Object* (to) sing.

3. It must be realised that phrases, and even whole sentences, may play the part of nouns, adjectives, and adverbs.

- e.g. (i) *Phrases used as Nouns* (Noun-equivalents).
  (Subject) *Playing games* is enjoyable.
  (Object) I like *to be amused*.
  - (ii) *Phrases used as Adjectives* (Adjective-equivalents).
  A man *sitting on a gate* spoke to me.
  (Enlargement of Subject "man".)
  I want a book *suitable for a child*.
  (Enlargement of Object "book".)
  - (iii) *Phrases used as Adverbs* (Adverb-equivalents).
  He ran faster than ever. He ran (for) a mile.
  He ran round the field.
  (Extension of Verb "ran".)

When sentences are part of a longer sentence they are called *Clauses*, and such sentences, acting as nouns, adjectives, and adverbs, are dealt with in the next chapter ("Clause Analysis").

4. When an infinitive is followed by its object, the phrase is called an Accusative and Infinitive.

    e.g. *Subject:* I.
         Verb: like.
         Object: to sing songs.

5. *The Absolute Construction or Nominative Absolute.*
This is fortunately rarely encountered, but when it occurs it must not be treated as part of the sentence at all; it must be labelled accordingly. It is best understood by an example.

    e.g. *The game being lost,* the spectators left the ground in disgust.

"The game being lost" has nothing to do with the subject, "spectators", yet "game" is nominative, so we have two subjects.

If this had been written "As the game was lost" it would have been an extension of the verb "left"; if it had been written "The spectators, seeing the game lost, left . . ." it would have been an enlargement of the subject, "spectators".

6. In some sentences "it" and "there" are merely introductory words, and do not therefore belong to the sentence when we analyse it.

    e.g. "*It* is true that he is intelligent." (= "That he is intelligent (subject) is true".)
    "*There* are two books here." (= "Two books (subject) are here".)

The latter example shows clearly that "there" is not an adverb in this case, as the books are "here" (so cannot be "there" also!). In such cases we omit "it" or "there" from the analysis, and state that they are introductory words.

II. Analysis of Longer Sentences

Analysis of longer sentences consisting of two or more clauses (a **Clause** is a sentence which is part of a longer sentence) is dealt with fully in the next chapter, as is also the distinction between phrases and clauses.

Occasionally, however, a compound sentence (a **Compound Sentence** is a sentence consisting of two or more sentences linked together by a co-ordinate conjunction, viz. "and", "or", "but") has to be analysed in detail. Every separate finite verb indicates a separate sentence, so "made" and "gave" indicate that there are two sentences linked by "and" in this example.

Sentence: They made Paul their leader *and* he was given money by them.
Subject: They.
Verb: made.
Object: Paul.
Complement: their leader.
Connective: and.
Subject: he.
Verb: was given.
Extension of Verb: by them.
Object: money (= Retained object).

This is an interesting and helpful example, as it shows that a verb can take both an object and a complement in the case of verbs of "making" (factitive verbs) and also shows a verb in the passive ("was given") that has a retained object.

PARSING

The chapters on the Parts of Speech (Chapters I–VIII) are an essential introduction to this type of exercise.

(*a*) **Parsing individual words**

We may be called upon to state the grammatical function of an individual word, or of various selected words, in a sentence or paragraph.

e.g. He goes *whistling*[1] everywhere; *whistling*[2] is *no doubt* an admirable accomplishment in any house *except mine*.

whistling[1]: present participle, qualifying "he".

whistling[2]: gerund; subject of "is".

no doubt: compound adverb (= doubtless), modifying verb "is".

except: preposition, governing "mine".

mine: possessive pronoun; object of "except".

(b) Parsing a complete sentence

We may be called upon to parse each word in a sentence, and the following example shows the details required for each part of speech.

Example:

Sentence: "He will go to Paris later and visit his uncle."

He—Pronoun, Personal, Singular, 3rd Person, Subjective or Nominative Case (because the doer of the action).

will—Verb, Auxiliary (helping to form a future tense with "go"), Active, Indicative Present.

go—Verb, Infinitive, forming Future Tense with "will".

to—Preposition (showing relation between "he" or "go" and "Paris").

Paris—Noun, Proper, Objective Case (because governed by preposition "to").

later—Adverb (modifying verb "go") of Time, Comparative Degree.

and—Conjunction, Co-ordinate (joining "go" and "visit").

visit—Verb, Infinitive, forming Future Tense with verb "will", which is understood.

his—Adjective (qualifying the noun "uncle"), Possessive.

uncle—Noun, Common, Singular, Objective Case (object or sufferer of verb "visit").

EXERCISES

A

Divide the following sentences into subject and predicate. Underline the finite verbs.

(a) Up the road came a horse galloping wildly.

(b) Mary and Jane, being alarmed, ran away fast.

(c) Working day and night, he never seems to rest.

(d) Come to my house as soon as possible.

(e) Do you consider success impossible?

(f) According to this book, we are wrong.

(g) At this moment he was seized by two men.

(h) Strange was the scene before him.

(i) Where can we find a house to let?

(j) The subject of this essay, a difficult one, requires thought.

B

In the following sentences write down words or phrases which are direct objects, indirect objects, or complements, indicating in brackets which each is.

(a) He immediately sent them a telegram.

(b) This problem seems difficult to solve.

(c) My sister enjoys playing the piano.

(d) I am teaching my friend chess.

(e) This prize was awarded me for Latin.

(f) Whom did you meet on the way here?

(g) Being unhappy, she planned to escape.

(h) They elected him to lead them.

C

In the following sentences write out phrases used as enlargements of subject or object, or as extensions of the verb, indicating in brackets how each is used.

(a) The man in dress clothes hailed the taxi waiting outside.

(b) For his efforts he was well and truly rewarded.

(c) Water to drink was found after a long search.

(d) Most people imprisoned in towns want a cottage in the country.

(e) The explosion at a nearby factory was heard by us all.

D

Analyse fully, setting analysis out in columns (or vertically):

(a) Working hard, he soon earned more money to spend.

(b) On the way home John and Peter lost their way twice.

(c) Mr. Smith taught my son Latin in vain for many years.

(d) When will you come with us to see the circus?

(e) French is taught us here by a professor from Paris.

(f) That rude boy makes himself a nuisance to everyone.

(*g*) The courageous lion-tamer was attacked by two lions simultaneously.

(*h*) Copy out this page carefully in this book before going home.

(*i*) Frequently the best seats in the theatre are booked in advance.

(*j*) A man convinced against his will is of the same opinion still.

E

Parse each word in the above sentences, or in any sentence or sentences selected from the above.

F

Say what part of speech each word in italics is in the following sentences, and what its function is in its sentence.

(*a*) *Before* it is *too* late we *should consider what* steps are essential *to prevent* war, and *so* prove *that* we wish *to avoid such* a catastrophe.

(*b*) *Without hesitating* he plunged *into* the water, and, *swimming as fast* as he *could*, he seized the *drowning* man *as* he was going *down*.

(*c*) The prisoner asked for *something to drink* and I hurried *to bring him* some water. *But* he found difficulty in *swallowing this*; he was extremely weak, *being* nothing *but* a skeleton.

CHAPTER XII

CLAUSE ANALYSIS

Having dealt with the detailed analysis of each word in a simple sentence, we now come to the problem of analysing into clauses the different parts of a long sentence in which are contained several shorter sentences.

The process of clause analysis is considered excellent training in the clear understanding of a lengthy sentence, though it must be admitted that this type of question is set by examiners chiefly because it is an exercise which is easy to mark, as the answer has a mathematical precision which is noticeably lacking in answers to other types of questions in English. A long-suffering student might be tempted to add that any long sentence requiring clause analysis to clarify its meaning would have been a better sentence if split up into two or more shorter sentences.

A *Clause*, as we have already seen, is a sentence which is part of a longer sentence, and a *Phrase* and a *Simple Sentence* have also already been defined in Chapter XI. There are several types of sentences consisting of two or more clauses, and the following definitions are necessary. In these we shall refer to (1) **Main or Principal Clauses,** which are those which express the main idea and ideas on which other clauses may depend, and which make sense on their own and could stand alone, and (2) **Dependent or Subordinate Clauses**, which, as their title implies, do not make complete sense by themselves but are dependent on, or subordinate to, the main clause, and so cannot stand alone.

e.g. The dog *bit* the visitor (Main).
because he *kicked* it (Dependent).

In the above example, notice that the finite verbs "bit" and "kicked" have been italicized. This is the secret of discovering in sentences made up of two or more clauses how many separate clauses are contained in the whole sentence, as each clause must have its own finite verb. Identifying and underlining the finite verbs will also prevent us from confusing clauses and phrases, and from taking a mere phrase to be a clause, since a phrase is a group of words that does not contain a finite verb.

e.g. (*a*) I *arrived* at the hotel, and I *booked* a room (two finite verbs, two clauses—both main).

(*b*) Arriving at the hotel, I *booked* a room (one finite verb only, so this is a simple sentence, "arriving at the hotel" being merely a phrase, though it conveys the same idea of meaning as the clause in (*a*)).

Clauses and phrases can each do the work of a noun, of an adjective, or of an adverb in a sentence, but it is essential in clause analysis that clauses and phrases should not be confused.

Types of Sentence

1. **A Complex Sentence** is a sentence containing one Main Clause, and one or more Dependent Clauses.

e.g. As it *was raining*, I *took* my umbrella, which I *had* recently *bought*.
Here are three clauses:
Main: "I took my umbrella"
Dependent: "as it was raining"
"which I had recently bought"

Dependent clauses are generally introduced by a conjunction, such as "as, that, when," etc. (It sometimes happens that there is a dependent clause dependent on a clause that is already dependent:

e.g. "which I had recently bought when I was in London".

Here "when I was in London" is dependent on the dependent clause "which I had recently bought", telling us when it was bought.)

The relationship between clauses can be shown by the graphic method, as follows:

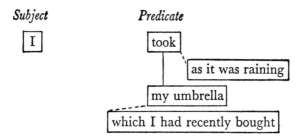

Subject *Predicate*

2. **A Compound Sentence** is the name given to any sentence containing more than one main clause. These sentences can be classified or subdivided as

(*a*) **Double Sentences**—two main clauses joined by a co-ordinating conjunction (i.e. "and", "but", "or").

e.g. I *bought* a book and (I) *read* it.

Note that the subject is sometimes omitted before a series of verbs to which the same subject applies.

(*b*) **Multiple Sentences**—three or more main clauses.

e.g. He *wrote* a letter, *addressed* an envelope, *stamped* it, and *posted* it.

A double or multiple sentence may be complex as well (i.e. may contain one or more dependent clauses in addition to its main clause).

e.g. He *wrote* a letter (while he *was waiting*) and posted it at the pillar box (that *was* at the end of the road).

In the above example the dependent clauses are, of course, those enclosed in brackets.

137

Types of Dependent Clause

Having learnt to distinguish between Main and Dependent Clauses, the next and final problem is to distinguish between the three kinds of work Dependent Clauses do. The fact that we already know (or should know) from earlier chapters what work Nouns, Adjectives, and Adverbs do should greatly help us, as the functions of Phrases and Dependent Clauses are precisely the functions of these three parts of speech.

There are therefore three types of Dependent Clause:

1. Noun Clauses (doing the work of a Noun).
2. Adjectival Clauses (doing the work of an Adjective).
3. Adverbial Clauses (doing the work of an Adverb) (subdivided into nine types).

e.g. A. *Simple Sentence.*
Subject: rats
Enlargement: observant (Adj.); possessing sharp eyes (Adj. Phrase)
Verb: see
Extension: often (Advb.) on entering my shed (Advb. Phrase)
Object: traps (Noun).

B. *Complex Sentence.*
rats
that *are* observant (Adj. Clause)

see
whenever they *enter* my shed (Advb. Clause)

what I *have prepared* for them (Noun Clause).

This example shows clearly how in B a whole clause with its finite verb has been substituted for a single word or for a phrase, having the same function as the word or phrase it has replaced.

If we substitute "on entering my shed" for the extension of verb in B, we have an Adverbial Phrase, as it is a group of words containing no finite verb. Similarly, "possessing sharp eyes" would be an Adjectival Phrase replacing "observant", and "preparations to catch them" would be a Noun Phrase, replacing "traps".

If we now have a clear grasp of the difference between

phrases and clauses, and of the three functions each can fulfil, the final stage is to examine in detail Noun, Adjectival, and Adverbial Clauses.

1. **Noun Clauses**

Noun Clauses are naturally used as Subject, Object, or Complement of a Verb; or as Object of a Preposition.

Many are preceded by the conjunction "that"; but "how", "when", "where", and "what" also introduce Noun Clauses. In the following examples the Noun Clauses are in brackets.

e.g. *Subject:*   (That he is ill) is obvious.
                   (What he says) is true.
                   (Where he lives) does not matter.
    Object: I think (that he is right).
                   We wonder (where he lives).
                   They heard (what you said).
                   He asked (how I did it).
Complement: The result is (what I expected).
Obj. of Prep.: I agree *with* (what you say).

Clauses that are in *apposition* to a subject, object, or complement (i.e. standing in the same grammatical relationship to the rest of the sentence as the subject, object, or complement does), are Noun Clauses.

e.g. You must learn the *rule* (that no one may smoke).
    (= You must learn that no one may smoke.)

Do not be tempted to think "that no one may smoke" is an Adjectival Clause describing "the rule" (one would not "smoke" a "rule", incidentally). "That no one may smoke" *is* "the rule", and can replace the word "rule".

Note that any direct statement or question is a Noun Clause.

e.g. He said: "What time is it?"
    "Are you ready?" he called.

Noun Phrases will, of course, have no finite verb.

e.g. *Shopping by post* often saves time (subject).
    I like *to live by the sea* (object).

2. Adjectival Clauses

These are like adjectives, used to qualify or describe a noun or pronoun.

> e.g. The man (*who* was begging) was arrested.
> The cat (*which* looked starved) was found by some children.
> Here is the student (*from whom* I borrowed a pen).
> Are these the books (*that* you want)?
> This is the house (*of which* I spoke).
> Here is the hotel (*at which* I am staying).
> You are wearing the same sort of hat (*as* I am wearing).
> The day (*when* I arrived) it was raining.
> I remember the street (*where* I met him).

Adjectival phrases fulfil the same function, but have no finite verb.

> e.g. The man *standing by the door* was waiting.
> A bush *planted in the corner* was covered with a mass of yellow flowers.

Notice that Noun, Adjectival, and Adverbial Clauses can begin with "that". The distinction between a Noun Clause in apposition and an Adjectival Clause has already been explained (i.e. the Adjectival Clause must describe the noun it refers to: the Noun Clause in apposition can replace the noun to which it is in apposition). Identification of all words, phrases, and clauses must always be by their function in each particular sentence. Such rare causes for confusion as parenthetical clauses (or "asides") are very unlikely to occur.

> e.g. The lion's claws, I noticed, were very sharp.

Here "I noticed" does not mean "that I noticed" but is a remark inserted by the speaker. If such an example is encountered, the "aside" should be classified separately as a "Parenthesis".

3. **Adverbial Clauses**

These are both numerous and varied, and must be sub-divided into their nine different kinds. It is a helpful plan to learn by heart the examples of each type, with their introductory conjunctions. Adverbial clauses and phrases limit or modify verbs, adjectives, and adverbs.

(i) *Cause* (as, because, since).

e.g. The boy was hungry (*as* he had had no lunch).
(*Because* I was delayed), I missed my train.
(*Since* you are so obstinate), you can go.
("Since" here = "because", and is nothing to do with time.)

(ii) *Comparison or Degree* (as, than).

e.g. He works as hard (*as* any student (works)).
The sun was red (*as* fire (is)).
No one looked prettier (than Mary (looked)).

Note that in clauses after "as", "than" in most cases the verb is omitted or understood. This is called an *elliptical* (or shortened) clause.

(iii) *Concession* (although, though, however).

e.g. (*Although* he worked hard) he failed in his examination.
I always enjoy flower-shows (*though* I have no garden).
(*However* tired you are), you must try to work.

(iv) *Condition* (if, unless).

e.g. (*If* you cannot swim), it is dangerous to go rowing alone.
He refused to work (*unless* I paid him in advance).

In some cases "if" is omitted, but understood.

e.g. (Had we been there), we should have protested.
(*If* we had been there).

(v) *Manner* (as).

e.g. Do exactly (*as* I do).
He looked (*as* if he were exhausted).
("as"—"in the same manner as") and must not be confused with ("as"—"since" or "because".)

(vi) *Place* (where, wherever).

e.g. I shall walk (*where* I choose).

Do not confuse with

(*a*) I know (*where* he lives)—Noun Clause.
(*b*) The house (*where* I was born)—Adj. Clause.

(vii) *Purpose* (so that, lest).

e.g. The burglar wore gloves (*so that* he would leave no finger-marks).

He would not fly (*lest* there should be an accident).

Note: The vital difference between Purpose and Result is that in the case of Purpose the purpose has not at the time been accomplished, whereas in Result clauses the purpose is or has been accomplished.

(viii) *Result* (so that, that).

e.g. He missed his train (*so that* he was late for work).

The goalkeeper was so slow (*that* the ball was in the net before he had moved).

(ix) *Time* (when, whenever, since).

e.g. I shall go out (*when* I am ready).

We have not seen him (*since* he came back).

Note: Adverbial phrases will, of course, have no finite verb.

e.g. He ran *as fast as possible.*

Worked Example of Clause Analysis

Sentence: Strolling by the river, I *noticed* a boy who *was swimming* near a boat in midstream and I *was* astonished to see, when I *looked* more closely, that he *was* apparently a cripple, as he *was moving* one leg only.

Rules: (1) Underline all the finite verbs (a verb, as we have seen, may consist of more than one word), and the number of these will determine the number of clauses.

(2) Set the clauses out in a column in the order in which they occur in the complete sentence, and number them.

(3) Decide which is the main clause, or which are the main clauses.

Notice that though clauses are usually separated by commas, this is not always so, and so commas cannot be taken as an infallible guide to the number of clauses.

Three columns are required as follows:

Clause	Kind	Function
1. Strolling by the river, I noticed a boy	Main Clause.	Makes a statement.
2. who was swimming near a boat in midstream.	Adjectival Clause. (subordinate to 1).	Qualifying "boy" in 1.
("and"—Co-ordinating conjunction, linking Main Clauses 1 and 3)		
3. I was astonished to see	Main Clause.	Makes a statement.
4. when I looked more closely	Adverbial Clause of Time (subordinate to 3).	Limiting "was" in 3.
5. that he was apparently a cripple,	Noun Clause (subordinate to 3).	Object of "to see" in 3.
6. as he was moving one leg only.	Adverbial Clause of Cause (subordinate to 5).	Limiting "was" in 5.

Notice that in the above example there are two main clauses and that the co-ordinating conjunction which is no part of either is indicated on a separate line.

Clause 6 is dependent on or subordinate to 5, an example of how a subordinate clause may be dependent on another subordinate clause, and not necessarily on a main clause.

Notes:

1. *Elliptical Clauses.*

In the case of elliptical clauses (i.e. clauses in which words have been omitted which are needed to complete the sense), the words omitted but understood must be supplied.

e.g. He caught and held the thief = He caught the thief (Main Clause).
(and = co-ordinating conjunction).
he held the thief (Main Clause).

2. Introductory "it" (see Chapter XI) may be misleading.

e.g. (It) is true that he is ill = That he is ill (Noun Clause) is true.

EXERCISES

A

Write down the finite verbs in the following sentences, then state which are Simple, Complex, Double or Multiple; or Double and Complex.

1. If he arrives at all in this weather, I shall be surprised.

2. The art of hand-writing is rapidly dying, owing to the invention of the typewriter.

3. Tell me when you are ready to start, and I will come too.

4. I went to the theatre last night and saw an amusing comedy.

5. He ran forward, stumbled and fell, uttering a cry.

B

Write down the phrase or phrases in each of the following sentences, and state what work each is doing (i.e. fulfilling the function of a noun, adjective, or adverb).

1. In the high wind the inn-sign swung to and fro.

2. In my opinion he expects to be promoted.

3. Collecting stamps is a hobby to be recommended.

4. People unable to read or write are now few in number and growing fewer.

5. Seizing a rope, the sailor threw it as far out to sea as possible.

6. To give up now means abandoning all hope.

C

Write down the finite verbs in the following sentences, then write out (*a*) the main clauses, and (*b*) the subordinate or dependent clauses, without stating of what kind they are.

1. Although he is not intelligent, he does his best.

2. It is easy to see that you are a foreigner.

3. Come with us, and we will show you where we live.

4. The policeman, who was passing, seized the thief.

5. "Don't believe him", he cried, rushing at his accuser.

6. I told him as he went out that Henry was looking for him.

7. As you are here, I will call him, because he wants to see you.
8. Are these the books that Mary wanted to borrow?
9. That he is ill is obvious.
10. If I had been there, I should have helped him.

D

Write out the dependent or subordinate clauses in the following sentences. State whether they are Noun or Adjective Clauses, and explain the function of each in its sentence.

1. I should like to know where you have put my book.
2. Which bicycle is yours? The one that is near the gate is mine.
3. Surely you can see that he is far from happy.
4. This is the time when he usually calls.
5. Charles, whose garden is next to mine, keeps bees.
6. The reason for my resigning is that I am dissatisfied.
7. That was the race in which he came last.
8. That pigs cannot fly is an obvious fact.
9. This is the exact spot where William the Conqueror landed.
10. I base my opinion on what I have read, and the news that cars are to be dearer surprises me.

E

Write out the adverbial clauses in the following sentences, and state what type of adverbial clause each is, and what word it is modifying.

1. Unless it rains, I shall play tennis tomorrow.
2. He ran so fast that he collapsed with exhaustion.
3. You should have acted as I advised you to act.
4. He worked wherever he could find work.
5. As you are going to the station, may I accompany you?
6. The policeman caught him as he was about to jump.
7. Whenever you can come, please telephone me.
8. I bought an alarm-clock so that I might wake early.
9. It is true no one works harder than you do.
10. He failed to pass his examination although he worked hard.

F

Analyse in three columns (Clause, Kind, and Function) the following:

1. The children tried to cross where the river was shallow, but when they got out of their depth they called for help, as they could

not swim, and a fisherman sitting on the bank heard them, so that they were saved.

2. Although many people think that writing a book is easy, they do not realise that authors have to work harder than most other people work to earn a living, and that many earn very little or even starve.

3. After I had waited for some days for an answer to the letter I had written to my friend whose house I wished to buy, I sent him a telegram so that he might get my offer in time, and he accepted it.

4. When we realise that rabbits do so much harm, the fact that there is such an outcry about their extermination by people who do not understand the problem as the farmers do, is surprising.

5. This country should build roads that will not only be straighter but will also be reserved for motorists, so that journeys by car will be quicker and safer because of the absence of corners and cyclists.

6. Should war break out, and if it is impossible to prevent it, I certainly shall not construct a shelter in my garden as I did in the last war, because it would be useless.

G

Construct sentences in which the clauses are of the type stipulated, and in the order indicated.

1. Adverbial Clause of Time, Main Clause, Adjectival Clause.

2. Main Clause, Noun Clause, Adverbial Clause of Concession.

3. Adverbial Clause of Condition, Main Clause, Adverbial (any).

4. Main Clause, Adverbial Clause of Manner, Adverbial Clause of Purpose.

5. Adverbial Clause of Cause, Main Clause, Adverbial Clause of Result.

6. Main Clause, Adverbial Clause of Place, Main Clause, Adjectival Clause.

7. Main Clause, Noun Clause as object of a preposition, Main Clause co-ordinate with first.

CHAPTER XIII

PUNCTUATION

Although it is impossible to lay down fixed rules for all questions of punctuation, there are certain basic rules that must be observed.

When speaking, we convey our meaning by changes of tone and pace, by pauses, and also often by gestures. When writing, however, we must rely on punctuation to make ourselves clearly understood. We can indicate changes of tone by question marks and exclamation marks, and pauses by other stops.

Our present system of punctuation dates from the fifteenth century, and before that date there was apparently no system of punctuation at all. Later there was an increasing tendency towards excessive punctuation, but modern writers try to avoid the too-frequent and unnecessary use of stops.

Modern punctuation is based partly on the tone and pace to be indicated, and partly on the grammatical relation of words, phrases, and clauses in a sentence.

Its object is to convey clearly the writer's meaning by avoiding ambiguity, and to show the expression he requires.

Punctuation can make all the difference to the meaning of a sentence, as the following examples will show:

You have lost your wallet. (Statement.)
You have lost your wallet? (Interrogation.)
You have lost your wallet! (Surprise.)

Another example of the power of punctuation is illustrated by the story of the critical inspector who wrote on the board: "The inspector said the teacher is a fool", and then called on Smith minor to provide the correct punctuation. The inspector was more surprised than pleased to be confronted with Smith's version, which read:

"The inspector," said the teacher, "is a fool!"

Just as speakers vary in their style of oratory, so writers vary in their style of writing and use of punctuation. There are, however, certain definite rules that must be learned and observed.

Overstopping is just as serious an error as understopping; and commas and other stops must not be sprinkled at random in a sentence like currants in a cake. There should be some definite reason for each stop we use.

If we think before we write, and do not construct sentences of excessive length, we shall avoid becoming confused in our punctuation.

We must remember, too, that it is equally important to indent each paragraph correctly, and to leave a space after a full stop (i.e. between sentences) so that sentences are clearly separated.

Meanwhile, the following general principles will be found a useful guide.

Kinds of Stops and Their Uses

I. **The Full Stop (or Period)** is used:

1. To indicate the end of a sentence (and note that a question mark and an exclamation mark have their own full stops, e.g. ? !):

e.g. It is true. Is it true? It is true!

2. To indicate an abbreviation.

e.g. M.A. (Master of Arts); etc. (*et cetera* = and others).
P.C. (Police Constable); i.e. (*id est* = that is).
Dr. (Doctor), Mr. (Mister), Messrs. (Messieurs).

Note: A full stop is optional if the last letter of the abbreviation is the same as the last letter of the word when written in full (e.g. Rd, St, *but* Feb., Mon.)

II. **The Colon** is used:

1. To introduce a quotation, from an actual speech or from a book.

e.g. The policeman said: "I advise you to move your car, sir, before you incur a fine."

As Bacon in his essay on "Books" remarked: "Reading maketh a full man."

Note: A comma may be used instead of a colon for this purpose, and there is an increasing tendency to employ this alternative stop when the quotation is short.

e.g. His lawyer said, "I agree."

2. (*a*) To introduce a list.

e.g. The village shop sold practically everything: groceries, sweets, tobacco, newspapers, fruit, vegetables, china, pots and pans, and bread.

(But no colon when list is simply object of a verb. e.g. "She bought groceries, vegetables, fruit, and newspapers at the shop".)

(*b*) To introduce a summary of a statement.

e.g. The facts are as follows: English and Mathematics are compulsory subjects, French and Latin are optional, and there will also be an interview.

3. To separate two strongly contrasted statements, when there is no conjunction.

e.g. Man proposes: God disposes.

4. To separate two co-ordinate clauses, the second of which explains or amplifies the first.

e.g. Every runner has his best distance: Jones was a sprinter.

III. **The Semi-Colon** is used:

1. To separate co-ordinate clauses when conjunctions, especially "and", are omitted.

> e.g. He is an excellent scholar; he is a promising athlete; he is a keen amateur actor.

2. In enumerations consisting of phrases or clauses—not of single words, dependent on the same main verb.

> e.g. She said that she was tired; that she hated her work; that she intended to leave.

3. To separate long clauses dealing with the same subject, when a pause longer than that indicated by a comma is required, especially when commas have already been used in the individual clauses.

> e.g. The house, empty for more than a year, obviously needed redecorating, if not modernising; but the garden, once a delight, was in an even worse state, with weeds everywhere.

4. To separate co-ordinate clauses joined by a conjunction developing an idea (moreover, nevertheless, otherwise, therefore).

> e.g. You must drink your milk; otherwise you will never grow strong.

Note: To sum up, the semi-colon, a longer pause than a comma, enables us to avoid three errors of style: the abruptness of a series of separate short sentences ending with full stops; the monotony of a long sentence consisting of clauses strung together with "and" or some other conjunction; and the confusion of a complicated sentence divided only by commas.

IV. **A Comma** is used:

1. To separate words of the same type in a list of three or more items, or to separate a series of phrases or clauses (two items joined by "and" do not constitute a list, e.g. "cats and dogs").

e.g. He kept cows, sheep, pigs, and poultry.
A strange, silent, solemn man.
Panting and puffing, running to and fro, they searched.
It seems that he is ill, that he is desperate, that he is starving.

Note: Most writers now omit the comma before the word "and" in a series (e.g. "Sheep, pigs and poultry"), but strictly speaking this does not convey the same equality of pause or connection, as "and" then links the last two words more closely.

It must be admitted, however, that to omit the comma in such cases is now the general practice.

If two adjectives refer to two different types of quality no comma is required.

e.g. A nice little boy. ("nice" = character; "little" = appearance, size.)

2. To mark off a person addressed.

e.g. I hope, Charles, you are wrong.
I agree, sir.

3. To mark off words in apposition. (In apposition = in same grammatical relation to the rest of the sentence. The second of two nouns in apposition explains or amplifies the first.)

e.g. Julius Caesar, Emperor of Rome, was assassinated.
Hardy, a great novelist, lived in Dorset.
My aunt, Mary. (But "My Aunt Mary" is merely one title.)

4. To mark off phrases beginning with a present participle ("-ing".)

e.g. Arriving at the entrance, he stopped.
(*but* "The train arriving now is for London".)

5. To mark off such words and phrases as: "therefore", "however", "of course", "in fact", "for instance".

e.g. I saw, however, that he was ill.

(But no comma after "however" when it means "in whatever way", e.g. However shall we escape?)

6. To mark off a phrase or clause which is parenthetical (i.e. which is an "aside", which could really be placed in brackets).

e.g. He is the man, I think, that did this.

Note: Asides are sometimes also separated by brackets or by dashes.

7. In such cases as the following, to show that a word is omitted but understood.

e.g. He went his way; I, mine (= I went mine).

8. To separate clauses in a sentence where a pause is essential, especially to separate adverbial clauses ("when, as, if, though, unless") from the main clauses.

Short clauses joined by "and" or "or" do not require a separating comma, nor do short co-ordinate clauses, short adverbial clauses, or noun clauses.

e.g. When we eventually arrived at the castle, the gates were about to be closed.
     If you can possibly come, I shall be delighted.
     Though he made a gallant effort, he was unable to reach the bank.
but: He laughed and shouted for joy. (Short Co-ord. Cl.)
     I will go when you like. (Short Advb. Cl.)
     We said that we were willing. (Noun Cl.)

Note: The final test when putting in commas in a sentence of two or more clauses is to read the whole sentence through, noting where the voice naturally pauses briefly to give clarity and sense.

Remember that a comma is required to separate a "who" or "which" clause that is parenthetical (i.e. an added detail), but that no comma precedes a "that" clause (i.e. a defining clause).

e.g. The man, who was very old, walked with slow steps.
     The book, which had a yellow cover, was on the table.
but: The man that wrote that was prejudiced.
     The book that I selected was boring.

V. **Inverted Commas (or Quotation Marks)** are used:

1. To enclose the actual words of a speaker, or of a quotation from a book.

e.g. He said: "I shall go if possible."
Bacon wrote: "Reading maketh a full man."

Note: If only a word or a phrase is quoted, there is no preceding colon (or comma).

e.g. He shouted "Fire!" several times.

A capital letter is not required for words or phrases in such cases as : "He pronounced the word 'formidable' wrongly," as "formidable" does not constitute a complete sentence, and is not an exclamation.

2. For the title of a book, play, etc.

e.g. Shakespeare's "Macbeth".

3. To indicate a foreign word, any quoted word, or slang, etc.

e.g. Their "tête-à-tête" lasted an hour.
The word "eligible" is wrongly used.
He described everything as "okay".

Quotation Within a Quotation: When a quotation occurs within another quotation, we must differentiate between them by the use of single and double inverted commas, single inverted commas being usually used for the included quotation.

e.g. Smith said: "Suddenly I heard a voice shout 'Who is there?' "
or Smith said: 'Suddenly I heard a voice shout "Who is there?" '

Notice that there is no punctuation required before a quotation within a quotation (i.e. between "shout" and "Who . . .").

Other Stops in Quotations: Note carefully the use of commas, full stops, and capitals in the following examples depending on whether the mark or question mark carries its own full stop, and is therefore not followed immediately by a comma.

e.g. (a) "You are right," he said. "We shall win."
(Comma after "right". Full stop after "said", and capital "W" for "We" starting new sentence.)

(b) "I think," he said, "that we should stop."
(Comma after "said", and small "t" for "that", as sentence is continued from "I think".)

(c) "Heavens!" he exclaimed.
"Are you ill?" he asked.
(No comma before "he", as full stops are already contained in exclamation and question marks.)

(d) It was Kipling who wrote of "lesser breeds without the law".
(Full stop outside inverted commas here, as it ends the sentence, not the quotation.)

Paragraphing in Conversation: A new paragraph should be started for each new speaker, however brief his speech.

e.g. "You hope to go there, then, Mr. Brown?" asked Henry.
"Yes," replied Brown.
"And will you stay long?"
"I can't say, but it is probable I shall remain there some weeks."

VI. **Question Marks**

Question marks are not required in indirect speech.

e.g. He asked them what he was to do.
("What am I to do?" was the actual question.)

VII. **Exclamation Marks**

Exclamation marks are not compulsory after an interjection, and a comma may be used if a sudden emotion or sudden pause is not indicated.

e.g. "Ah, my dear fellow," he said, shaking hands.
"Ah! My dear Brown!" he cried, greeting me effusively.

VIII. **A Dash** is used:

1. To indicate an aside, or an afterthought.

e.g. His account at the bank—and I am telling you this in strict confidence—is overdrawn.

They were all found guilty—including the son, of course.

2. To summarise a series of subjects or to expand a subject.

e.g. Men, women, children, boats—all were lost.

The Roman—man, woman, child—lives again in this book.

3. To indicate broken speech (i.e. hesitation).

e.g. I—er—think—er—that—er—you—er—are—er—right.

(Note: Dots may be used as an alternative.)

4. To show a sudden breaking off of a statement.

e.g. He eventually escaped—but I must tell you the rest of the story later.

5. To introduce an unexpected or emphasised ending.

e.g. When the great man, of whom we had heard so much, finally appeared, we were surprised to see—a dwarf.

6. To indicate the omission of a name, or of a word or part of a word.

e.g. Mr.——. A d—— fool!

IX. **Dots** are sometimes used as an alternative to dashes, to show broken speech, or to show a sudden breaking off of a statement.

e.g. The last act takes place in Spain . . . but you must see the play for yourself.

And so they sailed away . . .

X. **Brackets** are sometimes used instead of dashes to enclose a parenthesis (an additional remark, an example, or an aside), though they are best suited to mathematics, or technical articles.

e.g. His son (a complete fool, I fear) was also there.

XI. **A Hyphen** is used to form compound words.

e.g. Mother-in-law, bird-cage, semi-detached.

(Notice the difference between "the best-known remedy" and "the best known remedy".)

XII. **A Diæresis** sign is used when two vowels that are next to each other are to be pronounced separately, and is always placed over the second of the two vowels.

e.g. aërate (= a-erate).

Note: Both "Coöperation" and "Co-operation" are correct, the latter being more usual. Notice also: "no one".

XIII. **An Apostrophe** is used:

1. To show possession (possessive or genitive case).

e.g. the farmer's wife.

(For detailed use in this case see Chapter II.)

2. To indicate the omission of a letter or letters, which occurs in conversation and poetry.

e.g. It's a pity (= it is); I can't say (= cannot); o'er (= over).

Note: Never use an apostrophe in the possessive adjective "its" (e.g. the dog wagged its tail), or for the possessive pronoun "hers", "ours", "yours" (e.g. It is ours).

3. To form the plurals of letters and of numbers written in figures.

e.g. How many "c's" in "necessary"?
     Add three 9's. In the 1890's.

XIV. **Capital Letters**

1. Capital letters are used for proper names of people and places (e.g. John Smith, London), and titles (e.g. Duke of Gloucester); for countries, inhabitants, and languages (e.g. England, the English, a Londoner, I speak French), and for adjectives connected with countries, places, and people (e.g. an English garden, a London fog, a Dickensian character); for names of months and days (but the seasons are normally written with a small letter); for "God" and "Christ", and pronouns or adjectives referring to either word (e.g. God in His mercy . . .; Those who come unto Him), and for "Christianity" or "Christian" as noun or adjective, and the word "Bible".

2. In titles of books, plays, etc., the important words are usually given capitals.

e.g. "Three Men in a Boat".

3. Words used in a special sense require a distinguishing capital, and capitals are also used to give special emphasis.

e.g. What the Church says about this problem is important.

Notes: (a) Do not confuse "It was Admiral Nelson" (title of an individual) and "The many admirals whose portraits you see" ("admirals" used in a general sense, representing a class).

Similarly: "One of my favourite uncles, Uncle George."

(b) In verse, every line usually begins with a capital, but this is not a fixed rule.

(c) In the case of a "french window" and "french chalk" a small "f" is now generally employed.

Before attempting an exercise in punctuation, the passage should obviously be read through carefully several times, until the sense, and hence the requisite pauses, are quite clear to the reader.

Paragraphing—particularly if the extract contains conversation, where a fresh paragraph is required for each speaker—comes before punctuation, and paragraphs should be marked off first with brackets.

Inverted commas to enclose any conversation should then be inserted, followed next by any question marks, exclamation marks, and full stops, and then all necessary capital letters.

Finally, commas and any other necessary stops should be inserted.

There is no absolutely hard-and-fast rule for punctuation (no two pianists play a piece in exactly the same way), and as long as the final version conveys the meaning of the extract clearly and accurately to the reader, it is successfully punctuated.

The following example of the punctuation of a test passage may prove helpful. The paragraphing—in this case a fresh paragraph for each speaker—is indicated by brackets:

(do you mean to tell me that you have never read treasure island smith asked mr jones) (no sir i must admit i havent smith answered) (heavens then get hold of a copy at once and read it without delay snapped mr jones) (whos the author please sir inquired the boy timidly) (r l stevenson replied the master snorting contemptuously spelt with a v not a ph).

"Do you mean to tell me that you have never read 'Treasure Island', Smith?" asked Mr. Jones.

"No, sir, I must admit I haven't," Smith answered.

"Heavens! Get hold of a copy at once, and read it without delay," snapped Mr. Jones.

"Who's the author, please, sir?" inquired the boy timidly.

"R. L. Stevenson," replied the master, snorting contemptuously, "spelt with a 'v' and not with a 'ph'."

EXERCISES

A

Insert commas where necessary in the following sentences:

1. I need not however tell you the whole story.
2. However did you guess my dear that I wrote that?
3. Arriving at the station he booked a return ticket.
4. Jones our leader hesitated too long and lost his chance.
5. She said "You are right George".
6. Thomas is we consider unsuitable for this post.
7. They promised that they would tell him.
8. Here are our hats. I'll wear yours; you mine.
9. If you really believe that I will resign.
10. It seems to me therefore that he is a silly old fool.
11. This black and white sketch is a poor disappointing effort.
12. That is the book that I want.
13. A tall frail boy who looked ill sat down by me.
14. We decided eventually to go to the theatre though we had not booked any seats.
15. She bought eggs bacon and butter at the grocer's.
16. Men and women of all races were there.
17. He finally reached the distant shore and climbed up the cliffs with some difficulty.
18. Telephone me when you are in London.
19. Mary said that she was feeling tired irritable and unhappy.
20. He is as fat as a whale yet he skates and skis.

B

Insert colons, semi-colons, or dashes where necessary in the following sentences:

1. He strode up to his opponent his fists were clenched his face was red with anger.
2. My car, a 1930 model, is constantly breaking down but, unless purchase tax is removed, I certainly cannot buy a new one.
3. Charles has more brawn than brains Peter, though not so strong, has considerable intelligence.
4. The subjects for this examination are as follows English, French, and either Latin or Greek.
5. The new owner they say he is a millionaire moves into the castle next week.

6. We cannot possibly elect him captain he has none of the necessary qualities.

7. The truth of the matter is this he simply wants to avoid making any decisions.

8. Men, women, children and animals all were herded into the barn.

C

Change small letters to capital letters where necessary in the following sentences, and insert inverted commas where required.

1. Last monday i went with my uncle charles to portsmouth to see nelson's flagship h.m.s. victory.

2. Every day except sunday i travel by the southern railway from my home in beech avenue kingston on thames to waterloo station.

3. Old admiral brown, whose house is called trafalgar lives near land's end in cornwall, and spends his day reading the times.

4. In english lessons we are studying shakespeare's the merchant of venice, and in history we are learning the names of the presidents of the united states.

5. The christian religion bases its teaching on the bible. In england church and state work closely together.

6. Our local m.p. is also a j.p., and a vice-president of the surrey horticultural society. He likes to look out of his french windows at his beds of madame butterfly roses.

D

Insert inverted commas, any other necessary punctuation, and capitals where required, in the following:

1. Surely he exclaimed you are not going to give up hope yet.

2. He replied that is my affair mind your own business.

3. Help i am drowning the boy shouted throw me a rope.

4. The word subway sir explained the american means an underground railway in my country.

5. Are you sure you heard him say tomorrow i asked.

6. The saying there is no fool like an old fool certainly does not apply to you he added laughing.

7. We saw the film julius caesar one evening when we were crossing the atlantic in the queen elizabeth.

8. I said and not or i told him No you didn't he retorted.

9. I asked what was he wearing an overcoat or a mackintosh.

10. They enjoyed a tête-à-tête conversation.

E

Insert apostrophes where necessary.

1. Its only eight oclock. We arent late.
2. Thats the phone, isnt it? Its always ringing.
3. How many ts are there in your dogs name? Its hurt its paw.
4. Cant you tell me what nine 7s are?
5. These farmers cows wont be sold at Tuesdays market.
6. Whos left this book here? Whose is it? Yours or Joans?

F

Write out each of the following sentences in two ways to show that there can be a difference of meaning, depending on the way each version is punctuated.

1. The man I saw was ill.
2. You are pleased I suppose Mr. Brown remarked.
3. All my friends children go to that school.
4. What have you forgotten my love.
5. I told him you were wrong.
6. George said John shot Henry.
7. We were delighted to see him and you.
8. If you really think that there is nothing more to be done I shall go.

G

Punctuate correctly the following passages, using capital letters where required, and paragraphing where necessary.

1. At the entrance to a small hotel in the south of france a notice stated here english german spanish and italian are spoken an englishman entered and asked where is the interpreter there isnt one replied the manager then who speaks the languages mentioned the visitors was the reply.

2. The work of the thames conservancy board is varied and complex its main tasks are these to be water controllers water conservers water purveyors and water purifiers also to deal with land drainage pollution fishing and river traffic i wonder if users of this waterway boatmen fishermen factory owners and holiday makers realise what they owe to this organisation.

3. As i understand it said the chairman the question is why has the annual subscription been raised and not has the annual subscription been raised for this is a fait accompli as our friends across the

channel say never mind about the french cried a voice its my money im worried about.

4. The emperor napoleon was chatting one day with his wife the empress josephine can you tell me my dear he said suddenly what difference there is between a mirror and you no she replied well a mirror reflects without speaking and you speak without reflecting explained her husband laughing.

5. Weve been waiting a long time to see you mr white said the manager leaning forward in his chair where have you been may i ask its my rheumatism sir ive been crippled with it you know didnt you get my letter what letter i wrote last monday i did really explained the old man terrified by his employers stern tone well youre better now i suppose snapped sir duncan or you wouldnt have come.

6. It was in august or september i forget which that i first met marys brother in law a six foot guards officer who had fought in the boer war hes always saying the guards arent what they were she explained but take no notice of him it amuses him.

7. A pleasant looking youth aged about eighteen or nineteen offered to help us although he was obviously poor his clothes were ragged and his boots in holes he refused the half crown i offered its not money i want sir its work he explained what sort of work i asked anything no farm work i can drive a tractor plough and milk he answered his large dark rather sad looking eyes lighting up with enthusiasm.

CHAPTER XIV

ERRORS TO AVOID IN GRAMMAR, VOCABULARY, AND STYLE

A. Errors in Grammar and Syntax

(Syntax = the grammatical relationship of one word to another.) The following summary indicates the main errors that occur under this heading:

Note: Many errors have been dealt with already in the chapters on the Parts of Speech, and reference is made to these where necessary.

Errors are indicated by italics in the examples given.

1. Nouns

(*a*) The word "alternative" (=one or other of two things only) may now be used for more than one thing or idea, and to do this is no longer considered an error.

e.g. We have several alternatives.

(*b*) Confusing singular and plural of nouns with unusual plurals:

e.g. This phenome*na* is interesting.
(Correction: "phenomenon"—singular form.)

2. Pronouns

(*a*) Inconsistency in the use of pronouns when writing about animals.

e.g. He spoke to the dog *who* had evidently hurt its paw.
("Which" should replace "who" here. "Who" may be

used for animals if they are referred to as "he" or "she" and then the adjectives "his" or "her" will replace "its". "Whose" may be used at all times for the possessive.)

Note: "That" can be used for persons, animals, and things in a defining clause. e.g. The man (the dog, the house) that I saw was the one I was looking for.

(*b*) There is often confusion as to which word is the antecedent of a dative pronoun—the noun to which it refers—with consequent error in the number and person of the verb.

> e.g. Matthews is one of the best footballers that *has* ever played.
> ("Has" should be "have", as "that" refers to "footballers"; but "Matthews is the best footballer that I have seen" is, of course, correct.)

(*c*) Relative pronoun in wrong case, i.e. writing "who" for "whom" when it is the object of a verb, or of a preposition.

> e.g. (verb) The man, *who* I met frequently, looked ill.
> (preposition) The men to *who* I refer. *Who* was it written by?
> ("Whom" should be used in these examples.)

But be careful with parenthetical remarks or asides, which can be misleading when case of relative has to be decided. (See Chapter III: Relative Pronouns.)

(*d*) Wrong case in dealing with other pronouns.

> e.g. Let you and *I* go.
> ("I" should be "me", object of verb "let".)
> It is *him*.
> ("Him" should be "he", as verb "to be" cannot take an object.)

(*e*) Errors in number. (See also Chapter III: Distributive Pronouns.)

> (i) e.g. Anyone can leave *their* car here.
> (Should be "his"—or "his or her" to be pedantic —as "anyone" is singular.)

Similarly "one", "everyone", "everybody", "anybody", "somebody", "nobody", "each", "either", and "neither" are singular.

e.g. As to the two boys, neither was very intelligent.

Note: "None" can take singular or plural, and is more frequently used with the plural now.

e.g. None were lost.

(ii) e.g. We have samples in blue, red, and yellow. I prefer the *latter*.

("Latter" and "former" can be used only when speaking of two persons or things. Say "I prefer the last" or "the yellow ones".)

(iii) e.g. The two men greeted *one another*.
　　　　　The four men all hated *each other*.

(In the first example "each other" used in the case of one of two persons—should be used; in the second example "one another"—used in the case of one of more than two persons—should be used.)

(iv) e.g. Give me the poker or the tongs—*any* will do.
　　　　　Books, papers, magazines—*either* will do.

("Any" in the first example should be "either", used when speaking of one or two; "either" should be "any" in the second example, as "any" means any one of more than two.)

(*f*) Unnecessary "and".

e.g. This officer, serving abroad, *and* who was a captain (omit "and" here as unnecessary).

However, if one relative clause has already been used, "and" is quite correct.

e.g. This officer, who was serving abroad, and who was a captain, . . .

3. Adjectives

(*a*) Mistakes in use of Comparative and Superlative. These are dealt with in Chapter IV (Adjectives).

(*b*) Confusion in use of "any" and "any other".

e.g. This paper has the largest circulation of *any* newspaper.

("Other" must be inserted and the comparative used. Write: "This paper has a larger circulation than any other newspaper".)

(*c*) Confusion of Singular and Plural.

e.g. Those kind (sort) of experiments *are* dangerous.

("Kind" is singular. It is best to say "Experiments of that kind are dangerous", though "that kind of experiment is dangerous" is also correct.)

(*d*) The distributive adjectives ("each", "every", "either", "neither") require a verb in the singular, as they refer to only one member of a group.

e.g. Neither book *was* of any use (not "were").

(Either can be used only for each of two. Use "each" and "any" for one of more than two.)

e.g. Either book of these two is expensive.
Any book in that library is interesting.
Each man of the team of eleven receives a medal.
Each of us is willing to pay his share. (Do not write "our share!")

(*e*) Confusion of "its" and "it's".

e.g. The dog wagged *it's* tail.

("It's" is a contraction of "it is". None of the possessive adjectives have an apostrophe. We do not write "hi's pen", so why write "it's tail"?)

(*f*) "Due" is an adjective, and so must be used with its noun only as an epithet (e.g. with due respect), or predicatively (e.g. The money was due.). It is therefore wrong to use "due" in such cases as "Due to the rain, the harvest failed".

Here "Owing to the rain" or "On account of the rain" or "Because of . . ." should be used.

4. Verbs

(a) A verb must agree with its subject in number and person. This is called the concord of verb and subject. Mistakes are made through failure to understand what is the real subject of a verb.

We are often attracted by the noun or pronoun nearest to the verb, and so misled; e.g. Each of us *have* decided to go ("each" is subject, so write "has"). Some brushes, a paintbox, and a sheet of paper *is* required (several subjects, so write "are").

e.g. Either the cat or the dog *are* sure to be hungry.

(Write "is". "Or" indicates that only *one* of the animals is the subject here.)

e.g. A copy of the rules *were* given to each candidate.

(Say "was", as "copy" is the subject.)

e.g. Economics *are* an important subject.

(Say "is", as "Economics" is the name of one subject.)
Note: (i) If two nouns are combined to form one idea, the verb will be in the singular.

e.g. This bread and butter is too thick.

(ii) Collective nouns (see Chapter II) take a verb in the singular or plural according to whether we wish to indicate the whole, or individual members.

e.g. The Sports Committee meets on Monday.
 The committee are now taking their seats.

(b) Tenses must not be used in the wrong sequence, i.e. past tense, for example, must be followed in the same sentence by a past tense.

e.g. He stated that we *are* annoying him.
 ("are" should be "were".)

Similarly, "will" must be followed by "shall", and "would" by "should".

e.g. If you will allow me, I shall (not "should") be glad to help.

(*c*) Confusion of "shall" and "will". This has already been dealt with when discussing the Future Tense (Chapter V).

(*d*) Generally speaking, it is preferable for reasons of unity and sound, to avoid splitting an infinitive.

e.g. I used to frequently see him.

(Should be altered to "to see him frequently" or "frequently to see him").

(*e*) Confusion of Simple and Perfect Infinitives.

e.g. He had hoped to be the first man to *have climbed* that mountain ("to have climbed" should be replaced by the Simple Infinitive "to climb").

(*f*) Errors often occur through *Ellipsis* (i.e. omitting words needed to complete a construction, regarding them as understood).

e.g. I never have and never shall allow this.

Here "I never have" is completed by "allow", whereas we should say "I never have allowed"—and so must insert the past participle "allowed" after "have".

(*g*) *Some Problem Verbs.* (See Chapter V.)

(i) The Verb "to lie" (intransitive—no object) and the verb "to lay" (transitive—with object) are often confused.

e.g. I *laid* down on the grass (should be "lay"—no object), but "I laid myself down to die" is correct, "myself" being the object.

(ii) The Past Tense and Past Participle of the verb "to hang" = "hanged" for "death by hanging", e.g. He hanged himself. He has been hanged.

In all other cases the Past Tense and Past Participle is "hung".

e.g. I hung up the picture.
The picture was duly hung.
He hung by his arms on to a branch or from a branch.

(*h*) Loose or Unrelated Participle.

e.g. *Strolling* over the moors, an aeroplane landed near me.

("Strolling" must refer here to the subject of the sentence—and this is obviously absurd. Correct by inserting the real subject to which "strolling" refers, i.e. As I was strolling over the moors, . . .)

(*i*) Confusion of "will" and "shall" (i.e. of determination with futurity—see Chapter V).

e.g. I *will* drown; nobody *shall* save me.
(Correction: "I shall drown; nobody will save me.")

(*j*) Confusion of Gerund with Present Participle.

e.g. I do not like *him* being appointed.
I do not like *Tom* being appointed.

(In both cases "being" is the "act of being", a gerund or verbal noun, and so must be preceded by an adjective in the first example; and by a genitive in the second. Correction: "his being appointed" and "Tom's being appointed".)

5. Adverbs

(*a*) Misplacing of adverbs.

e.g. This racket needs mending *badly*.

(The position of "badly" implies that someone is to mend the racket unsatisfactorily.)

e.g. I can *only* lend you £10.

(Alter to: "I can lend you only £10" if the amount is to be limited; otherwise the sentence means that a loan, and not a gift, is offered.)

(*b*) Use of double negative when unnecessary.

e.g. I have no paper *nor* ink.
I should not wonder if it did *not* rain.

("nor" should be "or", and "if it rained" should replace "if it did not rain", as in each case there is originally a double, or unnecessary second, negative. Such examples as: "I never go *nowhere*" are too obvious and painful to require discussion.)

(*c*) Misuse of "that" and "quite".

e.g. I am not *that* stupid.

("that" is not an adverb. Correction: "as stupid as that", "stupid to that extent".)

e.g. He made *quite* a noise.

("quite" is not an adjective but an adverb, so cannot limit the noun "noise". Correction: "a considerable noise".)

(*d*) Confusion of "less" with "fewer", i.e. of quantity and size with mere number.

e.g. There were *less* than ten spectators.

(Say "fewer", for numbers, when there is no idea of measurement.)

e.g. It weighed *fewer* than two tons.

(Say "less' when a question of measurement of quantity.)

(*e*) Confusion of adverbs with adjectives.

e.g. He will do it *quicker* than I can.

("quicker" is comparative of adjective "quick". The adverb is "quickly", so write "more quickly".) Some adverbs and adjectives are absolutely similar, of course, such as "a fast train"; "I run fast". Note: "leisurely", an adjective or adverb.

(*f*) Misuse of "than" after "hardly", "scarcely".

e.g. Hardly had we got ashore *than* the boat sank.

("than" is for comparison. Correction: "when the boat sank"; "when"—conjunction adverb of time—is required here, but we can say "No sooner had we landed than the boat sank", as in this sentence the idea is one of comparison, not of time.)

6. Prepositions

(*a*) Failure to use objective case after all prepositions. (See Chapter VIII.)

(*b*) Confusion of "between" with "among".

e.g. Divide it *between* the six men, or *among* the two boys.

("between" and "among" should be interchanged, as "between" is used when referring to two things and "among" when referring to more than two. Also, as "between" must refer to two things, write: "There was a space between each tree and the next" or "after each tree". We cannot say merely "between each tree".)

(*c*) Wrong preposition used after certain adjectives, nouns, and verbs.

e.g. This picture is different *to* that.
    ("to" should be "from".)

We say "indifferent *to* pain", however. A good dictionary will give the correct preposition to use.

(*d*) Mistakes due to ellipsis or contraction (i.e. omitting as understood words that would normally be inserted).

e.g. This quality did not add, but rather detracted from, his character.

(The preposition "to" must be inserted after "add"; we do not "add from", and "from" would otherwise be understood as the omitted preposition.)

(*e*) Ending a sentence with a preposition is often ugly.

e.g. The address I am writing *to*.

("To which I am writing" is preferable.)

7. Conjunctions

(*a*) Confusion of adjective "like" with conjunction "as".

e.g. Do *like* I do.

("Like" should be replaced by "as", a conjunction joining clauses. Always use "as" when a verb follows, but the adjective "like" [= like to] must be used when a noun or pronoun only is referred to. e.g. A boy like him.)

(*b*) Misuse of object after "than".

e.g. He is bigger than *me*.

("me" should be "I", as the complete clause is "bigger than I am", and "than" is therefore a conjunction and not a preposition.)

(*c*) "Or" wrongly used after "neither".

e.g. Neither cats *or* dogs interested him.

("or" should be "nor", as "either" is followed by "or" and "neither" always by "nor".)

(*d*) Use of preposition "without" instead of conjunction "unless".

e.g. I shall not go *without* you accompany me.

("without" is a preposition, not a conjunction. The conjunction "unless" is required here to join clauses.)

(*e*) Misuse of "while".

e.g. General Smith made a speech *while* the Mayoress presented the prizes.

("while" should be replaced by "and" or "following which, after which", as the two events were not simultaneous, but consecutive.)

(*f*) Wrong position of pairs of co-relating conjunctions (i.e. either—or, neither—nor, not only—but also).

e.g. I shall *neither* buy a car nor a caravan.

(Each one of a pair of conjunctions must precede words that are the same part of speech. Correction: I shall buy neither a car nor a caravan.)

(*g*) Error due to omission of conjunction.

e.g. His work is no better, and indeed not so good as yours.

(We cannot say "no better *as*" so must insert "than" after "better".)

(*h*) Wrong use of "because".

e.g. The reason he failed is *because* he is ill.

(Write: "that" for "because".)

B. Errors in Vocabulary

Errors in the choice of words can be summed up under four headings:

(1) The use of colloquialisms, slang, and dialect words. (See Chapter IX: "Vocabulary".)

(2) The unnecessary use of words and phrases borrowed from foreign languages. (See Chapter IX: "Vocabulary".)

(3) The too frequent and inaccurate use of certain adjectives ("nice", "lovely", "awful", etc.), adverbs ("awfully", "terribly", etc.), and verbs ("have" and "get"). (See Chapter IX: "Vocabulary".)

(4) The confusion of a word with another that is very similar in sound.

This type of error is termed a malapropism, a word derived from the character Mrs. Malaprop in Sheridan's play *The Rivals*. The name Malaprop is simply a contraction of the French *mal à propos* (= ill-timed, coming at an unsuitable time), and her constant misuse of words is commemorated by this term. It was she who wanted her daughter to have "a *supercilious* knowledge of accounts", but she did not wish her "to be a *progeny* of learning".

"Supercilious" means "haughty, disdainful", and "superficial" (= on the surface, i.e. not deep) was the word she should have used.

"Progeny" means "children, descendants", and she meant "prodigy" (= a wonder, an extraordinary person or thing).

Further examples of this type of error are:

He lived in a *luxuriant* flat.

("Luxuriant" means "growing abundantly" and is used of trees, shrubs, and plants. It should be replaced by "luxurious" (= abounding in luxury).)

George was unfortunately a *congenial* idiot.
("Congenial" means "suited to, pleasing" and the word required is "congenital" = "from birth".)

C. Errors in Style and Expression

We may write a sentence that is grammatically correct and in which the spelling and the punctuation are correct, and yet it may not be a good sentence because of errors in style and expression.

Ambiguity (= having more than one meaning, of doubtful meaning).

Three things lead to ambiguity:

(*a*) Vague use of pronouns or possessive adjectives. e.g. Jones admitted frankly to Brown that he hated his employer. This could mean either that Jones hated his own employer, or that he hated Brown's employer. Sometimes the use of "the former" and "the latter" helps to avoid confusion. Often we must repeat a noun instead of employing a pronoun: e.g. If your dog has distemper, it will vanish rapidly after swallowing these powders. "It" seems to suggest "your dog will vanish". It would be clearer and safer to substitute "the distemper" or "the illness", or even the pronoun "this", and we shall then have to alter "swallowing" to "after it has swallowed".

(*b*) Failure to observe the rule of *Proximity*—the rule which demands that any qualifying word or words should be placed in proximity to (i.e. as close as possible) to the word or words qualified. e.g. The kitten was found by a small girl crying pitifully at the top of a tall tree ("crying . . ." should come after word "found").

(*c*) The omission of some necessary word. e.g. He gave her a watch, and her brother a book. (Insert "gave" after "and".) Would you like to try on the dress in the window? (Insert "that is" after "dress".)

Anachronism (= placing some event before or after its correct time, an error in computing time). The usual example quoted is Shakespeare's reference in "Julius Caesar" to a clock striking. Clocks had not been invented at that time, and certainly not striking clocks.

Clichés. Certain phrases, through continual use, have lost their effectiveness—especially those where some particular adjective is invariably attached to a particular noun, e.g. "dazzling beauty", "leaden feet", "flashing teeth", "sparkling eyes", etc.

These outworn phrases are often referred to as "clichés" (a French word meaning "stereotyped, in a fixed mould or die") or as "hackneyed" expressions. They should be avoided if possible—and many good modern orators and writers have successfully replaced them by new and more striking phrases—in speaking and writing good English, though force of habit often tempts us to use them.

Circumlocution or Periphrasis (= expressing something in an unnecessarily roundabout or indirect manner).

> e.g. "A mechanically-propelled road vehicle" for "car".
> "A rodent-preventive officer" for "rat-catcher".

Circumlocution is sometimes employed deliberately and amusingly by humorous writers.

Irrelevance. Sometimes, particularly in journalism, when a writer attempts to cram a number of facts into a limited space, one part of a sentence bears no relation in sense to the other part.

> e.g. Educated in France, Fortescue wrote his first accepted poem at the age of 18.

(The fact that Fortescue was educated in France was not the cause of his writing his first poem at the age of 18.)

This error is often referred to as a *"non sequitur"* (Latin for "it does not follow").

Pleonasm or Redundancy (= saying more than required, using more words than necessary).

> e.g. He was carrying a stick *in his hand.*

"In his hand" is unnecessary; it is unlikely that one would carry a stick in any other way.

Repetition or Tautology (= saying the same thing twice).

Although repetition can be used very effectively, particularly in poetry for emphasis or rhythm, it is nevertheless an error when used unnecessarily, without attaining any effect except monotony. Examples of tautology occur in such incorrect everyday phrases as "*frequently* in the habit of", "*mutually* attracted to each other", "*equally* as well as", "*free* and without charge".

Verbosity (= excessive and complicated wordiness). This is very similar to Circumlocution.

> e.g. "He was intoxicated with the exuberance of his own verbosity."

This can be expressed more clearly and simply by "He spoke at great length" or "He was carried away by his love of talking".

Mr. Micawber in Dickens's *David Copperfield* is the best-known offender in this respect.

EXERCISES

A

Point out the grammatical mistakes in each of the following sentences:

1. He was so exhausted he just laid down on the ground.

2. Due to the drought, my roses have failed this year.

3. The bird, who had an injured wing, did not move.

4. A few days' delay were enough to ruin my plans.

5. Caruso was one of the greatest singers that has ever visited England.

6. Between you and I, the witness is untrustworthy.

7. The drainage is poor: the water just lays on the lawn after a storm.

8. The millionaire bought the best of the two pictures for his collection.

9. The committee was unable to make up their minds.

10. I wish to thoroughly examine this document.
11. The skill and speed of the champion was too much for his opponent.
12. A fine collection of pictures were on view.
13. Smith was a better worker than any in his office.
14. Either of the three houses will suit me.
15. Whom do you think won the prize?
16. Physics are my favourite subject, though I like French.
17. A total eclipse of the sun is a phenomena not often seen.
18. Each of the climbers were carrying an axe.
19. Hardly had she sat down than she fainted.
20. I drunk the wine only to please my host.
21. There was a space of twenty yards between every lamp-post.
22. Let you and I volunteer to help him.
23. John, who I expected to be seriously ill, soon recovered.
24. Who did you meet at the party last night?
25. Running on to the pier, his ship had already sailed.
26. On behalf of we citizens of Hull I thank you.
27. What do you think of me learning to swim?
28. Which is the easier to learn—French, German, or Spanish?
29. Neither of the dogs were willing to let go of the stick.
30. Are you sure he is older than me?
31. He explained to me that he will soon be back.
32. Watch your instructor, and then do like he does.
33. These chairs were neither cheaper, or better than the others.
34. I am certain it is not him who is guilty.
35. He is a murderer, and deserves to be hung.
36. The two old ladies greeted one another with pleasure.
37. These kind of apples never keep well.
38. It is nine o'clock. When will we start?
39. In the hall was his stick and umbrella.
40. He ran quicker than I expected.
41. The unfortunate cat injured it's paw in a trap.
42. Everybody can try their luck in this game.
43. Shall you help Peter with his homework tonight?
44. I meant to have telephoned you yesterday.
45. The reason I forgot is because I lost my diary.
46. All the bystanders which saw the fight were interviewed.
47. Her numerous pet dogs were always quarrelling with each other.
48. I can only help you in the garden for a week.

49. Is this letter your's? Who is it addressed to?

50. There are less than twenty players to choose from, but I think these are the three best.

B

Re-write the following sentences, in which words and phrases occur in the wrong position, so that each sentence has its correct meaning.

1. This house needs re-decorating badly.

2. He uses the money I send him every day to get drunk.

3. The old lady got out of a car with a curiously-shaped bonnet.

4. The leader of the party called a halt for refreshments which lasted only a few minutes.

5. The trucks were pulled by ponies that were empty.

6. This kitten was found by a little girl crying at the top of an elm-tree.

7. I repaired the leak before any damage could be done on your advice.

8. That stone was erected at the place where William Rufus was killed to mark an historic spot.

9. I read my employer's letter announcing his retirement with glee.

10. Arsenal are at home to Aston Villa, who have won the cup seven times, in the third round.

C

The following sentences contain words wrongly used. Replace these by the correct word in each case.

1. This painter had the honour of having his picture hanged in the Royal Academy.

2. A mirage is nothing more than an optical allusion often encountered in deserts.

3. I am not sufficiently practicable to be able to make a greenhouse by myself.

4. Order your next suit from us. Gentlemen can be given fits at any time.

5. The conquerors marched under triumphant arches.

6. My sister gave up marrying to become a nurse.

7. I was at the cemetery for his internment—a sad ceremony.

8. When we breathe in we inhale: when we breathe out we expire.

9. All teachers of English should be properly certified.

10. When you leave hospital I advise you to go to some spa to effervesce.

D

Re-write the following sentences so that they are no longer ambiguous.

1. He told Smith that he did not love his wife.

2. Would you rather a lion attacked you or a tiger?

3. When he joins the army he will not have his mother to cook.

4. Bring us your luggage, and we will send it in all directions. (Advt.)

5. The committee may refuse membership to anyone they think proper.

6. After attending my classes for two years, this student knows practically nothing.

7. The huntsman injured his knee when his horse fell, and had to be destroyed.

8. I have just smoked one of your cigars, and shall in future smoke no others. (Advt.)

9. Don't go to other shops to be disappointed, but come to us. (Advt.)

10. My father gave me a bicycle and my sister a book.

11. Jones was as anxious to capture the burglar as his dog.

12. Would you like to try on that dress in the window?

E

Re-write the following sentences, omitting any unnecessary words.

1. He was offered the samples free, at no cost to himself.

2. You should not try to monopolise the conversation entirely.

3. This stamp is the only one of this design ever printed. It is absolutely unique.

4. We left the camp at dawn, and when we returned again it was dusk.

5. His wife offered voluntarily to cook for us during Mary's absence away from home.

6. I shall start beginning to plan my new garden soon. What an interesting and fascinating task it will be.

7. He is in the habit of visiting his aunt in Scotland regularly every month.

8. The subject of the lecture will be about France.

F

Re-write the following sentences in simpler English.

1. The newcomer stated that he was most gratified to make my acquaintance, and invited me to partake of some liquid refreshment.

2. An ornithological specimen in one's personal possession has a value equal to that of a pair of similar species ensconced in a shrub.

3. Given favourable meteorological conditions I intend to take some ambulatory exercise.

4. While indulging in an equestrian contest he lost his equilibrium and the frontal portion of his cranium came in violent contact with the terrestrial surface.

5. My nocturnal researches into historical matters indicated as essential by my history master have been neglected owing to a con-catenation of circumstances inimical to concentration.

6. After a considerable period of cerebral activity the ancient mariner replied in the negative to an inquiry by a uniformed representative of the law as to whether he was inebriated.

CHAPTER XV

SENTENCE AND PARAGRAPH CONSTRUCTION

The basic rule in constructing a sentence or a paragraph is that there should be unity of thought and clearness of expression.

If in the course of a sentence or paragraph we wander from one idea to another we shall achieve only confusion. Two disconnected ideas require two separate sentences or paragraphs. We must learn to think *before* we write, and not merely as we write.

There can be no fixed rule for the length of a sentence or paragraph. It is obvious that the longer our sentences or paragraphs are, the more danger there is of their becoming involved and difficult to comprehend.

On the other hand, if we always aimed to write only a succession of very short sentences and paragraphs, we should attain only monotony.

We should therefore aim at varying length, carefully avoiding excesses in either direction.

SENTENCE CONSTRUCTION

The problem of sentence construction calls for an examination of the following points:

1. Unity of Thought.
2. Order of Words (Periodic and Loose Sentences).
3. Emphasis.
4. Methods of Linking Sentences.

1. *Unity of Thought.*

We must at all costs avoid composing a sentence which changes from one idea to another, and expresses two disconnected ideas.

> e.g. "While we are discussing the subject of butterflies, how interesting it is to study the life of the moth."

This is obviously rather an extreme example, but it illustrates that change of thought which is called a *"non sequitur"* (Latin: "It does not follow", and it certainly does not in this example).

If we write "While on the subject of butterflies, we shall find it interesting to study their complete life-cycle from the egg to the final development of the winged insect", we have achieved unity.

We can, therefore, include a series of actions in one sentence if they are closely related and contribute to one idea.

> e.g. "Arriving at the office, Mr. Smith greeted his colleagues, hung up his coat and hat, and sat down at his desk to read his correspondence."

2. *Order of Words.*

Sentences other than those containing no subordinate clauses (e.g. He posted the letter on Thursday) are classified under two types, *Periodic* and *Loose*.

A *Periodic* sentence is one in which the main verb or main idea is purposely reserved for the concluding part of the sentence.

> e.g. If I can finish my work in time, and provided that I can borrow George's car, I will meet you at the station.

This device sustains and even increases interest until the very end of the sentence.

A *Loose* sentence is constructed to have the opposite effect, the main idea being expressed at once at the beginning of the sentence, followed by subordinate clauses or phrases.

e.g. I will meet you at the station, if I can finish my work in time, and provided that I can borrow George's car.

It must not be thought, however, that the periodic sentence must be cultivated to the exclusion of the loose.

The fact is that, though the periodic is more effective in sustaining interest, and is more forceful, the loose sentence is more natural, and often clearer.

To use one or the other exclusively would lead to monotony, and the best style will therefore vary in form, and employ some of each.

3. *Emphasis.*

Emphasis can be obtained by several devices.

(*a*) *By position.*

When we wish to give emphasis to a certain word or words, the most effective position for the selected word or words is the very beginning of a sentence, and the next most prominent position is at the end of a sentence.

In the sentence "It is said that almost instantaneous death is the result of a bite from this snake", the normal order of words does not particularly emphasise the words "instantaneous death".

If, however, we alter the order of words to "Almost instantaneous death is said to be the result of a bite from this snake", the emphasis on "instantaneous death" is far greater. We can also write "The result of a bite from this snake is said to be almost instantaneous death" to achieve stress on "instantaneous death".

In the case of adjectives, emphasis can be obtained by placing them out of their normal position (i.e. after the noun they qualify).

(*b*) *By repetition.*

e.g. This is a far, far wiser course to take.

(*c*) *By prefacing* the word to be emphasised by "It is".

e.g. It is today that we must act.

183

(*d*) *By contrast.*

e.g. We must act today, and not tomorrow.

Constant and unnecessary emphasis of individual words leads, like all repetition, to monotony. How artificial and exhausting, for example, a personal letter can be in which the writer (dare we say usually a female?) stresses every third or fourth word by underlining it.

4. *Sentence Linking (Synthesis).*

If we were to express a series of ideas by a succession of brief separate sentences, we should achieve a very monotonous effect, as in the following example:

"I ate my breakfast. I wrote some letters. I finished writing them at eleven o'clock. I then looked out of the window. I saw that it was raining. I looked for my umbrella. I set out for the post office."

The linking of a series of short sentences to form a single sentence is called synthesis (a "putting together of different elements"), which is the opposite process to analysis (a "taking apart"), in which each component part is examined.

Sentences may be linked in the following ways:

(*a*) By using *Conjunctions.*

    (i) Co-ordinating, e.g. and, then, so, therefore, but.
    (ii) Introducing subordinate adverbial clauses, e.g. if, as, when, where, because.

e.g. I took my umbrella. I set out for the post office.
    I took my umbrella *and* I set out for the post office.

(We must be careful, however, not to use conjunctions, particularly "and" and "then", again and again, or we shall achieve the monotony we are trying to avoid.)

The above co-ordinating conjunction "and" joins two main clauses, but we can also employ subordinate conjunctions to introduce dependent adverbial clauses.

e.g. It was raining. I looked for my umbrella.
As it was raining, I looked for my umbrella.

(*b*) By using *Relative Pronouns* (e.g. who, which, that, what, whom, whose) to construct clauses subordinate or dependent on the main idea or ideas.

e.g. I wrote some letters.
I finished writing them at eleven o'clock.
= I wrote some letters *which* I finished at eleven o'clock.

(Note: Sometimes an adjective or adjectives added to the noun will be sufficient.

e.g. I picked some roses. They were white and scented.
= I picked some scented white roses.)

(*c*) By using *Phrases*, particularly those employing the present participle (e.g. arriving), to replace sentences.

e.g. I ate my breakfast.
I wrote some letters.
= *Having* eaten my breakfast, I wrote some letters.

And phrases constructed with a preposition followed by a gerund, by a noun, or by an infinitive.

e.g. After breakfasting, on arriving, before starting, etc.
After breakfast, on my arrival, on account of the rain
(= because it was raining.)
In order to go (= so that I could go).

(*d*) We can also use a *semi-colon* to avoid the use of "and" to join co-ordinate clauses, especially in cases where it is desirable to avoid the use of too many conjunctions.

e.g. I ate my breakfast and wrote some letters, which I finished at eleven o'clock; I then looked out of the window and saw that it was raining.

But we must not employ semi-colons when asked to combine a series of short sentences into one complex sentence, as each semi-colon used introduces a separate sentence.

Having noted the methods we can employ to link a series of short sentences, we must be careful to avoid the excessive use of any one linking-device.

We are now ready to link up the example given at the beginning of this section, and it will be seen that there can be several different successful versions of this. If we are asked to construct one complex sentence, however, we cannot use semi-colons.

First we must underline the sentence or sentences in the original series containing the main ideas round which the new and longer sentence is to be built. Practice will soon enable us to distinguish ideas that are essential and that cannot be subordinated from those which are merely dependent and comparatively unimportant.

The number of short sentences given as an example is rather too great for the final longer sentence to be built round one idea, and in this case we can underline the two sentences "I wrote some letters" and "I saw that it was raining" as important ideas round which to build one complex sentence.

Suggested sentence: "*Having eaten* my breakfast, I wrote some letters, *which* I finished at eleven o'clock, *and when* I then looked out of the window I saw that it was raining, *so* I looked for my umbrella *before setting out* for the post office."

Note: Linking words and alterations are underlined.

PARAGRAPH CONSTRUCTION

A paragraph is a grouping together of a series of sentences—and they may be few or many in number—which are connected with the development of some single idea, or deal with some single topic.

Paragraphs achieve two objects: they ensure ease of comprehension by separating one theme from another; and the natural pause the eye and the mind make between one paragraph and the next provides a welcome interval and rest for both. How often do we abandon, or never even start, the reading of an article or essay whose paragraphs each take up a whole column or page. Our eyes convey in such cases a message to our minds that such paragraphs are mentally indigestible.

It has already been stated that the basic rules for sentence construction (i.e. unity of theme, clearness of expression, and avoidance of excessive length or repetition) apply equally to the paragraph.

It will be helpful to study in addition the following points:

1. Construction: Length and Emphasis.
2. Opening Paragraphs.
3. Linking Paragraphs: Development.
4. Concluding Paragraphs.

1. *Construction: Length and Emphasis.*

If we are given too many rules for the construction and length of a paragraph, we shall never attain a natural fluency.

Having laid down unity of theme as the main rule, we can simply state that the question of length is more or less a matter of the importance of the theme or topic with which the writer is dealing; a minor topic or point will obviously call for only a brief paragraph, a major point for a longer one.

In the construction of a paragraph there will be one basic or topic sentence round which the paragraph is built up, and as in the case of the sentence, the most effective position for this is either at the beginning or at the end of the paragraph.

If we place the topic sentence at the beginning, we can then devote the rest of the paragraph to developing the idea expressed—and this is the easier, if less effective, method.

If we place the topic sentence at the end, we shall have

to build up the paragraph to reach this climax—a method which is more difficult generally, but one which is very effective, particularly in an argument.

Here are brief examples of each method:

(*a*) Topic sentence at beginning of paragraph.

Joan of Arc turned the tide of battle. She, a mere child, crossed half a ravaged and robber-infested France to give her message to Charles VII at his Court; she led rough and disillusioned soldiers to battles for which she had had no training; reassuring them, she fought the English until she drove them back, and would have liberated all France had she not been abandoned, betrayed by those she led.

(*b*) Topic sentence at end of paragraph.

Though a mere child, she crossed half a ravaged and robber-infested France to give her message to Charles VII at his Court; rough and disillusioned soldiers were led by her to battles for which she had had no training; reassuring them, she fought the English until she drove them back, dispirited; truly, though she was to die for it, the Maid of Orleans saved the soul of France.

At all costs we must avoid the incoherent, wandering paragraph, which has no unity of theme or of objective, such as the following:

The cow is surely the most useful domestic animal in the world. My uncle has a small milking herd on his farm in Dorset, and one of the cows is called Priscilla, after me. I am very fond of cows; they are so docile, and look so pleasant feeding in the green meadows. They are found in nearly every country, except in very cold regions. They are ruminating animals.

2. *Opening Paragraphs.*

These will naturally vary according to the type of composition we are attempting.

The basic rule, however, is that the initial paragraph should attract the reader's attention, and prepare his mind for what is to follow. Brevity is a virtue, as a long opening paragraph often repels rather than attracts.

This can be accomplished by several methods, which again will vary according to the type of composition with which the writer is dealing; by beginning with a quotation, a proverb, or an illustrative anecdote; by opening with a definition of the subject; by indicating why the subject under discussion is of topical interest; by a challenging statement or opinion; by some startling contrast; by a paradox; by some personal experience, amusing or otherwise; by a statement of the writer's aims and intentions; and even by asking the reader a question.

If we cannot find a striking opening, we can at least try to write a clear and brief introduction which leads naturally to subsequent paragraphs.

Examples:

(*a*) Opening with a definition of the subject. This is suitable for essays on scientific subjects, and in many other discursive essays.

e.g. (Subject: "Oil").

Though vegetable oils play an important part in our food and medicines, it is the vast reservoirs of mineral oil beneath the earth's surface which have altered the riches and commercial balance of power in the twentieth century.

or (Subject: "The Cow").

To the naturalist, the cow is a ruminating animal; to the walker, it is an animal which makes a pleasing picture as it feeds in a field; to the town-dweller, it is a source of milk and cheese; to the humble peasant, it is his greatest treasure.

(*b*) Opening with some illustrative anecdote, or personal experience, amusing or otherwise.

e.g. (Subject: "Tipping").

An eccentric Victorian millionaire was reputed to have solved the problem of tipping by invariably rewarding services rendered with a farthing; when the victim expressed surprise, the donor habitually explained with solemnity: "That's quite all right. I never give less."

or (Subject: "Thrift").

My grandfather, who owned a chain of shops when he retired, invariably emptied his trouser pockets every night after winding the clock and put every copper he found in them into a large tin money-box. He kept up this habit until the day of his death.

(*c*) Opening with a startling paradox, a comparison, a bold personal statement of opinion or of what the writer is setting out to prove, or even by a challenging question to the reader. These are obviously suitable openings for any controversial subject.

e.g. (Subject: "Modern Ideas in Education").
"The child is father of the man."

or (Subject: "Winter").
Spring is a season of awakening, but Winter is far from being entirely a season of sleeping.

or (Subject: "The Future of Railways").
In twenty years' time a steam-engine will be almost as rare a sight as the mythical dodo bird, and in fifty, railways may have disappeared altogether.

or (Subject: "The Keeping of Pets").
An Englishman's home is no longer his castle, but his menagerie.

or (Subject: "The Value of Foreign Travel").
"What should they know of England
Who only England know?" Kipling has remarked.

(*d*) Opening by indicating why the subject under discussion is of topical interest.

e.g. (Subject: "Television").
The impact of television on our leisure is now as great as, if not greater than, that of the cinema or the wireless; its influence for good or bad is of vital importance to the present generation.

(*e*) Opening with a suitable quotation, proverb, and

epigrams are often most helpful, but do not quote from the prose or poetry of a well-known author unless you can do so accurately.

All quotations must obviously be relevant to the subject, and not be included merely to give an impression of wide knowledge or scholarship.

e.g. (Subject: "Optimism").

We are all familiar with the proverb "It is a long lane which has no turning", but the definition of a pessimist as "someone who has met an optimist" is perhaps less well-known.

or (Subject: "Exploration").
"Send here the bold, the seekers of the way—
The passionless, the unshakeable of soul!"

(Kipling)

or (Subject: "Genius").

Edison was probably nearer the truth than anyone else when he wrote "Genius is one per cent inspiration and ninety-nine per cent perspiration".

(*f*) Opening with a brief statement of the writer's aims.

e.g. (Subject: "Camping").

In this essay I propose to deal with the subject of camping under four headings: firstly, the growth of camping; secondly, the different types of camping; thirdly, preparations and requisites for camping; fourthly, the value of camping.

3. *Development: Linking Paragraphs.*

The main point to remember in linking paragraphs is that they really should be linked, and develop or follow logically the opening paragraph.

It is also essential to avoid monotony by varying the initial words of paragraphs, and by avoiding the constant use of the same linking word.

For this purpose it is a wise plan to make a note of useful words and phrases with which to open a paragraph (e.g. In addition; On the other hand; It must be admitted that; It is often stated that; In conclusion; To sum up).

As to the planning of the development of composition, this will naturally depend upon the nature of the composition. In descriptions, narratives, biographies, or expositions, the sequence of paragraphs follows a logical course; in the case of controversial or discursive subjects, some paragraphs may be devoted to amplification of introductory ideas, to examples, to comparisons, or to deductions. It is impossible, and indeed undesirable, to lay down fixed rules for the development of any composition other than one that is descriptive or narrative. The secret of writing fluently is to plan first and so to know with what points each developing paragraph will deal.

4. *Concluding Paragraphs.*

Like opening paragraphs, these will vary considerably with the type of composition with which we are dealing.

In dealing with scientific or political subjects, some forecast of possible future developments will make an excellent conclusion; in discursive or controversial essays, where an opinion or an argument has been developed, a summary of the matter that has been discussed and the writer's personal views on the topic will conclude suitably; in the case of a biographical study, some final assessment of the value of the work and influence of the person in question will be called for; in a composition descriptive of a particular action or series of actions, such as a visit, an excursion, or an adventure, the conclusion will present no problems, as we merely have to describe the final stage of the activity in question.

Whatever the topic, however, the concluding paragraph should avoid the error of excessive length, but that does not mean it should be abrupt. The essential thing is that it should really be a conclusion, rounding off the essay and making as much impression on the reader as the opening paragraph which attracted his attention. Sometimes a short challenging sentence makes an excellent conclusion, such as this example from an essay on "The Donkey": "Were we all to be more like the donkey in patience, humility and devotion, we should certainly be better human beings."

EXERCISES

A

Convert the following sentences into periodic sentences:

1. He reached the top of the hill with difficulty, so great was the force of the wind.

2. Napoleon failed, owing to the severity of the winter, to conquer Russia, though he captured Moscow.

3. It was not surprising Smith had to resign: he was incompetent and lazy; he was also dishonest.

4. It is an excellent idea to keep a diary to remind one of events and of friends, and it provides news for letters.

5. It is impossible to learn a foreign language, you will find, if you do not master its grammar.

B

Combine the following sentences in two different ways :

1. I woke up late. I missed my train.

2. Mary went to the sales. She bought a hat.

3. The captain ordered his crew to abandon ship. The ship was slowly sinking.

4. Here is a path through the forest. I discovered it yesterday. It leads to the mountain.

5. The speaker seemed nervous. He stuttered frequently. His audience was restless.

C

Combine the following simple sentences into one complex sentence:

1. At the entrance to the drive stood a lodge. Its walls were covered with ivy. There was a small garden in front of it. This was enclosed by a hedge. The garden was a mass of flowers.

2. I was walking in the park. It was a pleasant summer evening. I noticed a group of people. In the centre of the group a man was

standing on a box. He was an elderly man with a white beard. He was making a speech.

3. The climber had nearly reached the summit. His foot slipped. He lost his balance. He fell like a stone. A solitary tree grew below the rock. He managed to seize one of its branches. This saved his life.

4. It was necessary to hide. We entered the barn. We crawled behind some sacks. The sacks contained corn. Some soldiers entered soon afterwards. They carried out a search. The search was a hurried one. We escaped detection.

5. The stranger looked like a tramp. His clothes were shabby. His shoes were in holes. He carried a sack on his back. He walked fast. Sometimes he ran. He glanced back frequently. He seemed frightened.

D

Write an opening paragraph (of not fewer than 12 lines, and not more than 20) for each of the following subjects:

1. Diaries
2. Maps
3. Spring
4. London
5. Choosing a Career
6. Modern Art
7. A visit to the dentist
8. Keeping pets
9. Holidays abroad
10. Christmas presents
11. Hobbies
12. The Ideal House
13. Ghosts
14. Bells
15. Superstitions

E

Write one paragraph of not more than 20 lines on each of the following subjects, giving a brief summary suitable for a news item in a paper.

1. Lion escapes from Regent's Park Zoo.
2. Visitor tries to steal jewels from Tower of London.
3. The Thames freezes over for the first time since 1817.
4. New car engine revolutionises motoring.
5. Rich gold deposits discovered in Devonshire.
6. College is burnt down in students' "rag".

CHAPTER XVI

FIGURES OF SPEECH

A figure of speech is a broad term for the use of a word or phrase of a particular kind which heightens or clarifies the meaning of an idea.

Figures of speech draw attention to an idea by means of another idea, and they should strike the hearer or reader as having made an idea clearer and more forceful if they are used correctly and successfully.

Most figures of speech are based on the use of comparison, of contrast, or of emphasis. We frequently use figurative expressions in our daily conversation to emphasise some idea without consciously realising that we are doing so.

The commonest of all figures of speech are those based on actual or implied comparisons. We say "The wind cuts like a knife", "She is as quiet as a mouse", or "He is as slow as a tortoise". These comparisons are called Similes (Latin "similis" = like). Often we omit the more obvious comparisons conveyed by "like" or "as" and merely imply comparison, as when we say "He was a *lion* in battle", "She has a *stony* heart", or "They were *snowed under* with begging letters". (These implied or condensed comparisons are called Metaphors, i.e. a transfer or carrying of an idea.)

Figurative expressions are drawn from many sources. Many are connected with the scenes, events, occupations, and pastimes of everyday life (e.g. a cat and dog life, a silver lining, a bone of contention, to fall between two stools, to sit on the fence, to play second fiddle, to throw overboard, to pass muster, to pay the piper, to look a gift horse in the mouth, to throw up the sponge, to have a card up one's sleeve).

Some are based on comparisons with characters or events from Greek sources (e.g. Achilles' heel, the strength of Hercules, a Spartan, the sword of Damocles, to rest on one's laurels), or from Latin sources (e.g. to cross the Rubicon, Fabian tactics).

Many come from the Bible (e.g. a Job's comforter, a scapegoat, as old as Methuselah, a good Samaritan); others from literature (e.g. a gargantuan appetite, a quixotic action, a mad hatter, a Micawber), or from history (e.g. a little Hitler), and geography (e.g. to send coals to Newcastle, to set the Thames on fire), and a great number from miscellaneous traditions, legends, and customs (e.g. to shed crocodile tears, a white elephant, a swan-song, to throw down the gauntlet, as mad as a March hare).

In some cases two expressions have the same origin: "to buy a pig in a poke (= sack)", i.e. to buy something without seeing it, refers to an old trick of putting a cat in a sack and selling it as a pig; a custom that has given us also "to let the cat out of the bag", i.e. to reveal a secret.

I. **Figures based on Comparison or Resemblance**

(Simile, Metaphor, Personification, Apostrophe.)

1. Simile (= likeness): a comparison made between persons, animals, or things differing in most character-istics, but alike in one or more points, the words "like" or "as" being employed in the comparison.

e.g. He runs *like* a hare.

He is as deaf *as* a post.

Note: "Peter is like John" is a comparison, but *not* a simile, as both are boys. Similes are comparisons between *different* classes or types.

196

2. Metaphor (= transference): a similar comparison with the words "like" or "as" omitted—so it is an implied or condensed simile.

> e.g. Jones is a veritable *hare* on the running track.
> (i.e. He runs *like* a hare, as fast *as* a hare.)

Metaphors can be expressed by:

(a) *Nouns:* e.g. He is a *hare*.
(b) *Adjectives:* e.g. A *freezing* glance.
(c) *Verbs:* e.g. I am *bursting* with pride.
(d) *Adverbs:* e.g. He replied *hotly*.

Faulty Metaphors. A word used metaphorically to transfer an idea must be apt. The metaphorical use of "sprang" in the following sentence is not apt:

"Canals *sprang* up everywhere."

("Sprang" gives an idea of haste, but canals never "spring", and certainly do not "spring up".)

Mixed Metaphors. The use of two or more closely following metaphors or transferences of ideas is often disastrous, as the two metaphors must be closely linked and must deal with the same idea. The following are examples of mixed metaphors:

"Unless you wish to raise a hornet's nest about your ears, you should let sleeping dogs lie" ("hornet's nests" have no connection with "sleeping dogs").

"We should all pull together, and not ride roughshod over everybody." ("pull together" comes from rowing, or a tug-of-war; "ride roughshod" comes from riding horses.)

Note: *Allegories*, *Fables*, and *Parables* are really types of extended similes or sustained metaphors.

An *Allegory* is a long narrative metaphor, usually with a moral (e.g. Bunyan's "Pilgrim's Progress", recounting Christian's journey, which represents in reality the journey of a man's life).

A *Fable* is a narrative in which animals, birds, and insects—and even inanimate objects—represent human beings in their actions, and point a moral (e.g. "The Fox and the Grapes"; "The Fox, the Crow, and the Cheese").

A *Parable* is the term used for Biblical stories in the New Testament that teach a lesson or point a moral (e.g. The Parable of the Sower. The Story of the Prodigal Son).

3. Personification (= making into a person): attributing life and consequent actions to inanimate objects or abstract ideas.

e.g. The moonlight *crept* over the grass.
Murder *stalked* through the village.

4. Apostrophe (= an address): a special kind of personification, in which the object or idea is addressed as if a living person; or an address to an absent, and usually deceased, person. This occurs chiefly in poetry.

e.g. O cruel North Wind!
Hail, smiling Morn!
Milton, thou shouldst be living at this hour.

II. Figures based on Emphasis by Contrast or Surprise

(Antithesis, Epigram, Hyperbole, Paradox, Oxymoron.)

1. Antithesis (= placing against)—setting one word or idea against another.

e.g. More haste, less speed.
Prosperity discovers vice; adversity, virtue.

2. Epigram (= inscription): a pointed saying, often employing contrast. Most proverbs are epigrams, the essence of which should be brevity and unexpectedness.

e.g. Vulgarity is the conduct of other people.
There is no fool like an old fool.
All men are liars: women make them so.
Nothing succeeds like success (or excess).
Necessity is the mother of invention.

3. Hyperbole (= exaggeration): an exaggerated comparison.

e.g. He is as old as the hills.
His speech brought the house down.

4. Paradox (= a contradiction): an apparent contradiction of accepted facts, hence all the more striking by its truth.

e.g. The child is father of the man.
Our enemies are often our best friends.
(i.e. because they tell us the truth, often hidden and painful, about ourselves.)

5. Oxymoron (= sharp and dull): a contrast of exact opposites united in the same phrase, and so more compressed and sharper than a paradox.

e.g. One must often be cruel to be kind.
His honour rooted in dishonour stood.
(and phrases such as "bitter-sweet", "an open secret", etc.)

III. **Figures based on special Arrangement or Construction**

(Climax, Anti-climax, Transferred Epithet or Hypallage, Syllepsis, Zeugma, Chiasmus, Rhetorical Question.)

1. Climax (= a ladder): an arrangement or grading of ideas in an ascending scale.

e.g. I came, I saw, I conquered.
(JULIUS CAESAR.)
Some books are to be tasted, others, swallowed, and some few to be chewed and digested.
(BACON.)

2. Anti-climax or Bathos (= an arrangement of ideas with a final descent instead of ascent, as a surprise, i.e. an effect opposite to Climax).

e.g. I came, I saw—I ran away.

(Anti-climax is a favourite device of humorous writers; it is also frequently an unintentional error.)

3. Transferred Epithet or Hypallage: the transference of an adjective from the noun to which it really belongs to another noun.

> e.g. He lay all night on a sleepless pillow. (i.e. "He", and not "the pillow", was "sleepless"—and our attention is attracted by this transference.)

4. Syllepsis: a condensed sentence in which a word is deliberately used once only instead of being repeated, but is understood as repeated in the second case with a different sense.

> e.g. He lost his hat and his temper.

5. Zeugma (= yoking or joining): a condensed form which differs from syllepsis because the verb or adjective used refers to two different nouns, but is not really applicable, strictly speaking, to one of the nouns.

> e.g. With *seeing* eyes and ears, alert he stood.

6. Chiasmus: the contrasting of two balanced phrases, the order of words in one phrase being reversed in the other.

> e.g. Some courage showed, cowardice others chose.

7. Rhetorical Question or Interrogation: a form of question used for effect and emphasis, particularly in speeches, but not requiring any actual answer. This is an orator's device and the answer is meant to be self-evident.

> e.g. Too many manufacturers and retailers require too much profit. Is it any wonder that prices are too high?

IV. Figures based on Associated Ideas

(Metonymy, Synecdoche, Prolepsis.)

1. Metonymy (= transference of name): an idea expressed or represented by a conspicuous accompaniment that is not an actual part of the idea but a symbol of it.

> e.g. The *pen* is mightier than the *sword*.
> (i.e. Writers wield more power than soldiers. Books have more influence than weapons or armies.)

His pictures came under the *hammer*.
(i.e. His pictures were sold by auction.)

2. Synecdoche (= removal of a part): an idea expressed or represented by using a part for the whole. This is a closer association, therefore, than metonymy.

e.g. All *hands* on deck. (sailors)
Twenty *sail* of the line. (ships)

Sometimes the name of some prominent character from history or fiction is used to typify a class.

e.g. It would take a Solomon (= a person of great wisdom) to solve this problem.

3. Prolepsis (= anticipation): the use of a descriptive word or words prematurely, i.e. before the event or idea has reached the stage where the word used is really applicable.

e.g. So these two brothers and their *murdered* man rode past fair Florence.

(KEATS.)

(The man the brothers intended to murder was not then dead.)

The phrase "the doomed ship", when used before the ship has sunk, is another example.

V. Figures based on Emphasis by saying the opposite, or by indirect suggestion

(Irony, Sarcasm, Innuendo, Litotes, Euphemism.)

1. Irony (= simulated ignorance): conveying one's real meaning by saying the opposite.

e.g. Brutus is an honourable man.
(i.e. Mark Antony intended to convey the idea that Brutus had acted dishonourably.)

2. Sarcasm is very similar to irony, but is more obvious (or less cleverly concealed), and generally accompanied by emphasis of voice.

Irony is a rapier, sarcasm a bludgeon.

e.g. What! A *born linguist* like you cannot order a drink in French!

You *are* a wonderful fieldsman. (To someone who has dropped a catch.)

3. Innuendo: a depreciatory insinuation, i.e. expressing a criticism by an indirect suggestion, that often seems harmless at first.

e.g. During the last five years my butler has several times been sober.

(i.e. He is habitually drunk.)

4. Litotes (= belittling): a form of understatement employing an opposite idea, often a negative form.

e.g. She is far from stupid. ⎱
She is no fool. ⎰ = She is intelligent.

5. Euphemism (= speaking pleasantly): another form of understatement in which pleasant terms are used to describe an unpleasant fact.

e.g. He *passed away* (= died).
The dog was *put to sleep* (= painlessly killed).

Note: Do not confuse euphemism with Euphuism, a term used to describe flowery and over-refined language, such as that employed by Lyly in his book "Euphues" (1579) from which this term is derived.

VI. Figures based on the appeal or effect of sound

(Alliteration, Onomatopoeia, Pun.)

1. Alliteration (= repetition of letters): the use of a sequence of words beginning with the same sound, a device chiefly employed in verse.

e.g. The *w*ind in the *w*illows *w*hispers.
*A*pt *a*lliterations artful aid.

2. Onomatopoeia (= word-making): a term applied either to words which have been introduced to represent actual sounds, or to a skilful use of words which conveys the sounds connected with the subject with which the writer is dealing.

e.g. Such words as "cuckoo", "buzz", "boom", "bang", "clang" are onomatopoeic.

As an illustration of the skilful use of sounds closely allied with subject-matter, Tennyson's poem "The Brook" is an excellent and much quoted example:

> I chatter, chatter as I flow
> To join the brimming river;
> For men may come and men may go,
> But I go on for ever.

The hurrying, babbling progress of a brook can be clearly heard in this, thanks to the choice of word and rhythm.

3. Pun: a play on words of similar sound, but different meaning.

e.g. Is life worth living?
That depends upon the *liver*.

The poet Thomas Hood employed this device most successfully and amusingly.

> A cannon ball shot off his legs
> So he laid down his arms.

An excess of "punning" is, however, regarded as a literary or conversational crime.

EXERCISES

A

Complete the following sentences by adding a suitable simile:

(*a*) The new block of flats towered above the surrounding houses like . . .

(*b*) The branches of the trees clutched him in the darkness like . . .

(*c*) The fog came down suddenly over the fields like . . .

(*d*) The rain simply poured down, as if . . .

(*e*) The swan glided over the lake like . . .

(*f*) The woodpecker's beak tapped on the trunk like . . .

(*g*) The fat man climbed the hill, grunting and snorting like . . .

(*h*) The engineer emerged red-faced from the boiler-room like . . .

(*i*) The dew sparkled on the grass like . . .

(*j*) The sergeant strutted about in front of the squad of recruits like . . .

(*k*) The torn sail was as useless to the yachtsman as . . .

(*l*) The flames curled round the log like . . .

(*m*) He had small, protruding, beady eyes like . . .

B

Give comparisons suitable for use with the following adjectives:

stubborn, blind, green, slippery, timid, pale, sour, black, happy, proud, fat, deaf, thin, sharp, mad, dry, busy, old, straight, crooked.

C

Write sentences using each of the following words metaphorically:

(*a*) forest, thirst, field, key, fruit, door, seed, light, fire, arm, rain, neck, fast, head, flash, chain, body, anchor, branch, root, tower, sea, fog, gulf, herald, veil, path, harvest, river, mountain.

(*b*) black, rosy, iron, polished, ripe, golden, rough, oily, smiling, tender, cold, hot, merciless, thin, glowing.

(*c*) to launch, to plough, to crown, to strike, to catch, to run, to reap, to break, to plant, to prune.

D

Explain the meaning of the following figurative expressions, indicating their origin. Write a sentence for each expression to illustrate its correct use.

(*a*) out of the wood

a wet blanket

sour grapes

a scapegoat

a rough diamond

crocodile tears

to blow hot and cold

a silver lining

to strike oil

an underdog

a free lance

to lie low

castles in the air

a dark horse

to bury the hatchet

a swan-song

a flash in the pan

a bolt from the blue

to split hairs

to toe the line

a broken reed

to draw in one's horns

to cut the painter

a red-letter day

below the belt

a cat's paw

to hand on the torch	a turncoat
to sit on the fence	a blackleg
to sweep the board	at daggers drawn
a busman's holiday	a black sheep
to draw the long bow	a fly in the ointment
a dog in the manger	a storm in a teacup
to show the white feather	a white elephant

(b) to cross the Rubicon	a herculean task
a philistine	a Job's comforter
Hobson's choice	a Good Samaritan
a titanic struggle	his Achilles' heel
a quixotic action	Utopian schemes
a gargantuan appetite	to take French leave
to send to Coventry	a Judas
the sword of Damocles	a Gordian knot

E

Define the following, giving one example of each:

fable, rhetorical question, allegory, bathos, epigram, onomatopoeia, proverb, mixed metaphor.

F

Name and explain the figures of speech employed in the following sentences:

1. Our enemies are often our truest friends.
2. He crept up to his victim like a panther stalking a deer.
3. He fell asleep, and was laid to rest in the village churchyard.
4. Autumn puts on her russet mantle.
5. At twenty he was an apprentice, at thirty works manager, at forty a director.
6. The enemy were dispersed by the attack like chaff before the wind.
7. Over the cobbles he clattered and clashed in the dark inn-yard.
8. Cambridge men think they own the world; Oxford men know they do.
9. The butler handed the duke an obsequious cup of coffee.
10. The children nearly died of laughing at the clown's antics.
11. Late-comers to a play are so amusing, with their habit of treading on one's toes and muttering excuses which drown the actors' voices.

12. He can best be described as a busy idler.

13. To judge from his marks, this student is far from stupid.

14. He lives by his pen, and hopes one day to be a famous novelist.

15. Ah, Death, where is thy sting?

16. The new class seemed an intelligent collection of students; several of its members could write their names.

17. The burglar escaped with alacrity and a gold watch.

18. They shared the same roof for some years.

19. When Tom died they told the sexton, and the sexton tolled the bell.

20. The rebel was compelled to pocket his pride and had to toe the line with the rest of the committee.

N.B.—See also pp. 211–13 for further questions on figurative expressions.

CHAPTER XVII

PARAPHRASING

A paraphrase is defined in the dictionary as "the restatement of the sense of a passage in other words".

Paraphrasing is a valuable exercise for improving our use of words and for teaching us to express ideas clearly.

To a great extent paraphrasing is an exercise in translation. We shall not be called upon to paraphrase passages of modern English prose the meaning of which is already clear to any reader, but some proverb or epigram which by its brevity and imagery needs explanation in longer form for many of us; or passages of prose from earlier centuries whose style is often more involved than that of modern prose and whose vocabulary is sometimes more obscure; or, finally, some poem in which the poet's expression of his thoughts and verbal images call for simpler version in prose to convey clearly his ideas to ordinary reader.

Writing a paraphrase of some passage of prose or of a poem must not be confused with making a précis. In a précis we are trying to summarise, condensing the original into a minimum number of words; in a paraphrase we are trying to express more clearly and simply, and so almost more fully, the meaning of the original, and our paraphrase will almost certainly contain more words than the original.

It will be best to divide paraphrasing into three types: (1) paraphrasing of proverbs and epigrams and phrases; (2) paraphrasing of prose passages; and (3) paraphrasing of verse.

Firstly, however, the following main rules for paraphrasing should be followed:

1. Whatever the nature of the original version, a paraphrase should be written in modern English. (When paraphrasing verse, the paraphrase must be written in prose.)

2. Do not paraphrase word by word (such a system would lead to a most peculiar and probably very untrue and obscure result) but phrase by phrase, or sentence by sentence. You are paraphrasing thoughts and ideas, not individual words only.

3. Keep to the tense and person of the original, and do not change any of the original words unnecessarily, but replace them with your own words only when you think the original is not clear, or requires a more lengthy explanation.

Obviously, any obscure or difficult word must be replaced by a simpler word or by a phrase, and any archaic or obsolete word must be replaced by modern words. Remember, too, that many words have changed their original meaning as, for example, "presently", which in Shakespeare's day meant "at once".

4. Do not be tempted to add any ideas of your own to the original version you are paraphrasing.

5. Although you should attempt to retain the style of the original, you need not hesitate to break up long sentences and paragraphs into shorter ones if this is necessary to add to the clarity of your paraphrase.

6. Replace figurative expressions such as metaphors by their literal meaning as much as possible, but similes may be retained.

Examples

(1) Proverbs, Epigrams, and Phrases

Example: "Those who live in glass houses should not throw stones."

Taken literally, this obviously means that people who live in glass houses should not throw stones for fear of reprisals (which would obviously cause considerable damage to their unusual property!); but as few people as yet inhabit glass houses we must aim at expressing the real meaning of this statement in more general terms.

Paraphrase: "People should not criticise in others faults that they themselves possess", *or*

"People should not criticise faults in others when they themselves are also open to criticism."

Example: "Birds of a feather flock together."

Paraphrase: "Just as birds of similar species flock together, so people with similar tastes tend to associate with one another."

Example: "Nothing succeeds like success."

Paraphrase: "An initial success is usually a great encouragement to further successes," *or*

"One success is usually a stepping-stone to further successes."

Example: "A rolling stone gathers no moss."

Paraphrase: "A person who is frequently changing his occupation is unlikely to be successful."

Example: "Necessity is the mother of invention."

Paraphrase: "When faced by some problem it is essential to solve, Man is usually inspired to invent a solution."

(2) Prose Passages

Example: At home I betake me to my library, whence all at once I command and survey all my household. It is placed on the third storie of a tower. It was in times past the most unprofitable place of all my house. There I pass the greater part of my lives dayes, and weare out most hours of the day. The forme of it is round, and hath no flat side, but what serveth for my table and chair. It hathe three baye-windowes, of a farre-extending, rich and unresisted prospect. In winter I am less continually there: for my house (as the name of it importeth) is pearched upon an overpearing hillocke; and hath no part more subject to all wethers than this: which pleaseth me the more both because the accesse unto it is

209

somewhat troublesome and remote, and for the benefit of the exercise.

(Florio's translation of Montaigne's "Essais".)

Paraphrase: At home I retire to my library from which I can command a view of the whole house at once. It is situated on the third storey of a tower. It was formerly the least used room in all my house. I spend the greater part of my time there, and certainly most of the hours of daylight.

It is round in shape, except for a small alcove where my table and chair are placed. It has three bay-windows which give an extensive, uninterrupted, and pleasant view.

In winter I do not spend so much time there; for my house (as its name indicates) is situated on the summit of a small hill, and contains no room more affected by severe weather conditions than this one; a fact which I find all the more satisfactory, on account of the difficulty of access to it and its consequent seclusion, and because of the beneficial exercise obtained in climbing up to it.

(3) Verse Passages

Example:

> "This is the state of man: to-day he puts forth
> The tender leaves of hopes: to-morrow blossoms,
> And bears his blushing honours thick upon him;
> The third day comes a frost, a killing frost;
> And, when he thinks, good easy man, full surely
> His greatness is a-ripening, nips his root,
> And then he falls, as I do.

(SHAKESPEARE, *King Henry VIII.*)

Paraphrase: A man's life often follows this pattern: in his youth he is full of hope and ambition; next, success comes to him, and he receives many honours: then, just when he thinks contentedly he is about to attain complete success, suddenly misfortune overwhelms him and he loses everything, as I have done.

Example:

> "A man severe he was, and stern to view;
> I knew him well, and every truant knew;

Well had the boding tremblers learned to trace
The day's disasters in his morning face;
Full well they laughed with counterfeited glee
At all his jokes, for many a joke had he;
Full well the busy whisper, circling round,
Conveyed the dismal tidings when he frowned:
Yet he was kind; or if severe in aught,
The love he bore to learning was at fault.

(GOLDSMITH, *The Deserted Village.*)

Paraphrase: He was a severe man, with a stern expression. I knew him well, and so did all who played truant from his school; those with guilty consciences had learned to trace the disasters awaiting them from the look on his face as he appeared in the morning. The pupils laughed heartily with simulated amusement at every one of his numerous jokes; when he frowned in annoyance a whisper of warning ran rapidly round the class. He had, however, a kindly nature, and if he was severe at times it was because of his desire to uphold the dignity of learning.

EXERCISES

A

Paraphrase the following figurative expressions, making their meaning clear.

(i) His decision means he has burnt his boats.
I like to call a spade a spade.
My reply took the wind out of his sails.
She is too fond of playing to the gallery.
You have let the cat out of the bag.
This is a case of the pot calling the kettle black.
We have a bone to pick with him.
She will not like having to play second fiddle.
He is a wolf in sheep's clothing.
Mary is penny-wise and pound-foolish.

(ii) You must cut your coat according to your cloth.
Henry will always fall on his feet.
They are living in a fool's paradise.
We must try to pour oil on troubled waters.
He will never set the Thames on fire.

Charles is hand in glove with our opponents.
We must not make mountains out of molehills.
Don't spoil the ship for a ha'porth of tar.
He is trying to draw a red herring across the trail.
We must take the bull by the horns.

(iii) They have jumped out of the frying-pan into the fire.
You are robbing Peter to pay Paul.
They threw cold water on the proposal.
He has got hold of the wrong end of the stick.
Don't put all your eggs into one basket.
John is a square peg in a round hole.
You must avoid falling between two stools.
He seems to have a bee in his bonnet about motorists.
Be careful not to buy a pig in a poke.
To do this would be carrying coals to Newcastle.

(iv) They are too anxious to throw up the sponge when faced by opposition.
You are too fond of burning the candle at both ends.
I think you have an axe to grind in this case.
This is a case of diamond cut diamond.
He is at the end of his tether.

B

Paraphrase the following proverbs:

(i) A stitch in time saves nine.
A bird in the hand is worth two in the bush.
Set a thief to catch a thief.
It never rains but it pours.
New brooms sweep clean.
There's many a slip 'twixt the cup and the lip.
When in Rome do as Rome does.
There's no smoke without fire.
It's a long lane that has no turning.
Never look a gift-horse in the mouth.

(ii) Every cloud has a silver lining.
A burnt child dreads the fire.
There are none so deaf as those who will not hear.
Nothing venture, nothing have.
Distance lends enchantment to the view.
Least said, soonest mended.
It's no use crying over spilt milk.

Necessity knows no law.
Beggars cannot be choosers.
Discretion is the better part of valour.
Give a dog a bad name and you may as well hang him.

(iii) Fools rush in where angels fear to tread.
The darkest hour is just before the dawn.
Possession is nine-tenths of the law.
Rome was not built in a day.
Well begun is half done.
The road to Hell is paved with good intentions.
Too many cooks spoil the broth.
One man's meat is another man's poison.
Fine feathers make fine birds.
Still waters run deep.

C

Paraphrase the following passages of prose and verse, rewriting them in clear modern English.

(a) *Of Studies*

Studies serve for delight, for ornament, and for ability. Their chief use for delight, is in privateness and retiring; for ornament, is in discourse; and for ability, is in the judgment and disposition of business; for expert men can execute, and perhaps judge of particulars, one by one: but the general counsels, and the plots and marshalling of affairs come best from those that are learned. To spend too much time in studies, is sloth; to use them too much for ornament, is affectation; to make judgment wholly by their rules, is the humour of a scholar: they perfect nature, and are perfected by experience: for natural abilities are like natural plants, that need pruning by study; and studies themselves do give forth directions too much at large, except they be bounded in by experience.

FRANCIS BACON (1561–1626).

(b) *Of Travel*

When a traveller returneth home, let him not leave the countries where he hath travelled altogether behind him, but maintain a correspondence by letters with those of his acquaintance which are of most worth; and let his travel appear rather in his discourse than in his apparel or gesture; and in his discourse let him be rather advised in his answers than forward to tell stories: and let it appear that he doth not change his country manners for those of foreign parts; but only prick in some flowers of that he hath learned abroad into the customs of his own country.

FRANCIS BACON.

(c) The Man in Black

Though fond of many acquaintances, I desire an intimacy only with a few. The Man in Black, whom I have often mentioned, is one whose friendship I could wish to acquire, because he possesses my esteem. His manners, it is true, are tinctured with some strange inconsistencies; and he may be justly termed an humorist in a nation of humorists. Though he is generous even to profusion, he affects to be thought a prodigy of parsimony and prudence; though his conversation be replete with the most sordid and selfish maxims, his heart is dilated with the most unbounded love. I have known him profess himself a man-hater, while his cheek was glowing with compassion; and, while his looks were softened into pity, I have heard him use the language of the most unbounded ill-nature.

OLIVER GOLDSMITH (1728–1774).

(d) Stocktaking

I suppose myself to be worth about £500 clear in the world, and my goods of my house my own, and what is coming to me from Brampton, when my father dies, which God defer. But my greatest trouble is, that I have for this last half-year been a very great spendthrift in all manner of respects, that I am afraid to cast up my accounts, though I hope I am worth what I say above. But I will cast them up very shortly. I have newly taken a solemn oath about abstaining from plays and wine, which I am resolved to keep, according to the letter of the oath which I keep by me.

SAMUEL PEPYS (1633–1703).

(e) The Schoolmaster

God, of his goodness, hath fitted several men for several callings, that the necessity of Church and State, in all conditions, may be provided for. So that he who beholds the fabric thereof may say, God hewed out the stone, and appointed it to lie in this very place, for it would fit none other so well, and here it doth most excellent. And thus God mouldeth some for a schoolmaster's life, undertaking it with desire and delight, and discharging it with dexterity and happy success.

He studieth his scholars' natures as carefully as they their books; and ranks their dispositions into several forms. And though it may seem difficult for him in a great school to descend to all particulars, yet experienced schoolmasters may quickly make a grammar of boys' natures, and reduce them all—saving some few exceptions— to some three general rules.

THOMAS FULLER (1608–1661).

(f) New Clothes

So did go to the office in it, and sat all morning, the day looking as if it would be foul. At noon home to dinner, and there find my wife extraordinary fine, with her flowered gown that she made two years ago, and now laced exceeding pretty; and indeed was fine all over; and mighty earnest to go out though the day was very lowering; and she would have me put on my fine suit which I did. And so anon we went alone through the town with our new liveries of serge, and the horses' manes and tails tied with red ribbons, and the standards gilt with varnish, and all clean, and green reins, that people did mightily look upon us; and, the truth is, I did not see any coach more pretty, though more gay, than ours all the day.

SAMUEL PEPYS (1633–1703).

(g) The Village Preacher

A man he was to all the country dear,
And passing rich with forty pounds a-year.
Remote from towns he ran his godly race,
Nor e'er had changed, nor wished to change, his place;
Unpractised he to fawn, or seek for power,
By doctrines fashioned to the varying hour;
Far other aims his heart had learned to prize,
More skilled to raise the wretched than to rise.
His house was known to all the vagrant train—
He chid their wanderings, but relieved their pain;
The long-remembered beggar was his guest,
Whose beard descending swept his aged breast;
The ruined spendthrift, now no longer proud,
Claimed kindred there, and had his claims allowed;
The broken soldier, kindly bade to stay,
Sat by his fire, and talked the night away;

OLIVER GOLDSMITH.

(h) *Advice*

And these few precepts in thy memory
Look thou character. Give thy thoughts no tongue,
Nor any unproportion'd thought his act.
Be thou familiar, but by no means vulgar.
The friends thou hast, and their adoption tried,
Grapple them to thy soul with hoops of steel;
But do not dull thy palm with entertainment
Of each new-hatch'd, unfledged comrade. Beware
Of entrance to a quarrel; but, being in,
Bear it, that the opposer may beware of thee.
Give every man thine ear, but few thy voice:
Take each man's censure, but reserve thy judgment.
Costly thy habit as thy purse can buy,
But not express'd in fancy; rich, not gaudy:
For the apparel oft proclaims the man;

WILLIAM SHAKESPEARE.

(i) *To an Oak Tree*

Thou wast a bauble once, a cup and ball
Which babes might play with; and the thievish jay,
Seeking her food, with ease might have purloined
The auburn nut that held thee, swallowing down
Thy yet close-folded latitude of boughs
And all thine embryo vastness at a gulp.
But fate thy growth decreed; autumnal rains
Beneath thy parent tree mellowed the soil
Designed thy cradle; and a skipping deer,
With pointed hoof dibbling the glebe, prepared
The soft receptacle, in which, secure,
Thy rudiments should sleep the winter through.

WILLIAM COWPER.

(j) *The Sea*

Roll on, thou deep and dark-blue Ocean—roll!
Ten thousand fleets sweep over thee in vain;
Man marks the earth with ruin—his control
Stops with the shore;—upon the watery plain
The wrecks are all thy deed, nor doth remain

A shadow of man's ravage, save his own
When for a moment, like a drop of rain,
He sinks into thy depths with bubbling groan,
Without a grave, unknelled, uncoffined, and unknown.

LORD BYRON.

(k) *The Path of Duty*

Not once or twice in our rough island-story,
The path of duty was the way to glory:
He that walks it, only thirsting
For the right, and learns to deaden
Love of self, before his journey closes,
He shall find the stubborn thistle bursting
Into glossy purples, which outredden
All voluptuous garden roses.

ALFRED, LORD TENNYSON.

(l) *Hope*

Say not, the struggle naught availeth
The labour and the wounds are vain,
The enemy faints not, nor faileth
And as things have been they remain.

If hopes were dupes, fears may be liars;
It may be in yon smoke concealed,
Your comrades chase e'en now the fliers,
And, but for you, possess the field.

For while the tired waves, vainly breaking,
Seem here no painful inch to gain,
Far back, through creeks and inlets making,
Comes silent, flooding in, the main.

And not by eastern windows only,
When daylight comes, comes in the light,
In front, the sun climbs slow, how slowly,
But westward, look, the land is bright.

A. H. CLOUGH.

CHAPTER XVIII

INDIRECT OR REPORTED SPEECH

Direct Speech indicates the actual words used by a speaker. Indirect or Reported Speech is a report of the words used, given indirectly by another person, e.g.

Direct Speech: "I shall go to Bristol tomorrow."
Indirect or Reported Speech: He (the speaker, Mr. Brown) said that he would go to Bristol the next day.

We consciously or unconsciously use indirect speech when reporting statements in our everyday conversation or writing.

Reported speech exercises are particularly useful practice for journalism and for writing "minutes" or summaries of committee meetings, though there is an increasing tendency in modern popular journalism to give the actual spoken words of a speech or conversation in reporting an interview, to give a livelier, if less literary, impression. Reported speech is essential when making a précis of a story containing conversation, as conversation must not be reproduced in any such summary.

RULES

(a) Introduction.

Reported speech is introduced by a sentence with the verb in the past tense, e.g. The speaker (chairman, secretary, Mr. Brown, etc.) said that . . .

There is no need to repeat the introductory "He said" for subsequent sentences by the same speaker.

(b) Word Changes required in the body of the report.

It must be clearly understood that the original spoken words should not be changed unless some change is unavoidable, and that no alteration of fact or tone must be made when turning direct speech into indirect speech. Reported speech must not be confused with paraphrasing, in which we express the meaning of a passage in our own words.

The following necessary changes should be noted:

1. Verbs

Verbs will all be in the Third Person Singular or Plural, and Present and Future Tenses will all be changed to Past Tenses.

e.g. I see—he saw.
> we see—they saw, etc.

is—was	shall, will—should, would
are—were	may—might
has, have—had	can—could
have been—had been	was, were—had been

e.g. Mr. Brown: "I have read the letter, and I may answer it."

Reported: Mr. Brown said that he *had* read the letter, and he *might* answer it.

Note: "Was, were" need not be changed to "had been" when a state, not an action, is described.

e.g. "When I was a small boy, I was once attacked by a bull."

Reported: He said that when he was a small boy he had once been attacked by a bull.

2. Pronouns

Subject	*Object*
I—he, she	me—him, her
we—they	us—them
you—he, she, they	you—him, her, them

219

Similarly, the possessive adjectives "my, our, your" become "his, her; their; his, her, their".

> e.g. Mrs. Brown: "You have left your books behind, Children."
> *Reported:* Mrs. Brown told the children that *they* had left *their* books behind.

Note: As ambiguity (two different meanings) can often occur when "he", "his", etc., are written several times in the same sentence, this must be avoided either by repeating the nouns, or by using "the former", "the latter".

> e.g. Smith: "Brown, you have won your bet."
> *Reported:* Smith told Brown that the *latter* (not "he") had won his bet.
> *or* Smith told Brown that he, Brown, had won his bet.

3. Adjectives

this—that
these—those

> e.g. Mr. Jones: "I have brought this box purposely."
> *Reported:* Mr. Jones said that he had brought *that* box purposely.

4. Adverbs

now—then
today—that day
tomorrow—the next day, the following day
yesterday—the day before, the previous day
last night—the night before, the previous night
here—there

> e.g. Mr. Jones: "I have come here today to work."
> *Reported:* Mr. Jones said that he had come *there that* day to work.

(c) Punctuation.

Punctuation will alter in reported speech, as quotation marks, question marks, and exclamation marks will not be required.

e.g. Charles: "Where are you going, Henry?"
Reported: Charles asked Henry where he was going.

(d) Tone (or Emotion).

The verbs which we employ to introduce the remarks being reported must be varied to express the tone of commands, exclamations, and questions as accurately as possible.

e.g. *Questions:* He asked, inquired, requested . . .
   Answers: He answered, replied, retorted . . .
   Commands: He told, ordered, commanded, requested . . .
   Exclamations: ("Heavens!", "Pah!", etc.) The speaker expressed his disgust, etc. ("Hear! Hear!", "Shame!" etc.) At this point there were cries of approval, dissatisfaction, etc., from the audience.
   Hesitation: He stammered, stuttered, mumbled, etc.

Notes: 1. Such forms of address as "Sir", "Gentlemen", etc., will have to be omitted in reported speech.

2. Although it will be necessary to begin a new paragraph for every speaker, this will not be necessary if the speaker merely says "Yes" or "No", or makes some other brief exclamation. "Yes" can be expressed by ". . . replied in the affirmative" or ". . . expressed agreement"; "No" by ". . . replied in the negative" or ". . . expressed disagreement".

EXAMPLE

A.

(SCENE: *The Annual General Meeting of the Shareholders of the Wonderland Bus Company.*)

Chairman of Directors. I am able today, ladies and gentlemen, to give you a most satisfactory report. Profits this year have reached a new record. Only last month your directors completed the purchase of the Minor Bus Company, our rivals in this district. Final figures show a profit of £200,000, and I am happy to announce a dividend of 1 per cent. The balance will be placed in the reserve fund.

Shareholders. Shame! Whose reserve fund?

Chairman. I assure you that I am as sorry as you are that the dividend is so small, but we must have a large reserve this year for expenditure on development and research. I hope, therefore, that the directors' policy will have your full support.

Mr. Brown (rising). As spokesman for my fellow shareholders, I must point out that exactly the same excuse was made last year, and that you will have no support from us. We should like to know what you intend to do, in view of this dissatisfaction?

Report of Meeting (alterations and additions are in italics).

The Chairman, addressing the shareholders, *told* them that he *was* able *that day* to give *them* a most satisfactory report. Profits *that* year *had* reached a new record. Only *the previous* month *their* directors *had completed* the purchase of the Minor Bus Company, *the company*'s rivals in *that* district. Final figures *showed* a profit of £200,000, and *he was* happy to announce a dividend of 1 per cent. The balance *would be placed* in the reserve fund.

At this point he was interrupted by cries of dissatisfaction from the shareholders, some of whom inquired whose reserve fund was indicated. He assured them that *he was* as sorry as *they were* that the dividend *was* so small, but *the company* must have a large reserve *that* year for expenditure on development and research. *He hoped,* therefore, that the directors' policy *would have* the full support *of the shareholders.*

Mr. Brown, rising *to reply* as spokesman for *his* fellow shareholders, *said* that *he* must point out that exactly the same excuse *had been made the previous year,* and that the directors *would have* no support from *the shareholders. They would like* to *inquire* what *the directors intended* to do in view of *the shareholders'* dissatisfaction.

EXERCISES

Put into Reported Speech:

A

1. "Where are you and your friend going?" asked John of his sister.

2. "Sit down at once and open your books," shouted Mr. Jones to the class.

3. Mary said: "If you are going to the post now, please take my letter for me, Joan."

4. "How are you, Arthur?" exclaimed my aunt. "Have you been waiting for me long?"

5. "What luck! I have picked up a half-crown," cried the boy.

6. "Don't hit me, sir," begged the thief, dropping the bag. "I can explain everything if you will only listen, Colonel."

7. "It would be better to save your money," my father said to my brother.

8. "I shall arrive here at eight o'clock tomorrow, if I am not delayed," John assured his friends.

B

"Who are you?" said the Caterpillar.

Alice replied shyly: "I hardly know, just at present—I know who I was when I got up this morning, but I think I must have changed."

"What do you mean?" said the Caterpillar sternly. "Explain."

"I can't explain, I'm afraid, sir," said Alice. "I'm not myself today, you see."

"I don't see," said the Caterpillar.

C

(SCENE: *Annual Meeting of Muddlecombe Social and Sports Club*)

Chairman. I am very glad to see such a good attendance at this evening's meeting. I am sorry, however, to have to inform you that the Treasurer's report shows that we have a considerable deficit, due almost entirely to delay by many members in paying their subscriptions. I fully realise these are difficult times for us all, but I cannot consider the annual subscription of two guineas excessive. Surely you all realise that we cannot continue to offer you such excellent amenities if subscriptions are not paid punctually.

Voice from back. Have you paid yours?

D

"I understand that I wait for you in all circumstances?"

"You have my certificate in your hand with the rest, you know, and will reserve my place. Wait for nothing but to have my place occupied, and then for England!"

"Why, then," said Mr. Lorry, grasping his eager but so firm and steady hand, "it does not all depend on one old man, but I shall have a young and ardent man at my side."

"By the help of Heaven you shall! Promise me solemnly that nothing will influence you to alter the course on which we now stand pledged to each other."

"Nothing, Carton."

"Remember these words tomorrow. Change the course, or delay in it, and no life can possibly be saved, and many lives must inevitably be sacrificed."

"I will remember them."

E

(SCENE: *A suburban garden on a Monday morning in September*)

Mr. Black. Do you realise, Mr. White, that by lighting a bonfire in this corner every Monday you are not only making it impossible for my wife to hang out the washing but also damaging my fence?

Mr. White. I am very sorry, sir. I have only been here a few weeks, and as your wife has not complained, I did not realise until now that my bonfires are a nuisance.

Mrs. Black (joining her husband in the garden). Good morning, Mr. White. You must not blame Mr. White, George, as he is a bachelor and probably sends all his washing to the laundry.

Mr. White. Please accept my apologies. I will see that my bonfires do not endanger your washing or your fence in future.

Mrs. Black. Thank you, Mr. White. And now, George, as you are free today, you can hang out the washing, dear.

F

Speaker. "We have often been told that money is the root of all evil, but you will all agree with me that it is very difficult in these days of heavy taxation to accumulate enough to fall into temptation, if we honestly declare our salaries or trading profits. This state of affairs is an encouragement to dishonesty. I fully realise, as you do, that we must balance the budget, but what are we to do to prevent honest men from losing all hope or ambition, or from joining the ranks of the tax-dodgers?"

Convert into Direct Speech:

G

1. I told him I would come early on the following day.

2. The speaker asked all who were there to raise their hands if they agreed with him.

3. My friend expressed surprise that I had arrived so early that morning.

4. Mary asked her mother where she was going and if she might invite Joan to tea during her mother's absence.

5. Peter's uncle promised him that if he passed his examination he would take him the following week to any theatre he chose. Peter expressed his thanks and suggested a visit to a circus.

6. The shopkeeper asked the customer how he was, and remarked that it was a long time since he had last called at that shop. The customer explained that he had been ill, and that his doctor had not been willing to give him permission to go out before that week.

H

(Add, where necessary, stage directions for movements)

When Mrs. Smith entered the dining-room, she gave a cry of surprise and called to her husband to come at once, explaining that she suspected from the general state of disorder that a burglar had broken in there. Mr. Smith hurried in from the garden, and at first expressed agreement with his wife's suspicions. On closer inspection, however, he found the dog crouching in a corner, with a guilty look in its eyes, and he then suggested that that animal was the culprit.

Mrs. Smith then told her husband that if he had not left the sideboard open and the dog locked in the room, all that trouble would not have occurred.

CHAPTER XIX

PRÉCIS AND COMPREHENSION

PRÉCIS

The word "précis" is a word we have adopted from the French, and means "summary". We are consciously or unconsciously frequently making précis of articles or letters we have read, or of speeches or conversations we have heard.

This exercise in condensation is one of the most valuable exercises we can practise to improve our clarity of expression and economy of words. It is also obviously an excellent exercise in concentration and comprehension, since we cannot possibly make an accurate summary unless we have carefully studied and understood what we have read or heard.

For examination purposes we are usually required to make a précis of an article, of a speech, or sometimes of a story, in about a third of the length of the original.

It is obvious that before we begin any précis we must read through the original several times.

Too many rules, suggestions, and systems for writing a précis may cause the student to become confused and bewildered.

Certain basic rules must be laid down, however, and to these are added some suggestions which it is hoped will prove helpful.

1. Read the original through once without underlining anything or making any notes, to get a general impression.

2. Read the original a second time, *underlining* any

sentences or phrases that you consider contain ideas that it is essential to include in your summary, and then make a note of them. This will save constant re-reading to check essential points, and will form a basis for the notes that should now be made. A very important point must be stressed here, however: namely, that you must on no account be tempted simply to lift these underlined sentences and phrases word by word from their context and write them out unaltered to form a finished précis.

While it must be made clear that some of the original words, phrases, and sometimes even sentences, may be used in the final précis, it must be stressed that the final version will be much more satisfactory if written in your own words as a summary of the points that have been underlined and the notes that have been made. Have the courage, therefore, to sum up mainly in your own words, but on no account alter (or add to) the main ideas of the original.

3. If any paragraph of the original is particularly long, try to divide it into two parts at some natural point in the sense, in order to assimilate its ideas more easily as you make your own notes. The use of vertical lines or brackets to mark off separate ideas and points will be found very helpful.

4. Since all details that are not absolutely essential must be eliminated, it will be found helpful to carry out the following rules.

(a) Reduce sentences to phrases, and phrases to single words, where possible. Similarly, a series of kindred ideas may often be reduced to one central idea. Remember, however, that a satisfactory précis cannot be made by simply reducing the length of each sentence of the original. This would be farcical, as some sentences have to be retained almost in their entirety, while others can be eliminated altogether.

(b) Eliminate, unless it is absolutely necessary to retain them, any comparisons or illustrations the author or speaker employs to make some idea more vivid.

(*c*) Eliminate qualifying words, such as adjectives and adverbs, if possible: sometimes one adjective or adverb may be retained as essential to express the general idea of a series of adjectives or adverbs in the original.

> e.g. The golden, russet, scarlet, and even multi-coloured autumn leaves were gently falling now, sometimes seeming to hover in the air as they fell, to form a thick rustling carpet along the avenue.
>
> Précis: The falling autumn leaves formed a carpet along the avenue.

(*d*) Replace a series of nouns, if possible, by some collective word or words.

> e.g. Ploughmen and cowmen, and the farmers themselves; carpenters, mechanics, and other factory craftsmen; all were dissatisfied with this arbitrary ruling.
>
> Précis: Workers on the land and workers in the factory were dissatisfied with this ruling.

5. Keep to the arrangement of ideas of the original and summarise the ideas in that order.

6. Remember that the length of the final précis required is usually stated, so that to reduce the original to 100 words when 150 is the stipulated length is not a sign of skill but a serious error.

When you are ready to write out your rough copy from your notes (and a rough copy is essential before your final version is written), it may be helpful to work on the following principle to ensure that your rough copy is approximately the right length.

If you estimate the average number of words you write in a line, a definite number of lines can be allotted and marked off for a rough copy, which will eliminate much waste of time in counting and often cutting down or increasing the length of the final version. For example, if 160 words are required, and you write on the average 8 words to a line, the rough copy should occupy some 20 lines.

7. When making a précis of an article, keep to the tense or tenses of the original (unless you are definitely instructed in the case of an article in the present tense to write your précis in the past tense, as if it were reported speech).

If, however, the original is a speech (or a letter) in the first person singular or plural ("I" or "we") and in the present tense, the précis must be written out in the past tense, and in the third person ("he", "she", or "they"), prefaced by the words "The speaker said that . . .", i.e. in reported or indirect speech, which has already been explained in Chapter XVIII.

> e.g. "I feel that the average Englishman's home is no longer his castle, but his menagerie. The problem of pets has become a serious one from more than one aspect. The overcrowded streets and pavements in our cities and towns are infested by stray dogs or by dogs on leads; our suburban wild birds are being decimated by innumerable cats. It is also not an exaggeration to state that in many homes more affection and more food are lavished on the family pets than on the children. What are we going to do about this state of affairs?"
>
> Précis: The speaker said that the Englishman's love of keeping pets was causing serious problems. Dogs added to the congestion of our streets and pavements; suburban bird life was threatened by cats; excessive affection and food was lavished on pets. He wondered what action should be taken.

When summarising a story containing dialogue (direct speech), no actual spoken words must occur in the précis, but the conversation must be condensed and turned into reported or indirect speech.

> e.g. An old French peasant arrived in Paris and hailed a taxi. The taxi set off, and travelled at such a speed and on such an erratic course that it nearly collided with several other vehicles and only just avoided knocking down a policeman. "Take care", cried the terrified passenger, tapping on the window to attract the driver's

attention. "You are frightening me by going so fast. This is the first time I've travelled in a car."

"Sir," replied the driver, smiling, "I sympathise with you. This is the first time I've driven one!"

Précis: A Parisian taxi hailed by an old French peasant travelled so fast that several accidents were narrowly avoided, and the passenger requested the driver to take more care, as it was the first time he had travelled in a car, to which the driver replied that he sympathised with him, as it was the first time he had driven one.

In the case of some memorable or witty saying quoted in some article or speech (such as famous last words, a brilliant epigram, or an apt retort), the original words may be retained in quotation marks if they would lose all effect or interest if turned into indirect speech.

8. Unless you are called upon to write a précis of a very lengthy article or speech in which there is a marked change in theme, your final version should be written out in a single paragraph, to add to the impression of conciseness.

Finally, supply a suitable and brief title summarising the contents of the article, speech, or story you have condensed.

Example: Length: 220 words. Précis required in about 70 words (i.e. one-third of the original).

It is highly *questionable* on all available evidence *whether*, if the problems are realistically faced, *a case can be firmly made out* for general measures *against a single British wild bird* in present conditions.| *Rabbits*, to take one example, *are estimated to consume several million tons a year of crops and grazing*, besides ruining large acreages by eating out all the nourishing herbage and *occupying some hundreds of men* full time in making, installing, and maintaining rabbit fencing, in trapping, and in making good damage in such ways as replacing injured young trees.| *Rats, which destroy vast quantities of food* ready for human consumption, *spread disease* and do great damage on the farm and on game estates, *are probably an even greater burden.*| *Compared with either of these even the gross damage inflicted by any wild bird in Britain is a drop in the bucket.* It is fair to add, however, that *while the economic loss caused by wild birds has often been vastly exaggerated, there is no scientific evidence to support* the equally large *claims for benefits alleged to be given by wild birds in destroying* agricultural and garden *pests.* It would be wise to *assume* until much more contrary evidence can be brought forward *that wild birds do us very little harm and also very little good.*

(From E. M. Nicholson's *Birds and Man*, Collins.)

The original extract has first been divided up into the sections which deal with various aspects of the main theme. This will greatly facilitate clear thinking.

Next, the most important points have been underlined to facilitate a summary, though many of the phrases and sentences underlined will have to be severely "pruned" or even eventually omitted to keep the summary within the necessary limits.

A suitable title in this case must contain the word "British", and will of necessity be a little longer than usual to express the main theme.

"Is there a case against some British wild birds?" or "Are British wild birds harmful or helpful?" are two titles which cover the subject-matter fully, and the latter seems preferable for its brevity and general appeal.

In a title, capital letters may be used for all important words, or even for every word.

As a rough estimate of length in a first or rough draft, we should aim at 8 to 10 lines according to the average number of words per line of our writing, which will approximately equal 7 printed lines (at 10 words to a line).

ARE BRITISH WILD BIRDS HARMFUL OR HELPFUL?

It is doubtful if a case can be made out against any British wild bird. Rabbits consume several million tons a year of crops and grazing, and keep hundreds of men occupied in counter-measures. Rats, which destroy vast quantities of food and spread disease, are probably more destructive. Compared with these, our wild birds, on scientific evidence, do little damage, but their value as pest-destroyers is equally small. (70 words.)

Notice that some of the points underlined have had to be omitted or greatly condensed; the last sentence of the original, for example, merely sums up or repeats the idea of the previous sentence. Note also the value of reducing enumerations and phrases to one word, as has been done by using "counter-measures" and "pest-destroyers".

COMPREHENSION

In most examinations a variety of comprehension questions is set either on the passage chosen for précis, or on a separate passage selected for such a test.

This exercise is designed to see that the student has read the passage carefully and intelligently and has clearly grasped its general theme and detailed meaning; and that he has the ability to answer questions on it accurately and concisely.

To answer these questions, the chief requirements are clear thinking, a reasonable command of vocabulary, and a knowledge of the contents of the preceding chapters of this text-book.

The student may, for example, be asked to identify or comment on some figures of speech, especially similes and metaphors (Chapter XV, "Figures of Speech"), to explain the meaning or exemplify the use of some difficult words or phrases (Chapter XVII, "Paraphrasing"), to supply synonyms or antonyms, or a single word to replace a phrase (Chapter IX, "Vocabulary"), to select or identify various parts of speech (Chapters I to VIII), or even to analyse into clauses some part of the passage (Chapter XII, "Clause Analysis").

Remember particularly that long words or difficult phrases must never be explained by using equally long words or phrases of similar meaning. This is evasion, not explanation.

EXERCISES

A

Make a précis of the following passage, reducing it to about a third of its present length (i.e. to about 50 words).

On Friday, the 3rd day of August, 1492, Columbus set sail, a little before sunrise, in the presence of a vast crowd of spectators, who sent up their supplications to heaven for a prosperous issue of the voyage, which they wished rather than expected. Columbus steered directly for the Canary Islands, and arrived there without any occurrence deserving of notice. But even in the short run to the Canaries, the ships were found to be so crazy and ill-appointed as to be quite unsuitable for a navigation which was expected to be both long and dangerous. Columbus refitted them, however, to the best of his power, and having supplied himself with fresh provisions, he took his departure from Gomera, one of the most westerly of the Canary Islands, on the 6th day of September. Here the voyage of discovery may properly be said to begin; for Columbus, holding his course due west, left immediately the usual track of navigation, and sailed into unfrequented and unknown seas.

B

Summarise the following passage, reducing it to about a third of its present length (i.e. to about 80 words).

Charles the Fifth was then fifty-five years and eight months old; but he was already decrepit with premature old age. He was of about the middle height, and had been athletic and well-proportioned. Broad in the shoulders, deep in the chest, thin in the flank, very muscular in the arms and legs, he had been able to match himself with all competitors in the tourney and the ring, and to vanquish the bull with his own hand in the favourite national amusement of Spain.

He had been able in the field to do the duty of captain and soldier, to endure fatigue and exposure, and every privation except fasting. These personal advantages were now departed. Crippled in hands, knees, and legs, he supported himself with difficulty upon a crutch, with the aid of an attendant's shoulder. In face he had always been extremely ugly, and time had certainly not improved his physiognomy. His hair, once of a light colour, was now white with age, close-clipped and bristling; his beard was grey, coarse, and shaggy.

His forehead was spacious and commanding; the eye was dark blue, with an expression both majestic and benignant. His nose was aquiline but crooked. The lower part of his face was famous for its deformity. The under lip, a Burgundian inheritance, as faithfully transmitted as the duchy and county, was heavy and hanging; the lower jaw protruding so far beyond the upper that it was impossible for him to bring together the few fragments of teeth which still remained, or to speak a whole sentence in an intelligible voice.

C

1. Summarise the following passage, reducing it to about a third (i.e. 130 words).

It has been part of Nelson's prayer, that the British fleet might be distinguished by humanity in the victory which he expected. Setting an example himself, he twice gave orders to cease firing upon the *Redoubtable*, supposing that she had struck, because her great guns were silent; for, as she carried no flag, there was no means of instantly ascertaining the fact. From this ship, which he had thus twice spared, he received his death. A ball fired from her mizzen-top, which, in the then situation of the two vessels, was not more than fifteen yards from that part of the deck where he was standing, struck the epaulette on his left shoulder, about a quarter after one, just in the heat of action. He fell upon his face, on the spot which was covered with his poor secretary's blood. Hardy, who was a few steps from him, turning round, saw three men raising him up. "They have done for me at last, Hardy!" said he. "I hope not!" cried Hardy. "Yes," he replied; "my backbone is shot through!" Yet even now, not for a moment losing his presence of mind, he observed, as they were carrying him down the ladder, that the tiller-ropes, which had been shot away, were not yet replaced, and ordered that new ones should be rove immediately. Then, that he might not be seen by the crew, he took out his handkerchief, and covered his face and his stars. Had he but concealed these badges of honour from the enemy, England, perhaps, would not have had cause to receive with sorrow the news of the battle of Trafalgar. The cockpit was crowded with wounded and dying men, over whose bodies he was with some difficulty conveyed, and laid upon a pallet in the midshipmen's berth. It was soon perceived, upon examination, that the wound was mortal. This, however, was concealed from all, except Captain Hardy, the chaplain, and the medical attendants. He himself being certain from the sensation in his back, and the gush of blood he felt momently within his breast, that no human care could avail him, insisted that the surgeon should leave him, and attend to those to whom he might be useful. "For," said he, "you can do nothing for me."

2. Explain the meaning of the following words: humanity, ball, epaulette, tiller, pallet, berth, mortal, chaplain, momently, surgeon.

D

1. Summarise the following passage, using about 120 words.

Samuel Pepys was the creator of three remarkable, and still surviving, things. The first, in order of their making, was his *Diary*. The second was the civil administration of the Admiralty—the rule and order that still give permanence to the material
5 form, fighting traditions and transmitted knowledge of the Royal Navy. A century after Pepys' death, at a time when his achievement as a diarist was still unknown and his name almost forgotten, Lord Barham—the man who shares with him the honour of being England's greatest naval administrator—testified that there was
10 not a department of the Admiralty that was not governed by the rules he had laid down in the seventeenth century. It was Pepys who made the scabbard for the sword that Nelson, and the heirs of Nelson, used.

Pepys' third creative achievement sprang from the second.
15 He has been described as the father of the Civil Service. Here, too, his orders hold. The rules he laid down and the administrative principles he elucidated have become part of the continuing life of his country. His family may have grown somewhat large of late, but it is still governed by the moral standards, integrity and
20 tradition of inflexible service on which in his lifetime he insisted. It has become in the course of generations what he strove to make it: a permanent watchdog against corruption.

Yet the work for which Pepys is best remembered and loved remains his Diary. It extends to over a million and a quarter
25 words: the length of a dozen fair-sized novels. After three centuries, there is not a page in it that does not arrest the reader and quicken his perception of humanity. It is probably the most searching and honest record of a man's daily doings ever penned. It is also one of the most vivid. As historical material I know of

30 nothing with such power to recreate the thought and daily
minutiae of a vanished age. It is strange to reflect that this wonderful achievement should have been wrought at the end of crowded
days of labour—the record of which is to be found not in the
Diary but in Pepys' vast collection of naval and administrative
35 papers.

(From Arthur Bryant's *Samuel Pepys—the Man in the Making*,
Collins.)

2. Answer briefly the following questions.

(*a*) Of the three things of which Pepys was creator, which *two*
were related to one another?

(*b*) When was the greatness of Pepys' work first recognised, according to this passage?

(*c*) What in fact is meant by *the scabbard* (line 12)?

(*d*) Write *two* words to give the meaning of *family* (line 18).

(*e*) Where, according to the author, is the record of Pepys' work
to be found?

(*f*) What, according to the author, makes the *Diary* of special
importance to the historian?

(*g*) What one word names a quality which the author indicates as
being characteristic both of Pepys' administration and of his *Diary*?

(*h*) Find *single* words in the passage which mean the same as:

    (i) *brought to light and explained* (second paragraph).

    (ii) *not to be turned from its right form* (second paragraph).

    (iii) *observation and understanding* (third paragraph).

    (iv) *details* (third paragraph).

(Oxford Local Examinations, General Certificate of Education,
Ordinary Level, Summer Examination, 1953.)

E

    1. Summarise the following passage in about 100 words.

We are accustomed to consider winter the grave of the year,
but it is not so in reality. In the stripped trees, the mute birds, the
disconsolate gardens, the frosty ground, there is only an apparent
cessation of Nature's activities. Winter is a pause in music, but
5 during the pause the musicians are privately tuning their strings,
to prepare for the coming outburst. When the curtain falls on one
piece at the theatre, the people are busy behind the scenes making
arrangements for that which is to follow. Winter is such a pause,
such a fall of the curtain. Underground, beneath snow and frost,

10 next spring and summer are secretly getting ready. The roses
which young ladies will gather six months hence are already in
hand. In Nature, there is no such thing as paralysis. Each thing
flows into the other, as movement into movement in graceful
dances; Nature's colours blend in imperceptible gradation; all
15 her notes are in logical sequence. We go out into the garden and
notice that when the last leaves have fallen off the lilac and currant-
bushes the new buds are all ready, like performers at the side-
wings waiting their turn to come on. In plants, the life which in
June and July was exuberant in blossom and odour, has with-
20 drawn to the root, where it lies taking counsel with itself regarding the course of action to be adopted next season. The coming
spring is even now underground, and the first snows will hardly
have melted till it will peep out timorously in snowdrops; then,
bolder grown, will burst in crocuses, holding up their coloured
25 lamps; then, by fine gradations, the floral year will reach its noon,
the rose; then, by fine gradations, it will die in a sunset of hollyhocks and tiger-lilies; and so we come again to withered leaves
and falling snows.

2. Answer the following questions on this passage.

(a) Explain the exact meaning of *four* of the following words or
phrases as they occur in the above passage: disconsolate (l. 3);
imperceptible (l. 14); in logical sequence (l. 15); exuberant in
blossom and odour (l. 19); timorously (l. 23); fine gradations
(l. 26).

(b) Say what the following metaphors suggest to you: the grave
of the year (l. 1); a fall of the curtain (l. 9).

(c) Express in your own words the meaning of the sentence: "In
Nature, there is no such thing as paralysis" (l. 12).

(d) Define "cessation" and "pause" as used in l. 4 so as to bring
out the difference between them.

(e) What effect does the writer try to suggest in the last sentence
by the words "noon" and "sunset", and by the repetition of the
phrase "by fine gradations"?

(University of London General Certificate of Education, Ordinary
Level, Autumn 1955.)

F

1. Summarise, *in your own words* as far as possible, the argument
of the following passage (which contains about 500 words), reducing

it to about 170 words. At the end of your *précis* state the *exact* number of words you have used.

From the moment in her history that England became Channel-conscious she became Channel-minded, and she has remained so ever since. Bedded in her memory is the recollection of her first duty—to keep herself to herself. The phrase is characteristic of
5 her people. I have never met an English working man or woman who did not boast of keeping the neighbours at arm's length. To be ignorant of other people's affairs and to cast a veil of impenetrable secrecy about one's own is, to the average Englishman, the primary mark of respectability. The boast is usually quite un-
10 justified, but that is not the point; what we like to think ourselves is often more revealing than what we actually are. The immediate reaction of all English people to a foreign invader or a foreign idea is to make access as difficult as possible.

For anyone of English blood there is no more agreeable pastime
15 than to watch the people of cosmopolitan mind trying to induce the British to toe the line of simplification and standardisation. They are always so naïve, earnest, and plausible, and they invariably use all the wrong arguments. At one time it was the Channel Tunnel, which would make it easier for foreigners to
20 get to England. Periodically it is suggested that we should abolish an old-fashioned coinage and an archaic system of weights and measures, so that foreigners need no longer waste time and energy in attempting to work out half-crowns in terms of francs, or reduce square yards (by bundles of $30\frac{1}{4}$) to perches, roods, and
25 square miles, and thence to square kilometres. And from time to time persons intent on the amelioration of business facilities and numb to literary history implore us to jettison our English spelling in favour of something that would be easier for foreigners to understand and remember.

30 The British listen politely to all these arguments and do nothing about anything, and the cosmopolitan laments and deprecates their lack of logic. Yet the British are not so illogical as all that; they understand perfectly that these reforms would make things easier all round. But they do not want things made easier; they
35 want, instinctively and passionately and inarticulately want, everything to be kept difficult. Behind the barrier of the rod, pole, or perch, and the barbed entanglement of the letters *-ough* they retire as into a fortress. To make things too easy is to risk an

invasion, even if it is only an invasion of privacy. It is useless to
40 tell the Englishman that if the serried ranks of iron railings were
removed, his house and grounds, to say nothing of his public
parks, would appear much more attractive and be more accessible;
the very idea makes him uncomfortable. The only thing that will
inspire him to tear up his railings is the conviction that they are
45 needed to defend his moat against a still more serious invasion.

2. The following questions relate to the passage in Question 2.
Answer them as far as possible in complete statements *in your own
words*.

(*a*) Explain what the writer meant by (i) "Channel-conscious",
(ii) "Channel-minded" (l. 2).

(*b*) Show, by giving any one example of your own, that you
understand what the writer means by the statement "what we like
to think ourselves is often more revealing than what we actually are"
(ll. 10–11).

(*c*) Why does the writer consider that "to watch . . . standardisation" (ll. 15–16) is an *agreeable pastime*?

(*d*) Suggest any reasons other than those given by the writer for
the Englishman's attitude to the proposals referred to in the lines
20–29 ("Periodically . . . remember").

(*e*) Explain the phrase "The barbed entanglement of the letters
-ough" (l. 37).

3. (*a*) Explain the meanings, in their contexts, of *five* of the following words in the passage in Question 2: cosmopolitan (l. 15), standardisation (l. 16), naïve (l. 17), plausible (l. 18), amelioration
(l. 26), deprecates (l. 31), inarticulately (l. 35), conviction (l. 44).

(*b*) Explain *four* of the following metaphors, showing how the
literal meaning of the word or phrase throws light on the meaning in
the passage:

(i) at arm's length (l. 6), (ii) to toe the line (l. 16), (iii) jettison
(l. 27), (iv) barrier (l. 36), (v) serried ranks (l. 40), (vi) moat (l. 45).

(University of London General Certificate of Education, "O"
Level, 1953.)

G

1. Summarise, *in your own words* as far as possible, the argument of
the following passage (which contains about 500 words), reducing it
to about 170 words, and assign a short appropriate title. At the end
of your précis state the exact number of words you have used.

Round London and other large towns the approach of Easter sees the return of week-end walking-clubs, and other gregarious ramblers, to the footpaths and commons: though not all such associations hibernate like hedgehogs and bats, or retire to warmer
5 winter quarters like the swallows. The bait that draws town walkers to country footpaths appears to vary. Some clubs provide an agreeable combination of social intercourse with healthy physical exercise, and a not too exacting appreciation of the beauties of nature. With well-chosen companions there is always the refuge
10 of intellectual discussion when the lambs and the primroses become tedious. The return of the cuckoo can be alternated as a conversational topic with the return to the gold-standard, and, if the skylarks obtrude themselves too noisily, relief is found from them over the simple plenty of the luncheon table in some well-
15 chosen inn. Other walkers appear in groups and couples like sand-martins, rather than in flocks like May frogs, and many of them afford mild amusement to rustic dullards by their evident sense of being bound on a dramatic adventure. They can be heard speaking of walking as "tramping"; their collars are of ostenta-
20 tious looseness, they wear ski-ing boots, and their walking-sticks are of the stoutness of those preferred by Sir Harry Lauder.

From the visits of these more striking spring migrants, as from those of the field clubs which plan a walk with some specific pur-pose, and of single naturalists and country-lovers, certain definite
25 advantages arise. The more that footpaths are used in outlying places the less is the chance of their disappearing, in fact if not in right. Village mothers who send children to school across newly-ploughed fields have been heard to declare that "the going will be better when the Londoners come". In proportion as dwellers
30 in cities grow familiar with country villages they will be readier to help in such voluntary services as the preservation of historic ruins, or of other historic buildings which can be saved from ruin. They become interested in safeguarding the spots of beauty which have given them pleasure, and imbibe that fostering interest in
35 open spaces which leads to support of the work of the National Trust and its kindred organisations. They achieve a substantial public benefit in improving the fare and accommodation at remote village inns; many small innkeepers who profess complete inability to satisfy the needs of motorists can be encouraged to rise
40 to the demands of those who arrive modestly on foot.

On the other hand there are those who maintain that the ramblers do much harm to the face of the countryside during their visits, but it is not habitual walkers who every Easter strip the countryside of flower-roots and blossoms. Motorists are not guilt-
45 less of this offence, nor are humbler holiday trippers. The visits of both these classes into the lanes and woods where flowers grow most freely are occasionally raids, whereas walkers who come regularly learn to prefer to see the blossoms unravished.

2. The following questions relate to the passage above. Answer them as far as possible in complete sentences *in your own words*.

(a) Express briefly and in your own words what the writer means by "though not all such associations hibernate like hedgehogs and bats" (ll. 3–4), and show its connection in meaning with the first part of the sentence.

(b) Name briefly *three* benefits the writer thinks the visits of these walkers will bring to the countryside.

(c) What do you understand by the term "field clubs" (l. 23)? What different reasons do the field clubs and walking-clubs have for a visit to the country?

(d) What is the difference, in the writer's opinion, between the visits of the motorists and humbler holiday trippers on the one hand, and those of the walkers on the other? Quote an earlier passage which suggests the reason for this.

(e) Why do you think the writer used the word "modestly" in l. 40? Quote another word later in the passage used with the same sense, and related to this context.

3. (a) Explain the meanings, in their contexts, of the following words from the passage in Question 2: commons (l. 3), obtrude (l. 13), ostentatious (l. 19), migrants (l. 22), imbibe (l. 34), fostering (l. 34), kindred (l. 36), unravished (l. 48).

(b) (i) What does the writer mean by "gregarious" (l. 2)? Quote an expression later in the same paragraph which repeats the idea.

(ii) Explain clearly the meaning and appropriateness of the metaphor "spring migrants" (l. 22) in its context.

(University of London General Certificate of Education, Ordinary Level, Autumn 1951.)

H

1. Summarise, *in your own words* as far as possible, the argument of the following passage (which contains about 500 words), reducing it

to about 170 words. At the end of your *précis* state the *exact* number of words you have used.

From the earliest days of civilisation the lord of creation has been inclined to chafe at his inferiority to the meanest cabbage-white butterfly or house-sparrow in the matter of flight. Until the end of the nineteenth century nothing practical had come of
5 it, beyond the ability to drift precariously about in the cars of balloons. But in more than the literal sense it might have been said that flying was in the air. One of the commonest books about the future described how some man had worked out the plans of a completely efficient airship and thereby achieved power to impose
10 his own terms on the rest of the species. Meanwhile inventors were working out the design of flying-machines that never quite succeeded in flying. Even advanced thinkers were inclined to be sceptical whether the final product of these activities was likely to be anything more than an ingenious toy, and there were still
15 pious folk to deplore the presumption of those who invited the wrath of the Almighty by trying to improve upon his plan of creation.

It was the success of the brothers Wright in 1903 that at last manifested to the world that the age of flying had actually
20 dawned, and henceforth progress was astonishingly rapid. So implicit was the faith in any sort of mechanical improvement that nothing but delighted applause was excited, in 1909, by what might well have been regarded as one of the most ominous events in British history. A Frenchman, M. Blériot, undeterred by the
25 failure of a compatriot a few days earlier, succeeded in piloting his monoplane across the Channel and landing near Dover. Henceforth Britannia might lord it as she would over the waves— her iron walls were no protection against an enemy who could fly over them. War had been transferred to a third dimension.

30 The conquest of the air was undoubtedly the most spectacular feature of the early years of the reign of George V. In an incredibly short space of time the sight and sound of an aeroplane became familiar to dwellers on the route from Croydon to the Continent. Records for speed, height and distance were continually being
35 surpassed, while stunt flying began to be practised and the loop was successfully looped. With construction still in the experimental stage, the life of a leading airman was held on the most pre-

carious tenure, although the number of prominent casualties
served only to increase the thrills of this new chase after speed.
40 The cult of the thrill followed inevitably from this universal speed-
ing up, and answered the need for some stimulus violent enough
to impress itself upon nerves dulled by long routine and absence
of sensation. It was most unlikely that a nice discrimination would
be fostered under such conditions, and the result was a sensational
45 age, one of crazes and panics in every department of life, in politics
and journalism, in art and the employment of leisure.

2. The following questions relate to the passage above. Answer
them as far as possible in complete statements *in your own words*.

(*a*) Explain the point of the reference to "the meanest cabbage-
white butterfly or house-sparrow" (ll. 3–4).

(*b*) What is meant by "the literal sense" (l. 6), and how does
the writer show that "flying was in the air" (l. 7) in another sense?

(*c*) Why might Blériot's flight across the Channel have been regarded as "one of the most ominous events in British history" (ll.
23–24), and why did people nevertheless receive it with "delighted
applause" (l. 22)?

(*d*) What were the conditions referred to in l. 44, and why would
they be unlikely to foster a "nice discrimination" (l. 43)?

3. Explain the meanings, in their contexts, of *five* of the following
words or phrases in the passage above.

chafe (l. 2), sceptical (l. 13), pious folk (l. 15), deplore the presumption (l. 15), undeterred (l. 24), compatriot (l. 25), precarious tenure
(l. 37), cult (l. 40).
(University of London, General Certificate of Education, Ordinary
Level, Summer 1953.)

I

1. Summarise the following passage in your own words, reducing
it to not more than 170 words. At the end of your summary state the
number of words you have used.

Buildings created by man tell us much about nations and individuals, and even about the nature of the part of the earth
where they dwell.

There are islands in the Pacific where one of your prime aims
5 in life is to escape being killed in your bed the next time your
house is blown down by a hurricane. The hurricanes come at

intervals of a few years; even earthquakes are quite on the cards; and then, however your house may have been built, it is bound to come down. The natural result is that people building in these
10 localities do not attempt to put up massive or imposing buildings: it is far better to have one side of a light match-box fall in on your head while you sleep than to be crushed beneath the weight of a handsomely vaulted roof of marble or alabaster. So the houses are built lightly of wood, and are never more than one storey high.
15 If large buildings, such as hospitals, have to be built, they are made with a rich abundance of doors, so that, as soon as disaster threatens, all the more helpless inmates can be swiftly carried out into the open. The architecture of places like this has a vivid eloquence of its own. To the reconnoitring eyes on every approach-
20 ing ship it cries aloud the severe conditions of living on that island.

All architecture talks to the beholder, although not always so loudly. The earliest Egyptian buildings, for example, speak freely about both sacred and secular things. Even if we had not known it in other ways, we should have learned from these buildings
25 what a serious affair the Egyptian thought it if his body were not left in a safe place after death. When a man died, his soul, unless he had been good, lived on as a tenant of the bodies of various beasts. If he had been good, his soul left him for the time, spent three thousand years with the god Osiris, and then came back to
30 the human body that it had left at death. Naturally an Egyptian architect, having to design a tomb, made sure that it would last at least three thousand years, and so shelter and preserve the body which the soul would at last re-enter. Those are the reasons for the fantastic solidity of a pyramid.

35 The chief secular thing that the greatest Egyptian architecture expressed was probably a cruel and primitive pride of conquest. In about the seventeenth century B.C. the rulers of Egypt believed in war as a business, necessary to the life of the nation, and not as a dire occasional necessity only. They made frequent raids on
40 their neighbours, and, bringing back hordes of them alive, they used them as slaves. No country had ever had at its disposal such a plentiful supply of cheap labour, and the Egyptians were so thrilled with their achievement that they determined to com-memorate it for all time in their architecture. For this reason they
45 chose to build in such a way as could be attempted only by those who could command an unprecedented multitude of unpaid

workmen. It was to prove to the world that they had this multitude
of slave workers in their power that they deliberately chose to
build with such purposeless massiveness. The best and truest art
50 takes pride in using the simplest means to reach its ends. The art
that created the Pyramids has merely shown the world how little
it achieved in proportion to all the toil that went to their building.

2. Answer the following questions. All references in brackets are
to lines in the passage in Question 2.

(a) (i) Give a word of equivalent meaning for *prime* (l. 4, where it
is an adjective); write a sentence in which *prime* is used as a different
part of speech, and state the meaning it has in your sentence.

(ii) Explain the precise meaning of *unprecedented* (l. 46).

(iii) What does the word *hordes* (l. 40) suggest that the word
crowds would not?

(b) For each of the following phrases give an expression equivalent
in meaning:

(i) quite on the cards (l. 7).

(ii) to the reconnoitring eyes (l. 19).

(iii) a dire occasional necessity (l. 39).

(iv) with such purposeless massiveness (l. 49).

(University of London Matriculation, June 1948.)

J

1. Summarise, reducing it to about 160–180 words, the following
passage (which contains about 500 words), and assigning a short
appropriate title. You are advised to devote about 15 minutes to
reading the passage, and about 30 minutes to writing the précis.
Count the number of words you use, and write the number at the
end of your précis. You are asked to be especially accurate in this.

When I look at our Western civilisation, I find myself dividing
people according to the way they think about work. One group
look upon it as a hateful necessity, whose only use is to make
money for them. They feel that only when the day's labour is
5 over can they really begin to live and be themselves. The other
group look on their work as an opportunity for enjoyment and
self-fulfilment. They only want to make money so that they may
devote themselves more single-mindedly to their work.

The first group is not made up solely of people doing very hard
10 and uninteresting work. It includes a great many well-off people
who do practically no work at all. The rich man who lives idly on

his income, the man who gambles in the hope of getting money without working for it, the woman who marries for the mere sake of being comfortably established for life—all these look on money
15 as something that saves them from the curse of work. Except that they have had better luck, their outlook is that of the factory hand whose daily work is one long round of toil. For them, work is something hateful, and money is desirable because it represents a way of escape from work.

20 The second group includes the artists, scholars, and scientists— the people really devoured with the passion for making and discovering things. It includes also the old-fashioned craftsmen, taking a real pride and pleasure in turning out a good job of work. It includes also those skilled mechanics and engineers who genuinely
25 love the complicated beauty of the machines they use and look after. Then there are those professional people in whom we recognise a clear spiritual vocation—those doctors, nurses, priests, actors, teachers, whose work is something more to them than a mere means of livelihood; seamen who, for all they may grumble
30 at the hardships of the sea, return to it again and again; farmers and farm workers who devotedly serve the land and the beasts they tend; and those comparatively rare women to whom the nurture of children is a full-time and absorbing intellectual and emotional interest.

35 But we must also admit that, of late, the second group of workers has become more and more infected with the outlook of the first. Agriculture has been directed, not to serving the land, but to bleeding it white in the interest of money-making. Certain members of the medical profession are less interested in preserving
40 their patients' health than in exploiting their weaknesses for profit. Some writers openly admit that their sole aim is the manufacture of best sellers. And if we exclaim indignantly that this kind of conduct is bad for the work, the individual, and the community, we must also confess that we ourselves have been only too ready to
45 acquiesce in these commercial standards, not only in trade, but in the professions and public services as well.

DOROTHY SAYERS.

2. The following questions are based on the passage above. Answer them briefly, and as far as possible in complete statements in your own words.

(*a*) "Except . . . luck" (ll. 15–16). In what respect has their luck been better?

(*b*) What sort of work does the author refer to as a "curse" and "something hateful" (ll. 15 and 18)? Give *two* examples of this kind of occupation.

(*c*) "something more . . . livelihood" (ll. 28–29). In the author's opinion, what can a man's work give to him, in addition to his livelihood?

(*d*) "infected" (l. 36). What are the symptoms, in the author's opinion, of this infection?

3. (*a*) Explain carefully the meanings, in their contexts, of *five* of the following words and phrases: civilisation (l. 1), established (l. 14), spiritual vocation (l. 27), serve the land (l. 31), bleeding it white (l. 38), manufacture (l. 41), acquiesce in these commercial standards (l. 45).

(*b*) Show briefly (in not more than *five* lines) how the argument of the passage is carried on from one paragraph to the next. If the passage had contained a fifth paragraph, what would you have expected its content to be? Give reasons.

(University of London General Certificate of Education Ordinary Level, Midsummer 1950.)

CHAPTER XX

APPRECIATION OF PROSE

Style: In order to help us develop standards of judgment we must consider the question of style.

Every writer has his or her own particular style which is closely connected with his or her own particular personality and intellectual gifts, though a writer's style is sometimes noticeably influenced by other writers. Indeed, literature would be very monotonous if all authors cultivated the same style of writing.

Some writers prefer simple everyday language, using short words whenever possible; others prefer a more complicated and varied vocabulary, using longer words; some prefer short sentences, and a loose construction; others, long sentences and the frequent use of periodic sentences; some aim at short paragraphs and directness; others at lengthy paragraphs and a less direct approach with digressions and much detail. Some styles are forceful, others restful, some lively or humorous and some dramatic, some moving, others tedious. There are many other ways in which styles will be found to differ, for much depends on the subject with which the writer is dealing and on the impression he or she wishes to convey.

Here are a few brief examples of widely differing styles:

1. BUNYAN: *The Pilgrim's Progress.*

"As I walked through the wilderness of this world I lighted on a certain place where was a den, and I laid me down in that place to sleep; and as I slept I dreamed a dream. I dreamed, and behold I saw a man clothed with rags, standing in a certain place, with his face from his own house, a book in his hand and a great burden upon his back. I looked, and saw him open the book, and read therein, and as he read, he wept and trembled."

Here is a simple, concise, clear style, employing the "loose" sentence.

Defoe's *Robinson Crusoe* and Swift's *Gulliver's Travels* exemplify the same plain style, avoiding long words and long sentences, comparisons, details, and digressions.

2. MACAULAY: Essay on "Oliver Goldsmith".

"But there are rivers of which the water when first drawn is turbid and noisome, but becomes pellucid as crystal, and delicious to the taste, if it be suffered to stand till it has deposited a sediment; and such a river is a type of the mind of Goldsmith. His first thoughts on every subject were confused even to absurdity; but they required only a little time to work themselves clear. When he wrote they had that time; and therefore his readers pronounced him a man of genius; but when he talked he talked nonsense, and made himself the laughing stock of his hearers."

Here is a richer style, that of an orator, with finely constructed and balanced sentences (both "loose" and periodic sentences are employed), and a rich vocabulary. Gibbon, author of *The Decline and Fall of the Roman Empire*, had a similar style and he tells of the effort he made to find "the middle tone between a dull chronicle and a rhetorical declamation". Lytton Strachey is equally rewarding as a stylist in his historical work, and Southey's *Life of Nelson* also exemplifies it.

3. CARLYLE: *The French Revolution.*

"Louis Tournay smites, brave Aubin Bonnemere (also an old soldier) seconding him: the chain yields, breaks; the huge Drawbridge slams down, thundering: Glorious: and yet, alas, it is still but the outworks.

"How the great Bastille Clock ticks (inaudible) in its inner court there, at its ease, hour after hour; as if nothing special for it or the world, were passing! It tolled One when the firing began, and is now pointing towards Five, and still the firing slakes not. Far down, in their vaults, the seven Prisoners hear muffled din as of earthquakes; their Turnkeys answer vaguely."

This style is essentially Carlyle's own—forceful, abrupt. He is like a painter painting a picture with a series of sudden splashes of colour. Notice his use of capital letters, of parentheses, and of exclamations.

4. Dickens: *David Copperfield.*

"The first objects that assume a distinct presence before me, as I look far back, into the blank of my infancy, are my mother with her pretty hair, and youthful shape, and Peggotty with no shape at all, and eyes so dark that they seemed to darken their whole neighbourhood in her face, and cheeks and arms so hard and red that I wondered the birds didn't peck her in preference to apples.

"I believe I can remember these two at a little distance apart, dwarfed to my sight by stooping down or kneeling on the floor, and I going unsteadily from the one to the other. I have an impression in my mind which I cannot distinguish from actual remembrance, of the touch of Peggotty's forefinger as she used to hold it out to me, and of its being roughened by needlework, like a pocket nutmeg-grater."

Notice the long opening sentence (and Dickens often employed long paragraphs also), the detailed description, with comparisons and contrasts, the whimsical touch at the end, so typical of Dickens. Dickens could be grave or gay, could handle dialogue brilliantly, and above all, whatever his faults of exaggeration, long-windedness, or excess of sentimentality, he could tell an enthralling story as few have done before or since.

5. Leigh Hunt: Essays, "The Cat by the Fire".

"A blazing fire, a warm rug, candles lit and curtains drawn, the kettle on for tea, and finally, the cat before you, attracting your attention—it is a sense which everybody likes unless he has a morbid aversion to cats! which is not common.

"The cat purrs, as if it applauded our consideration—and gently moves its tail. What an odd expression of the power to be irritable and the will to be pleased there is in its face, as it looks up at us!

"Now she proceeds to clean herself all over, having a just sense of the demands of her elegant person—beginning judiciously with her paws, and fetching amazing tongues at her hind-hips."

This final example, though there are many more styles, is of a pleasant, colloquial style that gives the impression that the author is actually talking to his reader. This style has charm, it is light in touch, and avoids excessive length of word or sentence, or complicated construction. The essays of Addison, Lamb, Goldsmith, and Mary Russell Mitford—and among modern essays those of E. V. Lucas, Harold Nicolson, and Robert Lynd—exemplify this style.

Appreciation

We are not concerned in this chapter with the appreciation of a complete novel, essay, or play, as this is dealt with in Chapter XXIX ("Reviews"), but with the examination of a short selected passage of prose typical of the style of its author.

The points we should study may be summed up as follows:

1. What type of sentences or paragraphs is employed?
   Are they predominantly long or short, or do they vary?
   Is the periodic or loose sentence employed equally, or is one type preferred?
   Is the rhythm of the writer's prose jerky or smooth?
   Are ideas presented in a roundabout or direct manner?
   Does the style employed suit the theme?

2. What type of vocabulary or diction (the choice and use of words) does the writer employ? Is it rich and varied?

 Does he delight in long words and phrases, or employ the simplest language to express himself?

3. Are comparisons (similes and metaphors) and other figures of speech employed?

 What other effects, such as contrast, emphasis, questions, or exclamations are employed?

4. Does the writer employ detailed enumeration or select only salient points in descriptions?

 If there is humour,* is it successfully employed?

 If there is an appeal to the emotions, is it carried to excess?

5. Does the writer write objectively (i.e. impersonally, with no intrusion of his own feelings or views) or subjectively (i.e. with a personal approach)?

6. What is the main impression and atmosphere the extract conveys?

EXERCISES

Write a brief appreciation of the style of each of the following extracts, and comment on the contrast of styles in each section.

A

1. I have an almost feminine partiality for old china. When I go to see any great house, I inquire for the china-closet, and next for the picture-gallery. I cannot defend the order of preference, but by saying that we have all some taste or other, of too ancient a date

---

* Remember, in appreciating humour, that humour can be of many types: (1) Humour based on amusing events, scenes, or characters; (2) humour based on exaggeration in presentation; (3) humour based on understatement in presentation (e.g. "I shot his pipe out of his mouth. He seemed upset."); (4) humour based on the unexpected (e.g. "Who on earth are you?" "I am engaged to your daughter, sir"); (5) humour based on innuendo (e.g. "In his first race as a jockey he was not in the saddle when his horse passed the winning-post"); (6) humour based on mock gravity—the use of long words to describe simple things and events; (7) humour based on witty dialogue.

to admit of our remembering distinctly that it was an acquired one. I can call to mind the first play, and the first exhibition, that I was taken to; but I am not conscious of a time when china jars and saucers were introduced into my imagination.

I had no repugnance then—why should I now have?—to those little, lawless, azure-tinctured grotesques, that, under the notion of men and women, float about uncircumscribed by any element, in that world before perspective—a china tea-cup.

I like to see my old friends—whom distance cannot diminish—figuring up in the air (so they appear to our optics), yet on *terra firma* still—for so we must in courtesy interpret that speck of deeper blue which the decorous artist, to prevent absurdity, had made to spring up beneath their sandals.

Old China, CHARLES LAMB (1775–1834).

2. As Sir Roger is landlord to the whole congregation, he keeps them in very good order, and will suffer nobody to sleep in it besides himself; for if by chance he has been surprised into a short nap at sermon, upon recovering out of it he stands up and looks about him, and if he sees anybody else nodding, either wakes them himself, or sends his servants to them. Several other of the old knight's particularities break out upon these occasions: sometimes he will be lengthening out a verse in the singing-psalms, half a minute after the rest of the congregation have done with it; sometimes when he is pleased with the matter of his devotion, he pronounces Amen three or four times to the same prayer; and sometimes stands up when everybody else is upon their knees, to count the congregation, or see if any of his tenants are missing.

I was yesterday very much surprised to hear my old friend, in the midst of the service, calling out to one John Matthews to mind what he was about, and not disturb the congregation. This John Matthews, it seems, is remarkable for being an idle fellow, and at that time was kicking his heels for his diversion. This authority of the knight, though exerted in that odd manner which accompanies him in all circumstances of life, has a very good effect upon the parish, who are not polite enough to see anything ridiculous in his behaviour; besides that the general good sense and worthiness of his character make his friends observe these little singularities as foils that rather set off than blemish his good qualities.

Sir Roger De Coverley, JOSEPH ADDISON (1672–1719).

B

1. Adam walked round by the rick-yard, at present empty of ricks, to the little wooden gate leading into the garden—once the well-tended kitchen garden of a manor-house; now, but for the handsome brick wall with stone coping that ran along one side of it, a true farmhouse garden, with hardy perennial flowers, unpruned fruit-trees, and kitchen vegetables growing together in careless, half-neglected abundance. In that leafy, flowery, bushy time, to look for any one in this garden was like playing at "hide-and-seek". There were the tall hollyhocks beginning to flower, and dazzle the eye with their pink, white, and yellow; there were the syringas and Gueldres roses, all large and disorderly for want of trimming; there were leafy walls of scarlet beans and late peas; there was a row of bushy filberts in one direction, and in another a huge apple-tree making a barren circle under its low-spreading boughs. But what signified a barren patch or two? The garden was so large. There was always a super-fluity of broad beans—it took nine or ten of Adam's strides to get to the end of the uncut grass walk that ran by the side of them; and as for other vegetables, there was so much more room than was necessary for them, that in the rotation of crops a large flourishing bed of ground-sel was of yearly occurrence on one spot or other. The very rose-trees, at which Adam stopped to pluck one, looked as if they grew wild; they were all huddled together in bushy masses, now flaunting with wide open petals, almost all of them of the streaked pink-and-white kind, which doubtless dated from the union of the houses of York and Lancaster.

Adam Bede, GEORGE ELIOT (1819–80).

2. Then I made my way, by a stony road, towards the manor-house; and presently could see its gables at the end of a pleasant avenue of limes; but no track led thither. The gate was wired up, and the drive overgrown with grass. Soon, however, I found a farm-road which led up to the house from the village. On the left of the manor lay prosperous barns and byres, full of sleek pigs and busy crested fowls. The teams came clanking home across the water-meadows. The house itself became more and more beautiful as I approached. It was surrounded by a moat, and here, close at hand, stood an ancient chapel, in seemly repair. All round the house grew dense thickets of sprawling laurels, which rose in luxuriance from the edge of the water. Then I crossed a little bridge with a broken parapet; and in front of me stood the house itself. I have seldom seen a more perfectly propor-

tioned or exquisitely coloured building. There were three gables in the front, the central one holding a beautiful oriel window, with a fine oak door below. The whole was built of a pale red brick, covered with a grey lichen that cast a shimmering light over the front. Tall chimneys of solid grace rose from a stone-shingled roof. The coigns, parapets and mullions were all of a delicately-tinted orange stone. To the right lay a big walled garden, full of flowers growing with careless richness, the whole bounded by the moat, and looking out across the broad green water-meadows, beyond which the low hills rose softly in gentle curves and dingles.

The Thread of Gold, A. C. Benson (1862–1925).

C

1. "Whisht, gudewife!" exclaimed the Smith. "Is this a time, or is this a day, to be singing your ranting fule sangs in?"

"And you, ye doil'd dotard," replied his gentle helpmate, her wrath, which had hitherto wandered abroad over the whole assembly, being at once and violently impelled into its natural channel, "*ye* stand there hammering dog-heads for fules that will never snap them at a Highlandman, instead of earning bread for your family and shoeing this winsome young gentleman's horse that's just come frae the North! I'se warrant him nane of your whingeing King George folk, but a gallant Gordon, at the least o' him."

The eyes of the assembly were now turned upon Waverley, who took the opportunity to beg the smith to shoe his guide's horse with all speed, as he wished to proceed on his journey. The smith's eyes rested on him with a look of displeasure and suspicion, not lessened by the eagerness with which his wife enforced Waverley's mandate. "D'ye hear what the weel-favoured young gentleman says, ye drunken ne'er-do-good?"

"And what may your name be, sir?" quoth Mucklewrath.

"It is of no consequence to you, my friend, provided I pay your labour."

doil'd = stupid.
whingeing = whining.

Waverley, Sir Walter Scott (1771–1832).

2. "Look out, Gerard."
"Ay. What will they do next?"
"We shall soon know."

"Shall I wait for you, or cut down the first that opens the door?'

"Wait for me, lest we strike the same and waste a blow. Alas! we cannot afford that."

Dead silence.

Sudden came into the room a thing that made them start and their hearts quiver.

And what was it? A moonbeam.

Even so can this machine, the body, by the soul's action be strung up to start and quiver. The sudden ray shot keen and pure into that shamble.

Its calm, cold, silvery soul traversed the apartment in a stream of no great volume; for the window was narrow.

After the first tremor Gerard whispered, "Courage, Denys! God's eye is on us even here." And he fell upon his knees with his face turned towards the window.

The moon drew a broad stripe of light across the door, and on that his eyes were glued. Presently he whispered, "Gerard!"

Gerard looked and raised his sword.

Acutely as they had listened they had heard of late no sound on the stair. Yet there—on the door-post, at the edge of the stream of moonlight, were the tips of the fingers of a hand.

The nails glistened.

The Cloister and The Hearth, CHARLES READE (1814–84).

D

1. "Cab!" said Mr. Pickwick.

"Here you are, sir," shouted a strange specimen of the human race, in a sackcloth coat, and apron of the same, who, with a brass label and number round his neck, looked as if he were catalogued in some collection of rarities. This was the waterman. "Here you are, sir. Now, then, fust cab!"

"Golden Cross," said Mr. Pickwick.

"Only a bob's vorth, Tommy," cried the driver, sulkily, for the information of his friend the waterman, as the cab drove off.

"How old is that horse, my friend?" inquired Mr. Pickwick, rubbing his nose with the shilling he had reserved for the fare.

"Forty-two," replied the driver, eyeing him askant.

"What!" ejaculated Mr. Pickwick, laying his hand upon his notebook. The driver reiterated his former statement. Mr. Pickwick looked very hard at the man's face; but his features were immovable, so he noted down the fact forthwith.

"And how long do you keep him out at a time?" inquired Mr. Pickwick, searching for further information.

"Two or three veeks," replied the man.

"Weeks!" said Mr. Pickwick in astonishment—and out came the note-book again.

The Pickwick Papers, Charles Dickens (1812–70).

2. His bicycle was now very old, and it is one of the concomitants of a bicycle's senility that its free-wheel should one day obstinately cease to be free. It corresponds to that epoch in human decay when an old gentleman loses an incisor tooth. It happened just as Mr. Polly was approaching Mr. Rusper's shop, and the untoward chance of a motor-car trying to pass a wagon on the wrong side gave Mr. Polly no choice but to get on to the pavement and dismount. He was always accustomed to take his time and step off his left pedal at its lowest point, but the jamming of the free-wheel gear made that lowest moment a transitory one, and the pedal was lifting his foot for another revolution before he realised what had happened. Before he could dismount according to his habit the pedal had to make a revolution, and before it could make a revolution Mr. Polly found himself among the various sonorous things with which Mr. Rusper adorned the front of his shop—zinc dustbins, household pails, lawn-mowers, rakes, spades, and all manner of clattering things.

The History of Mr. Polly, H. G. WELLS (1866–1946).

SECTION III

COMPOSITION

CHAPTER XXI

DESCRIPTIONS OF THINGS

We have already discussed and attempted brief "dictionary" definitions in Chapter IX ("Vocabulary").

Now, as a first step in the more ambitious exercise of Composition, the student will find it an excellent training in clarity of expression and logical arrangement of facts to attempt short descriptions of everyday appliances, machines, etc.

It is advisable to attempt descriptions of some simple objects first (e.g. a fountain-pen, a watering-can, an umbrella, a wheelbarrow, a bicycle-pump) before dealing with objects with more complicated mechanism (e.g. a typewriter, a lawn-mower, a sewing-machine, a bicycle, etc.).

(a) **Description of Simple Objects**

Method is essential in describing even the simplest object, and it will be found that the following system provides the most satisfactory result.

1. Give a brief general definition.

2. Deal with the structure of the object, dividing it into its main separate parts, and pointing out the purpose or function of each.

Take the parts in order of importance, starting with the basic part to which other parts are attached.

Details of shape and size are often obviously important, but details of colour and material can be omitted if unimportant.

3. Add any accessories you feel to be important, such as details of the self-filling mechanism of a fountain-pen. The pocket clip of the pen, on the other hand, is not vitally important if the time and space of your description are limited.

Here is a student's description, limited to a maximum of twenty lines, of a fountain-pen.

A FOUNTAIN-PEN

A fountain-pen is a type of pen which carries its own supply of ink.

It consists of three main parts: a barrel, a nib, and a filling mechanism.

The barrel is cylindrical in shape, about $\frac{1}{4}$ in. in diameter and varying in length from about 3 in. to 7 in., and is usually made of some plastic material. The barrel encloses a rubber tube which holds the ink supply.

The nib, a small pointed piece of gold or other metal, is inserted into the open end of the barrel, with a plastic ink-feed which controls the flow of ink to the nib. The nib is covered by a protective cap, which can be slipped on to the other end of the barrel when not required as a protection.

The filling mechanism consists either of a lever on the side of the barrel or of a plunger, protected by a small cap, at the top of the barrel.

Here is a brief description by a student of a wheelbarrow.

A WHEELBARROW

A wheelbarrow is a contrivance to enable heavy loads of earth, sand, stone, etc., to be moved from one place to another by pushing or pulling it (by hand), without mechanical aid.

A large shallow open box is fixed on two shafts, the rear ends of which project to form handles, while a wheel is mounted on an axle fixed between the projecting front ends of the shafts. At the rear end of the box, and at right-angles to the shaft, are two legs which support the barrow in a horizontal position when it is stationary.

It can be constructed of either wood or metal.

(b) **Description of Machines, etc.**

In the case of a machine it will, of course, be necessary to describe the actual working of those parts which move by hand or mechanical propulsion.

For example, in describing the action of a lawn-mower, after describing the position, mounting, and type of blades employed, we could say:

"When the machine is propelled forward, the blades mounted on the axle between the wheels rotate rapidly and, pressing the grass against the fixed blade, cut it at the desired height, which is fixed by the setting of the roller.

"At the same time the rotating blades, aided by a curved metal guard at the rear of the mower, throw the grass cuttings into the container mounted at the front of the machine to collect them."

It will be found advisable to make notes first, in order to avoid omission of any essential details, and to ensure that details are arranged in their right order. A rough draft is nearly always necessary before a satisfactory final effort can be achieved. A second attempt will enable us to "prune" our description, cutting down the number of words used, especially by the judicious use of the right descriptive adjectives, of constructions with the present participle (i.e. "moving", "turning", "lifting", etc.), and of relative clauses. We must make sure, however, that relative clauses come next to their antecedent nouns, and avoid loose participle constructions, such as "pushing from behind, the machine moves forward".

EXERCISES

A

Describe in not more than 12 lines or 100 words:

1. An electric torch.	5. A tennis-racket.
2. A pen-knife.	6. A teapot.
3. A pillar-box.	7. A garden roller.
4. A pair of scissors.	8. A cooker (gas or electric).

9. A watering-can.
10. A deck-chair.
11. A watch.

12. An umbrella.
13. A telephone kiosk.
14. A piano.

B

Describe in not more than 20 lines or 150 words, explaining the principle on which each works:

1. A bicycle-pump.
2. A typewriter.
3. A gramophone.
4. A wireless-set.
5. A bicycle.
6. A tram.
7. A motor-car.
8. A railway engine.
9. A passenger-ship.
10. A sewing-machine.

11. A television-set.
12. An aeroplane.
13. A vacuum-cleaner.
14. An electric washing-machine.
15. A cigarette-lighter.
16. A thermometer.
17. A rifle, or a revolver.
18. A camera.
19. A mouse-trap.
20. A bicycle-bell.

21. Traffic-lights.
22. Canal or river lock-gates.

CHAPTER XXII

DESCRIPTIONS OF PERSONS AND ANIMALS, AND PLACES AND SCENES

In the previous chapter we have dealt with the description of inanimate objects. These objects have been of a fixed type, each having exactly the same characteristics as all other objects in their particular class. When we are dealing with places or persons, however, each place or person has a different appearance and character.

As in the case of inanimate objects, such descriptions are an excellent test of our powers of observation, but we must cultivate also the gift of selection—that is, we must select or emphasise just those points which are of most value in making an effective picture or portrait, rather than make a lengthy and dull catalogue of every detail.

The effectiveness of a description can also be increased by the use of interesting comparisons, but we must try to employ similes which are striking and unusual rather than those which are now commonplace through too frequent use, and so are lacking in effect.

Finally, we come to the problem of the style in which the description is to be presented.

There are two main types of descriptive writing, the objective style and the subjective style.

The term *objective* is used for the type of description in which the writer aims at presenting an impersonal and purely factual description (i.e. he is writing solely with the presentation of facts as his *object*), and to do this the third person is used (e.g. "Bussage is a small village in the

Cotswolds, some five miles north of Stroud. It consists of some fifty houses and cottages grouped round the intersections of two roads at the head of the Toadsmoor Valley. The church and the village inn are the only buildings of note, the remainder being mostly typical Cotswold cottages.")

The term "*subjective*" is used to denote a descriptive style in which the writer inserts his personal views or impressions, employing when he does so the first person singular (e.g. "At first sight the village did not seem to me to differ from the many other charming, peaceful villages which shelter in the Cotswold valleys. I was soon to discover my mistake. It was a fortunate meeting with the Vicar whom I met as I strolled down the narrow, winding main street of attractive, solid Cotswold houses and cottages, that led to my discovery of one of the finest Elizabethan manor houses in the country").

The scene is "subjected" to the author's personal view, and he expresses the impression it makes on him.

This latter style generally appeals more to the reader than the impersonal objective style, just as an oil-painting appeals more vividly to the eye than a black-and-white photograph or drawing. We not unnaturally find a skilled writer's subjective description of a scene or person more colourful and interesting than the entirely factual and objective description of a guide-book or a dictionary of biography. The personal approach must not be allowed, however, to intrude to excess, to the point where it is tedious or where it obscures the clarity of the description.

The constant use of "I" or "we" can become as monotonous as the excessive use of "one".

There is a third method of presentation that is often used effectively by journalists, and this is to suggest to the reader that he or she is visiting the scene, in person, or is being given guidance as to how to view it, and to achieve this the second person is used (e.g. "You suddenly turn a corner and see . . . You must not fail to visit . . . You would hardly expect to find . . . It will surprise you to discover . . ."). It is probably best to leave this method to the experienced journalist.

The desirability of avoiding the use of "one", which tends to become monotonously frequent, has already been discussed in Chapter III.

It will be necessary to discuss the description of people separately from that of places, as the method of approach will naturally differ in some respects. While it would be wrong to lay down rigid rules or to draw up a fixed formula for the description of people or places, the following notes and examples may be helpful as a general guide to planning such descriptions.

DESCRIPTIONS OF PERSONS (AND ANIMALS)

In the case of a person, and also in the case of an animal (particularly when we are describing some animal kept as a pet), we have to describe not only physical appearance (and in the case of a person, the way in which he or she is dressed) but also character and habits (unless we are specifically asked for a description of physical characteristics only).

If we take the description of an animal first as offering a simpler exercise, the following contrasting descriptions of a dormouse—the first purely objective, impersonal, and factual; the second subjective, personal, and less formal—will serve to show the difference between these two descriptive styles. Notice that when we are talking of a pet that has been given a pet name we refer to it as "he" or "she".

THE DORMOUSE

A dormouse is very similar in appearance both to a squirrel and a mouse, but is in size much smaller than a mouse.

It is about five inches in length from its nose to the tip of its tail, and its tail is nearly equal in length to its body, and is bushy and tufted like that of a squirrel.

It has a rather large head compared with the size of its body, with a blunt muzzle, prominent eyes, rounded ears, and long whiskers.

Its body is covered with light tawny-coloured fur, which is yellowish white on the underside.

It sleeps heavily during the day in summer, usually in a nest of grass, and becomes active at night, when it goes in search of nuts and berries; in winter it hibernates in a nest underground or under moss, feeding occasionally on a store of nuts laid up for this purpose.

It is found in most woodland areas of England and Wales.

Our Dormouse

I found Donald, our pet dormouse, when I was reclining with my back against a tree after a spring walk in our local woods.

He was the first dormouse I had ever seen, and when this tawny little mixture of miniature squirrel and mouse softly crept on to my hand, I was amused to see that his furry tail, some two and a half inches in length, was as long as his plump body. He stared at me for a moment with his large, appealing eyes, his rounded ears erect, then promptly snuggled down in the palm of my hand and dozed off in the hot sun.

As he seemed both lonely and lost, I took him home to the family, and though my mother and sister protested at first, they soon grew devoted to him, and christened him Donald.

Donald slept all the first day in a box lined with cotton-wool under the kitchen sink.

On consulting a nature-study book, we learnt that dormice sleep during the day, and forage at night for their food of nuts and berries, that in winter, except for a very occasional awakening to feed from their winter store, they sleep all the time in some underground retreat.

Provided with nuts and fruit to nibble, Donald scampered happily about at night. In the daytime no attempt was made to keep doors or windows shut, but he slept soundly till dusk in his beloved box.

Visitors were enchanted by him—and if removed from his

bed to be shown off he invariably fell asleep in the palm of some admirer's warm hand.

Donald stayed with us till the following spring, when we felt he should be given a chance to return to his native woods, a decision which was not unopposed but which was influenced by my sister's wish to adopt a stray kitten.

I felt his life would be in greater danger from the kitten than from the perils of the wilds that he had forgotten. Accordingly, we all accompanied Donald on his last journey, and when he was ceremonially released in a glade of bluebells and scampered into some young bracken, we turned away hastily and somewhat sheepishly dabbed at our eyes with our handkerchiefs as we retraced our steps.

In the case of persons we must avoid the sort of description we might find outside a police station when a missing or wanted person is sought. This is solely concerned with physical appearance, mannerisms, and occupation. It has the cold accuracy and detail of a black-and-white photograph and lacks the colour and warmth of a painting; we should know nothing of the person's character or personality.

A detailed catalogue of physical characteristics and of clothing will be unnecessary and confusing; it is the writer's task to select just those details which will bring the person described to life in the reader's imagination. Nothing is gained by mentioning that a person has ears, but if that person has prominent ears or only one ear, the fact is of interest.

The following plan is given as a guide rather than a rule for this type of composition.

1. General description (age, build, occupation).

2. Most interesting or striking details of appearance.

3. Character, habits, peculiarities. An anecdote is often valuable.

Here is a brief example in which this order of presentation is employed.

Professor X

When I knew him, Professor X had retired for some years from his post as history lecturer, and must have been well over seventy years of age. Unlike many of his profession, he always held himself impressively upright, and as he was well over six feet in height, he looked more like an ex-Guards officer than a professor.

He had a long and rather pale, cadaverous face, with piercing blue eyes surmounted by extremely bushy white eyebrows. His hair was as white and luxuriant as his eyebrows, and not content with this, he cultivated a trim white moustache and beard, the latter cut to a sharp point.

His clothes were as neat as his appearance, but old-fashioned. He almost invariably wore a fawn Norfolk jacket, a bow-tie, and a bright yellow waistcoat adorned by a massive watch-chain; trousers he scorned, preferring knickerbockers and rough grey stockings.

Whenever he went out, in summer or winter, he put on a faded black-and-white straw hat, which, it was rumoured, was a relic of his undergraduate days.

I never met a more energetic or cheerful man; he did everything from talking to gardening with speed and urgency and seemed tireless. He was essentially a kindly man, and his perpetual smile had made permanent wrinkles at the corners of his eyes.

He had an amusing, high-pitched voice, and a laugh which seemed to explode internally and shake him silently long after the first explosion.

He was a delightful mixture of deep learning and childlike simplicity; of efficiency and absent-mindedness.

I can see him now with his genial smile, and eyebrows raised enquiringly as I pointed out to him on one occasion that he was pumping up the front tyre of his bicycle, whereas the rear tyre was the one in need of attention. "Really, dear boy?" he protested in surprise. "Don't they intercommunicate?"

And here is J. B. Priestley's description of the young schoolmaster, Inigo Jollifant, in *The Good Companions*.

He is a thin loose-limbed youth, a trifle above medium height. His face does not suggest the successful preparatory-school master. It seems rather too fantastic. A long lock of hair falls perpetually across his right eyebrow; his nose itself is long, wandering and whimsical, and his grey eyes are set unusually wide apart and have in them a curious gleam. He wears a blue pullover, no coat, a generous bow-tie, and baggy and rather discoloured flannel trousers. He is smoking a ridiculously long cherry-wood pipe. There is about him the air of one who is ready to fail gloriously at almost anything. We realise at once that his History, French, English Literature, his cricket and football, are dashing but sketchy. At this moment he is ostensibly engaged in writing an elaborate essay—in a manner of the early Stevenson—entitled *The Last Knapsack*, an essay that he began many weeks ago, in the middle of the long vacation. His right hand grasps a fountain pen and there is a writing-block on his knees, but never a word does he set down. He blows out clouds of smoke, keeps his feet on the window-sill, and balances his chair at a still more alarming angle.

DESCRIPTIONS OF PLACES AND SCENES

In describing places we must decide, as in the description of persons, whether we are going to write an objective or subjective description, and the order in which we are going to present our facts once we have selected them.

When describing a limited scene, such as a room, we must (as in all descriptions) proceed from general impressions to details (such as the colour scheme and furniture). It will also help to subdivide the room into sections (such as the centre, the fireplace, walls, windows, etc.).

In *David Copperfield*, Dickens depicts a bedroom in Mr. Peggotty's converted boat-dwelling with a few telling strokes of his pen:

"It was the completest and most desirable bedroom ever seen—in the stern of the vessel; with a little looking-glass, just the right height for me, nailed against the wall, and framed with oyster-shells; a little bed, which there was just room enough to get into; and a nosegay of seaweed in a blue mug on the table. The walls were whitewashed as white as milk, and the patchwork counterpane made my eyes quite ache with its brightness."

For the description of a building, such as a church or a castle, the plan will differ. The following example will prove helpful.

A CATHEDRAL

1. General remarks about its position, size, and age.
2. Details of its history and development, and styles of architecture.
3. Exterior: tower, spire, or dome; main entrance.
4. Interior: main or central aisle, windows, pillars, roof, altar, side chapels, crypt.
5. Monuments, tombs, and any other points of special interest.

If we are describing the cathedral subjectively, and not merely objectively, there will be, as in all such descriptions, an additional paragraph in conclusion in which we sum up our final personal impressions.

In descriptions of cities, towns, and villages, the first paragraph must be devoted to indicating the geographical position and general surroundings of the place to be described. When this locality has some special claim to fame (for historical, architectural, cultural, or industrial reasons), this can also be indicated briefly in the opening paragraph.

> e.g. The town of Rye, one of the two Sussex ports that were added to the original Cinque Ports of Kent, is built on a hill a few miles from the boundary of the two counties and nearly a mile now from the sea to which it owes its fame.

The reader wants to know the location of a place in order to take an interest in subsequent details and to form a complete picture in his mind.

Next, in cases where past events have influenced the

position and development of a place, a brief summary of its history will be required.

Then will come a detailed description of the place and of its inhabitants and activities; and finally any further interesting details.

DESCRIPTION OF A TOWN OR VILLAGE

1. Its geographical position, size, and activities. Indicate briefly any particular appeal or feature which makes it well known.

2. A brief summary of its past history and development.

3. Detailed description. Its chief street(s) and buildings.

4. Detailed facts about the occupations and activities of the inhabitants. Any local industries.

5. Any further interesting details (i.e. any unusual customs or distinguished inhabitants).

6. Final personal impressions, if a subjective description.

PAINSWICK

Painswick, one of the most attractive of all Cotswold villages, is situated high on the western side of the road leading from Stroud to Cheltenham and looks down on a valley of beechwoods. Just to the north of this village, or little town— it has now some 2,500 inhabitants—stands Painswick Beacon, with its wonderful view of the valley of the Severn, but to most tourists Painswick is best known for its famous churchyard yew trees, one hundred in number.

A village undoubtedly existed here in Roman times, and it was a village of some local importance in the Middle Ages as the centre of a sheep-rearing area, sheep whose wool was later to be in great demand for Cotswold cloth.

Its long main street is lined with typical Cotswold stone houses and cottages, their gardens bounded by the picturesque mortarless walls of this region.

The fifteenth-century church stands in the centre of the village and has an impressive spire, and walls still marked in places by shot and reddened by fire from a skirmish in the Civil War. Its peal of twelve bells is one of the finest in England. The surrounding churchyard is entered through an ancient gatehouse, and contains the celebrated hundred yew trees, some more than one hundred and fifty years old. Many local inhabitants claim that there are only ninety-nine yew trees, and that all attempts to get the hundredth to grow successfully have failed. By the wall there stands a famous pair of stocks with a stone seat behind for the victim.

The old grey Court House, with its tall chimneys and many gables, is another notable feature to be visited.

Painswick is an excellent touring centre; the many people that have chosen this district to retire to have made it a popular residential area; the remainder of its inhabitants are chiefly engaged in agriculture; and artists abound in the summer.

Henry VIII brought Anne Boleyn to this district when he came hunting in 1536, and here at a later date this tragic queen is said to have been kept in custody at a local farmhouse while awaiting execution. It is a tribute to the beauty of this valley that a nearby village is called Paradise.

This scheme will differ slightly in the case of the description of a general scene rather than of a specific place, as the historical element will not enter into the scheme unless the scene was or is a battleground or the scene of some other notable event, and as the scene is presumably viewed from one spot, the writer must deal separately with the background, middle distance, and foreground.

Here is an example of a suggested plan for this type of description, which will be more effective if a subjective approach is employed.

THE SEVERN ESTUARY

1. The point from which the scene is observed.
2. Background or distant scene.
3. Middle distance or centre of scene.
4. Foreground.
5. Any special personal impressions.

In some cases there will be movement and sounds to describe to give added effect to the word-picture.

A subjective approach is essential in those cases where

we are asked to describe a personal visit to a certain building or place. The first paragraph can, in such cases, deal with the circumstances of our visit, and the final paragraph can sum up our personal impressions.

The personal touch is particularly necessary in describing such places as museums, zoos, gardens, and factories, as it helps to avoid the dullness of a merely factual description, which could develop into a catalogue of contents.

When dealing with such complex subjects as these, it is best first to divide the numerous exhibits into their main sections, and then to select only those details in each section that we consider of most interest.

The describing of visits can hardly be classified as the narration of personal experiences or adventures, as the description of the scene or place visited is our main purpose, but the visit must be arranged in logical order, just as a story must have a beginning, development, and end.

Here is a student's description of a visit to the London Zoological Gardens. This subject is not as easy as it first appears to be, for it is essential in such a case to avoid a mere catalogue of birds and beasts and the mistake of employing with monotonous frequency "and", "and then", and "next", and such common descriptive adjectives as "interesting", "beautiful", "huge", and "amusing".

A Visit to the Zoo

The statement that the inhabitants of a city never get to know it half as well as a stranger does is certainly true in my case.

I have lived in London for nearly twenty years, but I have to confess with shame that when a visitor from France persuaded me to accompany her last week on a visit to the Zoological Gardens in Regent's Park it was the first time I had ever visited them.

We arrived at the Zoo as early as possible in the morning, which proved a wise plan, as the motor-coach now makes possible a daily invasion in summer of some thousands of school children from all parts of the country, and once these arrive it is sometimes difficult to see the animals, or, as Marcelle, my Parisian friend, remarked, to decide which are in reality the wild animals.

Early mistakes convinced us that it is essential to plan one's itinerary with the aid of a guide-map, as the grounds are surprisingly extensive and the exhibits very numerous, and nothing is more exhausting than having continually to retrace one's steps to find some animal or group of animals that has eluded one's first tour of inspection.

The exhibits, attractively set among lawns and flower-beds, are divided into four main sections; animals, birds, reptiles, and fish—and to give a comprehensive list of all those we saw would require much time and serve little purpose.

In the animal section we admired the nobility and grace of movement of the lions, tigers, and leopards; surveyed the mountainous elephants and ponderous hippopotamuses—the smell from the latters' tropical bath was distinctly pungent—and marvelled at the height of the giraffes and the massive strength of the yak and the buffalo. Next we envied the aquatic skill of the seals and sea-lions. By the time we reached the monkeys the crowd of youthful admirers outside their cages was so unruly that Marcelle suggested we should study their antics instead.

The animals that most appealed to my companion were two of the smallest: firstly, the darting, bright-eyed mongoose, and secondly, a small black-and-white kitten—not an official exhibit at all—that was playing in front of the giraffe's cage, to the annoyance of the fifteen-foot occupant, which lowered its six-foot neck to within a few inches of its feline rival.

The aviaries present every type of exhibit from birds of prey and sea-birds to birds of brilliant or strange plumage, notable amongst which are naturally the parrots and parakeets. The exhibit that delighted us most, however, was the brightly-lit and specially heated aviary where incredibly small and delicate humming-birds hovered on whirring wings above tropical ferns and flowers, rivalling the latter in their dazzling colours.

Having completed our inspection of the animals and birds by lunch-time, we decided to eat our sandwiches on a seat on the Mappin Terraces, a range of artificial hills constructed in concrete. At its highest point this terrace houses mountain-goats and mountain-deer; on its lower slopes, provided with suitable caves, live the bears, both the polar and brown species. What attracts the crowds most to this terrace, however, is the emperor penguins, which inhabit an enclosure with a large pond at the foot of the terrace. To see these unusual creatures, with their beady, inquisitive eyes and puffed-out yellow chests, waddling pompously on shore like aldermen, is a laughable sight; in contrast, when they enter the water they become marvels of stream-lined speed—an incredible trans-formation.

After lunch we made our way to the Reptile House. Snakes do not appeal to everyone, and they did not attract Marcelle, yet I must confess I found a certain fascination in their smooth and silent movements. It is little wonder their prey is taken unawares, and struck down before there is any time for realisa-tion of the approach of danger.

Finally, somewhat exhausted by now and glad to pay an additional entrance fee to escape from the growing crowds, we visited the aquarium.

Its dark, cool depths were very restful after the glare of the sun, and the sight of fish of all sizes, shapes and colours gliding effortlessly through the clear water of their tanks gave us a sense of peace after the jostling of the sightseers. Watching the fantastic little sea-horses manoeuvring among the weeds, I felt transported temporarily to a marine fairyland.

As we made our way home I could not help wondering, despite the interest and pleasure such a fascinating collection gives to those who visit it, whether the majority of the animals and birds we had seen should ever be kept in captivity. It is often said that they are only too pleased merely to eat and sleep unmolested by the enemies and problems that would confront them in their natural state, but, as Marcelle remarked, it would be interesting to have the animals' own opinion of this theory.

Here, from *People and Things*, is Harold Nicolson's description of a nocturnal visit he paid to the Zoo.

Last night, after the rain, I went to Regent's Park. For on Thursday nights the Zoo, as you know, is open till eleven, and there are little lights of green and blue and gold twinkling in the trees, and the great Mappin Terraces are lit by searchlights. It had rained yesterday and the paths were almost deserted. I had the place to myself. And I have seldom passed a happier evening.

First I came to the cage of the lemurs. There was a mother lemur with a long striped tail like a lamp-brush and on her back a young lemur who clung on tight while his mother, with reckless indifference to the principles of infant welfare, leapt from perch to perch. For dear life did the little baby cling; at any moment I expected a catastrophe. But the mother went on leaping away gratuitously, jumping wildly from north to south. "Don't do it," I said to her. But, such is the known obstinancy of lemurs, she continued her senseless and cruel acrobatics. And high up in the corner two black lemurs crouched like goblins in disapproving protest.

I passed on to Monkey Hill. Now I have seen it written that the searchlights and the band are bad for monkeys and that it is cruel to keep the things awake at night. This, I feel sure, is an exaggeration. For last night, merely because it had been raining, Monkey Hill was completely deserted. Not a baboon was to be seen. Upon the terraces remained only a few pieces of damp biscuit, ignored and wasted. If the baboons can go indoors because their terrace is damp, they could go indoors if they felt sleepy. I doubt whether any monkey need stay out on Thursday evenings merely because it feels it would be rude to go to bed.

The deer, on the other hand, seemed to enjoy the soft night air. High up upon the Mappin Terraces the antelopes strode with dignity, their shadows flung sharply against the rock as they moved. They stood there sharp cut as the animals in Noah's Ark and around them the night spread wide, giving to the encircling shape of Regent's Park the immensities of wide prairies and uncharted forests. Here were the Polar bears, glistening, sinuous, like huge wet ferrets, and here a condor roosting sulkily in a weeping willow.

By the time I had reached the bird-house I could hear the bark of the sea-lions. I asked the keeper whether he would feed them. They are amiable men, these keepers, and he disappeared behind a door, returning with a whole dish of herrings. We went out to the pond of the sea-lions, which was isolated from the rest of the park within the circle of its own searchlight. Great forms swayed out from the black shadow of the rocks and plunged glistening into the light. In a moment the pond had ceased to be a pond and had become an angry sea, lashed into fury among the rocks. And then the fish were finished, and the sea lions flopped back into the shadow, and the sea became a pond again. The band played "God Save the King", and we began to leave.

In cases where a club or society has to be described, its official meeting-place could be dealt with first, and then its activities, and possibly in conclusion some of its interesting members.

The various plans and suggestions given in this chapter may seem to compel the writer to give a stereotyped description, but their purpose is merely to show the importance of considering things in their right order. So many students put down their ideas together in the order in which they occur to them and so achieve a confusing jumble. It is obvious that we can appreciate a building more by first knowing its history, and that we should consider the exterior before the interior, yet this order is not always adhered to.

EXERCISES

Persons and Animals (a description of character, mannerisms, etc., may be included).

1. One of your own relatives, or a close friend.

2. An animal or bird kept by you or by some acquaintance as a pet.

3. Your lecturer or teacher.

4. Your local clergyman, doctor, policeman, postman, or milkman, or any local shopkeeper.

5. The animal or bird that interests you most at a zoo.

6. An eccentric, amusing, or unusual character you have met.

7. A film-star, actor or actress, sportsman or sportswoman you admire.

8. A foreigner you know.

9. An insect, including some remarks about its life-cycle.
10. Any distinguished person, past or present.

Places and Scenes

1. The room in which you are now sitting or your own room at home.
2. The house or flat in which you live.
3. The city, town, village, and district in which you live.
4. An historic cathedral, church, castle, or residence.
5. A museum, an art gallery, or an exhibition you have visited.
6. Your garden, or some garden or park you have visited.
7. The school or college where you are studying or have studied.
8. A view which greatly impressed you.
9. Any place where you have spent a holiday.
10. A busy airport or railway-terminus or port.
11. The scene in a town or in the country on a snowy day.
12. An interesting shop or street or square.
13. A market-place or fair-ground or factory.
14. A wood or field in winter, spring, summer, or autumn.
15. An historic city, town, or village.

CHAPTER XXIII

DESCRIPTION OF PROCESSES AND ACTIONS

Having practised descriptions of objects, places, people, and animals, the next valuable training in logical arrangement of facts and in clear expression is the description of processes or methods of carrying out some operation, or of playing some game.

There are several styles from which to select. Most descriptions in technical and scientific books and journals are written in a formal and impersonal style, i.e. giving direct instructions (e.g. "To keep the car battery in good order, see that the correct level of distilled water is maintained in each cell. Grease the terminals whenever necessary").

Next comes the slightly more personal style, addressing the reader as "you" when giving advice (e.g. "When erecting a tent, you should be careful to choose a dry and level site"), or the description of what you yourself would do personally in a certain case (e.g. "If I had to mend a puncture in a bicycle-tyre, I should first——"). Remember "I *should*", "we *should*"—but "he *would*", "they *would*", is the correct conditional tense.

Finally, when writing up experiments we have carried out personally, we generally use the past tense, and "I" or "we" (e.g. "I (we) dissolved a small quantity of the salt in a beaker of water"—though we can describe the experiment impersonally and say "A small quantity of the salt was dissolved in a beaker of water").

Whichever style is selected as suitable for a particular description, it is important to remember to be consistent and not to wander from one style to another (i.e. from "I" to "we" or to "you").

Connecting words and phrases should be varied by ringing the changes on "secondly", "next", "following this", "then", etc., and the use of long technical words should be avoided whenever possible.

The logical method is to divide all actions up into three parts:

1. Preparations.
2. Main action.
3. Any additional remarks.

The first sentences or paragraph of the description of a process or activity must be devoted in many cases to indicating the apparatus, equipment, or tools necessary to the carrying out of the process in question.

Though the erection of a tent does not require any apparatus or tools other than a wooden mallet for driving in the tent-pegs, the mending of a puncture in a bicycle tyre will require a repair outfit, tyre-levers, and a pump.

Here are examples of three different styles of description:

ERECTING A TENT

First, I should select a suitably level and dry site, protected if possible from the prevailing wind by trees or a hedge. The site should not, however, be under trees, as these have the disadvantage of dripping in wet weather, and also, owing to their spreading roots, often make the ground hard and uneven.

Having chosen a suitable site, and decided which way the tent was to face in order to avoid having the opening facing the prevailing wind—as this wind is usually the west wind in summer, the tent will generally face the east and the morning sun—I should set out the tent-poles, canvas, guy-ropes, and pegs in readiness, with a mallet or hammer for driving in the pegs.

I should erect the front pole, placing this in position with the canvas and guy-ropes already attached to it if I had to erect the tent unaided, so that I could at once peg in and adjust the guy-ropes to hold the pole firmly in position.

Next I should stretch out the top of the tent and attach the canvas to the rear pole, which I should place in line with the front pole, and then secure by guy-ropes.

Finally, I should attach the remaining guy-ropes to the sides of the tent, and adjust them correctly after first pegging them down.

MENDING A PUNCTURE

In order to mend a puncture in a bicycle tyre you require tyre-levers, a puncture repair outfit, and a bicycle pump.

First you unscrew the valve of the inner tube, and remove this tube from the outer tube with the aid of tyre-levers.

Next you replace the valve and inflate the inner tube with a bicycle pump to locate the exact place where the tube has been punctured.

If you cannot locate this by the eye or by observing the point where air is escaping, you immerse the tube in water, when the bubbles created by escaping air will indicate the puncture.

You then clean a small circular space round the puncture, using sandpaper if necessary, apply adhesive solution and cover the prepared area with a suitable rubber patch, pressing this on firmly. You must allow a few minutes for the solution to set, and then dust the patch with french chalk to ensure that the inner tube cannot stick to the outer tube, in which it can now be replaced.

Finally, you replace the valve, and inflate the tyre, allowing a minute or so to elapse to make sure that no air is now escaping, before you remount the bicycle to test the tyre under running conditions.

Sports and Pastimes

The first paragraph of a description of how to play some game must be devoted to the conditions and equipment required.

Here, for example, is a brief description of the game of table tennis.

TABLE TENNIS

This game, once known as "Ping-pong", is played chiefly indoors.

The requirements for this game are: a rectangular table, a net, rackets, and a ball.

The table should be 9 ft. long by 5 ft. wide and 2 ft. 6 in. above the floor for official recognition, and preferably of a dark colour edged with a white line.

The net, $6\frac{3}{4}$ in. high, should divide the playing surface into two courts of equal size.

The rackets may be of any material, size, shape, or weight, but they are usually of wood or cork, often surfaced with rubber, and circular in shape, some 9 in. in diameter with a short handle about 6 in. long.

The ball is hollow, white in colour, and is made of celluloid, and should be $4\frac{1}{2}$ in. to $4\frac{3}{4}$ in. in circumference.

Either two or four persons may play this game.

To serve, the ball must first touch the server's court and then, passing over the net, touch the receiving court.

Service is changed at every five points, and a point is gained by a player when his opponent fails to serve or to return the ball so that it passes over the net and touches the court opposite to him.

Games are of 21 points up, and if both sides are level at 20 they continue until one gets 2 points ahead.

As an example of how *not* to explain a game, the following attempt to describe the game of cricket is noteworthy:

"You have two sides: one out in the field, one in. Each man in the side that is in goes out, and when he is out comes in, and the next man in goes out until he is out. When all are out the side that has been out comes in and the side that has been in goes out, and tries to get those coming in out. Then, when both sides have been in and out, the game ends."

Although confusing, this description is at least concise. It must be admitted, however, that cricket is not an easy game to describe, with its ambiguous terms "in" and "out".

How to Make Something

In this type of exercise, the first paragraph should give details of the materials and tools that will be required.

It is important to check carefully that no important part, moving or otherwise, has been omitted. One student, under the stress of examination nerves, omitted to put any door in a rabbit-hutch.

It is advisable to state the function of any moving parts.

There is no reason why in the case of any complicated construction there should not be a diagram added to give added clarity, and it is quite permissible and even essential in certain cases to state that certain parts must be purchased ready-made, such as the lens, view-finder, and shutter-mechanism of a camera.

EXERCISES

Processes

Describe clearly in not more than 25 lines or 200 words:

1. How to lay and light a fire.
2. How to replace a burnt-out electric fuse.
3. How to dial a telephone number.
4. How to send a telegram.
5. How to lay a concrete path.
6. How to prepare distilled water.
7. How to plant a standard rose tree.
8. How to start a stamp-collection.
9. How to take and develop a photograph.
10. How to plan a small garden.
11. How to change the wheel on a car.
12. How to make a rabbit-hutch, a boat or a box-camera.
13. How to bisect an angle using only a pair of compasses.
14. How to sail a small sailing-boat single-handed.
15. How to lay a table for lunch when guests are expected.
16. How you would furnish a bed-sitting-room of your own.

17. How you would make a cake, or an omelet.

18. What you would do if your house caught on fire.

19. How you would save a drowning person if you could swim.

20. What you would do if you heard a burglar downstairs during the night.

Sports and Pastimes

Describe clearly in not more than 30 lines or 250 words how the game of (a) Association football, (b) Rugby football, (c) lawn-tennis, (d) hockey, (e) net-ball, (f) basket-ball, (g) baseball or rounders, (h) golf, (i) bowls, (j) billiards, (k) snooker, (l) bridge or whist, is played.

CHAPTER XXIV

DESCRIPTIONS OF EVENTS
(PERSONAL EXPERIENCES)

This heading covers a wide variety of events, such as the description of a walk or of a journey; the description of an excursion or of a holiday; the description of some spectacle such as a football match or a theatrical performance, or of some ceremony or procession, such as a prize-giving or a military parade; or the description of some personal adventure.

This type of composition should present few difficulties, as the order in which facts are to be presented is entirely straightforward, being the chronological order (i.e. the correct time sequence) in which the events occurred.

Such compositions will, however, not be entirely a matter of listing actions in their order of occurrence, as some description of the scenic background and of people will be necessary.

Also, as we have already seen in Chapter XXII, a purely objective description of events that is merely a dull chain of facts will not appeal as much as one in which the writer's personal feelings and views are expressed.

We must try to select details which are unusual and which distinguish the event described from other similar events.

As a rough guide to the planning of this type of composition, here are some preliminary notes for the description of (a) A personal experience: "A Steamer Trip on the Thames"; (b) A personal adventure: "Cut off by the Tide"; and (c) A natural phenomenon: "A Storm".

(a) *A Steamer Trip on the Thames*

    1. Circumstances of excursion: i.e. Steamer trip in summer holidays from Westminster to Windsor. Companion or companions, if any.

    2. Brief description of steamer.

    3. Outward journey. Scenery. Places of interest passed on the way. Negotiating locks.

    4. Windsor: description of visit to the town, including the Castle and Eton College.

    5. Return journey.

    6. Any additional points or incidents that were of particular interest to the writer. Final impressions.

(b) *Cut off by the Tide*

    1. Where and when did incident occur? Companions, if any?

    2. Reason for climbing cliffs at low tide (in search of birds' eggs, or rare flowers). Description of climb and any discoveries.

    3. Discovery that incoming tide has cut off descent to sands, and that steepness of cliffs makes an ascent equally impossible.

    4. Calls for help and signals with handkerchief or shirt. Long interval with no result. Occupants of small boat eventually reply to signal.

    5. Rescue by coastguards with rope lowered from cliff top.

(c) *A Storm*

    1. When and where the particular storm took place.

    2. Preliminary signs and warnings of approaching storm.

    3. Development of storm.

    4. Climax.

    5. After-effects.

The description of personal experiences is excellent preliminary training for short-story writing, and there is no reason why some dialogue should not be introduced, as it tends not only to relieve the monotony of uninterrupted narrative writing but also gives additional life to a story. Dialogue must not, however, be employed to excess at this stage, and must be introduced only if it is relevant and conveys more vividly some particular point.

Here is a student's description of a camping experience.

A NIGHT UNDER CANVAS

Two years ago, before I was called up to do my National Service in the month of September, I decided to spend my last fortnight of freedom on a cycle tour of North Wales.

A school-friend agreed to join me, and suggested that we should carry light-weight tents and try camping, an experience new to both of us.

We went by rail from London to Chester, and spent a day in that interesting old city, where we purchased tents, sleeping-bags and a stove. As there was a threat of rain, we felt it wise, if cowardly, to spend our first night at a small inn on the road to Rhyl.

The next morning dawned gloriously fine, and we reached Llandudno by the excellent coast-road in time for lunch.

After climbing up the Great Orme in the afternoon to admire the wonderful panorama of coast and inland mountains to be seen from its summit, we remounted our bicycles and made our way to Conway. After tea and an inspection of the impressive and historic castle we made our way leisurely inland up the lovely valley of the Conway, with the firm intention of camping for the night at the first suitable farm we encountered after passing through Llanrwst.

We passed several farms about whose suitability we could not agree, but eventually came to what we both considered an ideal spot—a small farm situated half-way down a lane leading to the river.

Dismounting, we wheeled our bicycles into the farmyard, and, watched suspiciously by two Welsh sheepdogs, I knocked nervously at the door.

A cheerful, voluble little man, whom I took to be the farmer, answered my knock eventually, and readily granted us permission to camp in one of his fields. "Camp where you like, man," he said, "but close the gates, see, and mind the bull by the river."

We thanked him, and made our way to a sheltered stubble field, surrounded by protecting hedges. Here we proceeded to erect our small tents and lay out our sleeping-bags, remembering to avoid a site under trees or facing the prevailing wind, and looking most carefully in every direction to assure ourselves that no bull was present in this particular field.

Dusk was now falling rapidly. We had rashly delayed our choice of a camping-ground in our search for the ideal, and as we had forgotten to bring a torch, and there was little moonlight to be expected, it was obvious that we must light our small paraffin stove and cook our supper as soon as possible.

At this point we discovered that neither of us had any matches, and this entailed a hasty return to the farmhouse to borrow some from our friend the farmer; half-way back my companion remembered we had fetched neither water nor milk. Another knock at the door, and the long-suffering farmer's wife gave us supplies of both.

It was now too late to prepare anything ambitious, so after a meal of bread and cheese washed down by cocoa brewed in semi-darkness, we gladly slipped into our sleeping-bags, and leaving the tent-flaps open to enable us to enjoy the evening scents, we soon fell asleep despite the mournful piping of the curlews and the hooting of owls.

It must have been well after midnight, judging by the moonlight which was now shining into the tent, when I was awakened suddenly by a strange snorting noise that was too loud and too near to be my companion snoring in his adjoining tent.

Before I could crawl out of my sleeping-bag to investigate, the tent collapsed on me, and I was literally flattened by what seemed to be a thundering herd of elephants passing over me.

A mighty crash followed, which I recognised as the collapse of our bicycles, parked upright against each other outside our tents, and then the whirlwind seemed to die away.

Slowly regaining courage and the use of my limbs, I crawled out from the collapsed canvas, just in time to catch a glimpse, in the bright light of a full moon, of a large black bull vanishing through the half-open gate of our field.

My unsympathetic companion, awakened by the noise, emerged unscathed from his tent, and, scanning the scene of the disaster, burst into a roar of most ill-timed laughter. The next hour was spent in restoring some sort of order in my tent, and in mutual recriminations about the carelessness of the person who had l·ft the gate open.

After a short period of fitful sleep, I was aroused by the rays of the early sun, and, peering out of my tent, I was relieved to see nothing more hostile than a few foraging rabbits and pheasants.

Waking my companion, I suggested an early call at the farm to fetch eggs for a sumptuous breakfast to help me forget the nocturnal disturbance.

The farmer's wife greeted us with a motherly smile. "Owen, bach, fetch half a dozen eggs for the gentlemen," she called to her small son who was playing in the yard.

Owen soon returned, and carefully handed me six eggs from his pockets. His hands were, I noticed, completely covered with red spots. His mother observed my surprise.

"It's only the measles," she said apologetically. "They'll soon pass."

As we sat on the river bank, enjoying our fried eggs and bacon while butterflies flitted idyllically around us in the warm sunshine, my companion said suddenly:

"Don't you think camping is a great life?"

Despite the sufferings of the night and the shadow of measles, I was compelled to agree.

In Charlotte Brontë's novel, *Jane Eyre*, there is a dramatic account by Jane of how she saved her master, Mr. Rochester, from being burnt to death.

"I hardly know whether I had slept or not; at any rate, I started wide awake on hearing a vague murmur, peculiar and lugubrious, which sounded, I thought, just above me. I wished I had kept my candle burning: the night was drearily dark; my spirits were depressed. I rose and sat up in bed, listening. The sound was hushed.

I tried again to sleep; but my heart beat anxiously, my inward tranquillity was broken. The clock, far down in the hall, struck two. Just then it seemed my chamber-door was touched; as if fingers had swept the panels in groping a way along the dark gallery outside. I said, "Who is there?" Nothing answered. I was chilled with fear.

All at once I remembered that it might be Pilot: who, when the kitchen-door chanced to be left open, not unfrequently found his way up to the threshold of Mr. Rochester's chamber: I had seen him lying there myself, in the mornings. The idea calmed me somewhat: I lay down. Silence composes the nerves; and as an unbroken hush now reigned again through the whole house, I began to feel the return of slumber. But it was not fated that I should sleep that night. A dream had scarcely approached my ear, when it fled affrighted, scared by a marrow-freezing incident enough.

This was a demoniac laugh—low, suppressed, and deep— uttered, as it seemed, at the very key-hole of my chamber door. The head of my bed was near the door, and I thought at first the goblin-laughter stood at my bedside—or rather, crouched by my pillow; but I rose, looked round, and could see nothing; while, as I still gazed, the unnatural sound was reiterated: and I knew it came from behind the panels. My first impulse was to rise and fasten the bolt; my next, again to cry out, "Who is there?"

Something gurgled and moaned. Ere long, steps retreated up the gallery towards the third storey staircase: a door had lately been made to shut in that staircase; I heard it open and close, and all was still. Impossible now to remain longer by myself: I must go to Mrs. Fairfax. I hurried on my frock and a shawl; I withdrew the bolt and opened the door with a trembling hand. There was a candle burning just outside, left on the matting in the gallery. I was surprised at this circumstance: but still more was I amazed to perceive the air quite dim, as if filled with smoke; and, while looking to the right hand and left, to find whence these blue wreaths issued, I became further aware of a strong smell of burning.

Something creaked: it was a door ajar; and that door was Mr. Rochester's, and the smoke rushed in a cloud from thence. In an instant, I was within the chamber. Tongues of flame darted round the bed; the curtains were on fire. In the midst of blaze and vapour, Mr. Rochester lay stretched motionless, in deep sleep.

"Wake! wake!" I cried—I shook him, but he only murmured and turned: the smoke had stupefied him. Not a moment could be lost: the very sheets were kindling. I rushed to his basin and ewer; fortunately one was wide and the other deep, and both were filled with water. I heaved them up, deluged the bed and its occupant, flew back to my own room, brought my own water-jug, baptized the couch afresh, and, by God's aid, succeeded in extinguishing the flames which were devouring it.

The hiss of the quenched element, the breakage of a pitcher which I flung from my hand when I had emptied it, and, above all, the splash of the shower-bath I had liberally bestowed, roused Mr. Rochester at last. Though it was now dark, I knew he was awake; because I heard him fulminating strange anathemas at finding himself lying in a pool of water.

EXERCISES

A

Describe in detail:

1. An interesting day-excursion you have made by train or car.
2. Any walking- or cycling-tour you have undertaken.
3. An interesting ceremony or procession you have seen.
4. Your first visit to a theatre.
5. An exciting game or sporting or athletic event you have seen or in which you took part.
6. The plot of a film or play which you particularly enjoyed.
7. A summer holiday which was memorable or unusual.
8. A thunderstorm, or a snowstorm, or a fog in which you were caught.
9. An unusual adventure or experience you have had.
10. An amusing experience you have had.
11. Your first journey in an aeroplane, trip on a steamer, or voyage in a liner.
12. A walk in the country, at any season.
13. A visit you have paid to some foreign country.
14. A visit to a dentist or a photographer.

15. A typical day in your life at school or college, or in your present occupation.

16. The most memorable day in your life.

B

Write:

1. The story of your own life.
2. The autobiography of a coin or of a postage-stamp.
3. The autobiography of a book.
4. The autobiography of any bird or animal.
5. The story of a lion's escape from a zoo, recounted (*a*) by the lion, (*b*) by the housewife in whose garden he was recaptured, (*c*) by the keeper who recaptured it.

CHAPTER XXV

LETTER WRITING

Letter writing can be divided into two main sections:
I. Formal Correspondence.
II. Informal or Private Correspondence.

I. FORMAL CORRESPONDENCE

This can be subdivided into:

(i) (a) Letters to a firm, making inquiries or complaints.

(b) Letters from a firm, giving information or dealing with complaints.

(ii) Circular letters.

(iii) Letters of application for a post (employment).

(iv) Letters to a person who is not a close acquaintance, making some formal request or inquiry.

(v) Letters on some topic to a newspaper or magazine.

(vi) Formal Invitations and Acceptances in connection with some function. These are not really letters, but some notes on this more social than literary art may prove useful.

Letter Headings

Note the following points in the examples which follow:

(a) *The Address* of the writer is placed at the top *right-hand* side of the page.

Each line of the address should be indented (i.e. placed farther to the right than the previous line).

Commas are required at the end of each line of the address except the last, when a full-stop is necessary. (A comma after the number of a house is optional.)

(*b*) *The Date* is placed under the address and should be written in full, and not abbreviated (1st, 2nd, 3rd, 4th, etc., are not abbreviations so no full-stop is required after the "st", etc.).

(*c*) The name and address of the recipient or addressee is placed on the *left-hand* side of the page, starting on the line below that used for the date.

Note the following:

Messrs. T. Brown & Co., Ltd.
The Johnson Box Company, Ltd.
The Secretary, or The Manager, Messrs. Brown, Jones, Ltd.
A. B. Jameson, Esq., or Mr. A. B. Jameson.
Sir T. Knight, D.S.O., M.A.
The Rev. E. Church.
The Rt. Hon. A. Hall, M.P.
Dr. J. Smart, or J. Smart, Esq., M.D.

Titles and decorations awarded by the State are placed before University degrees.

e.g. A. B. Smith, Esq., D.S.O., M.A.

Never write both "Mr." (abbreviation of "Mister" and "Esq." (abbreviation for "Esquire").

e.g. Mr. J. Smith, Esq.

"Messrs." is an abbreviation of the French "Messieurs" (= "Gentlemen"). It is not used when addressing a limited company, when the name is impersonal.

e.g. Messrs. Black and Green,
    but: The General Trading Co. Ltd.,
      Fairways Ltd.

(d) A filing reference number (e.g. F.C./21) is often placed by business firms in the top left-hand corner of a letter.

Salutations and Conclusions

The following table is a general guide to the customary openings and closures in formal letters.

Type	Salutation	Conclusion
1. *Business*		
(a) Individual	Dear Sir, (Dear Madam)	
(b) Firm	Dear Sirs, (Mesdames)	Yours faithfully,
(c) Board	Dear Sirs, *or* Gentlemen,	
(d) Circular	Dear Sir or Madam,	
2. *Miscellaneous*		
Between equals, or to a distant acquaintance	Dear Mr. X, (Dear Mrs. X)	Yours truly, *or* Yours sincerely,
3. *To a Newspaper, etc.*		
i.e. The Editor or Editress	Dear Sir, *or* Sir, (Dear Madam, or Madam)	Yours truly, *or* Yours etc.

Note: "Yours obediently" and "Yours respectfully" are now no longer used. Government communications often conclude with "Your obedient Servant" as a formality.

Signature

(i) Even if you are a genius, a doctor, a lawyer, or a managing director, your signature should be legible, as it is of importance to the recipient to be able to identify the writer of the letter.

To aid in this identification, especially in cases where there could be confusion (i.e. brothers), a Christian name in full is included. In cases of a father and son with the same Christian names "Senior" or "Junior" can be added, as appropriate, to identify the writer. In the case of possible doubt as to whether the writer is a man or woman "Mrs." or "Miss" can be added in brackets.

When letters are signed on behalf of a higher authority, taking legal responsibility (i.e. by a manager or secretary on behalf of his firm) the abbreviation "per pro", or simply "p.p." is written, with the name of the firm just above the signature of the writer. (Latin: "per procurationem" = "by the action of".) "Per" may be used alone when a person is writing for somebody else, but without undertaking any legal responsibility.

(ii) Remember that "Yours" must start with a capital letter. Avoid ending a letter with a present participle construction.

e.g. Hoping to receive an early reply,
Yours faithfully,

Here you have no finite verb, and it is not therefore a sentence; nor have you indicated clearly who is hoping.

Write: "I hope to receive an early reply.
Yours faithfully,"

or "Hoping to receive an early reply,
I am,
Yours faithfully,"

Contents or Body of the Letter

(i) The body of the letter should begin on the line below the salutation and should be indented, as should all subsequent paragraphs, which should be indented uniformly (i.e. at an equal distance from the margin).

(ii) A contents- or topic-heading is often placed in the centre of the line below the salutation and above the body of a business letter, especially if the letter is about a matter already under discussion. This heading is underlined.

e.g. Dear Sir,

<u>Fire Insurance Claim</u>

(iii) An excellent and simple principle to adopt in the writing of business and every other type of formal letter is to divide the letter into three parts.

1. Reason for writing (one paragraph).
2. Details (one or more paragraphs).
3. Any action suggested or required in consequence (one paragraph).

This system makes for clarity and brevity, the two essentials of a business letter.

(iv) Politeness, however difficult in certain circumstances, is a virtue which pays dividends. Courtesy is likely to be repaid by courtesy, and often disarms the impolite and softens the hard heart; firmness can be combined with politeness, which must not be confused with servility.

(v) Use "we", and not "I", when a letter is written on behalf of a firm.

(vi) Business jargon, pomposity, long-windedness, and slang must all be avoided. Business jargon, once so popular, is now giving way to plain English, e.g.

Commercial Jargon	*Plain English*
inst., or instant	of this month
ult., or ultimo	of last month
prox., or proximo	of next month
We are in receipt of your esteemed communication	We have received your letter
Yours of 2nd May to hand We hereby beg to inform you	We wish to inform you
"Re" (Latin: "Concerning the matter")	With reference to

(i) **Letters to, and from, a firm**

(a) *Example of a letter to a firm:*

2, Fir Avenue,
Old Malden,
Surrey.
20th April, 1955.

Garden Supplies, Ltd.,
Victor Street,
London, S.W.4.

Dear Sirs,

I purchased a Cutall lawn-mower from you on the 14th March and I regret to say that it has proved most unsatisfactory.

The machine is the 12″ Junior model, and although it has been regularly oiled and most carefully used it is running extremely noisily, and is not cutting at all cleanly. In addition, the adjusting screws appear to be faulty, having no effect on the setting of the blades.

I should be glad if you would arrange as soon as possible either to collect the machine for overhaul, or to replace it under guarantee.

Yours faithfully,
R. B. Low.

(b) *Example of a letter from a firm:*

Garden Supplies, Ltd.,
Victor Street,
London, S.W.4.
21st April, 1955.

R. B. Low, Esq.,
2, Fir Avenue,
Old Malden,
Surrey.

Dear Sir,

We have received your letter of the 20th April and regret to learn that the Cutall Junior lawn-mower you recently purchased from us has proved unsatisfactory.

We have dealt with this firm over a long period, and have

always found their machines most reliable. You will appreciate the fact that faults in components or assembly are inevitable occasionally in any mass-produced article, despite careful checking, and the machine you have purchased may be one of the very small number that have developed faults.

We will arrange to collect your machine for a free overhaul on Tuesday next, 24th April. Should it still prove unsatisfactory after this, we will replace it by a new machine of the same type.

Yours faithfully,
p.p. Garden Supplies, Ltd.,
A. J. Cutt
(Manager).

(ii) Circular Letters

Circular letters play an important part in business, and also in political and community life. They may be used to announce the opening of some new business premises or of some trade exhibition; or to draw attention to a sale or special offer by some firm; or to enlist support for some political campaign, charitable cause, or social club.

The circular will begin "Dear Sir (or Madam)"—unless the appeal is addressed exclusively to one sex.

The address of the addressee will not be required above the salutation.

The same plan as that already indicated for other business letters will be most suitable, i.e. an opening giving the reason for writing, followed by details, and a concluding paragraph suggesting the action the sender hopes the recipient will take.

A business circular is usually signed by the managing director of the firm in question; a circular on behalf of a committee is signed by the secretary.

A circular must be interesting and appealing in its wording, and its objective must be clearly stated. Above all, it must not be long-winded, or the reader will consign it, after a casual glance, to the wastepaper-basket.

Here is an example of a business circular:

> Home Heaters, Ltd.,
> Clarence Street,
> Newton.
> 1st October, 1957.

Dear Sir or Madam,

With the approach of winter, with its attendant colds and chills, we feel sure you will be considering the problem of maintaining satisfactory standards of warmth in your home.

We are the main agents in Newton for all the leading makers of heating appliances, and are organising a special Home Heating Week, beginning on Monday next, 7th October, at our showrooms, where the latest types of domestic boilers, fires, and radiators will be on view. A highly-qualified heating engineer will be in attendance throughout the week, to answer queries and give advice on your heating problems.

May we, therefore, invite you to visit this display, and express the hope that we may have an opportunity of placing our experience at your disposal?

> Yours faithfully,
> p.p. Home Heaters Limited,
> J. J. Therm
> (Managing Director).

(iii) **Letters of Application**

Plan carefully the order in which you set out your information (i.e. education, qualifications, and experience).

Testimonials should, if possible, not all be connected with your school career.

Further references (or referees) can be given if required.

Avoid both self-praise and humility. Do not include such obvious (and servile) remarks as "Should you be so good as to offer me the vacancy, I shall carry out my duties to the best of my endeavour (or make every effort to fill the post to your satisfaction)". Of course you will, or else you will shortly be applying again elsewhere. Also, do not say condescendingly, "I should be pleased to attend an interview if required". You *must* attend an interview if required, and will be one of a few fortunate ones if you are requested to do so.

Example:

Advertisement:

Clerk (male), age 20–25, required by Chartered Accountants, Wooltown, for audit department. Some experience essential. Write giving full particulars, stating age, experience, and salary, to Box X123, *Comet* Office, Wooltown.

<table>
<tr><td></td><td>1, Earl Road,</td></tr>
<tr><td>Box X123,</td><td>Wooltown,</td></tr>
<tr><td>*Comet* Office,</td><td>Yorkshire.</td></tr>
<tr><td>Wooltown.</td><td>2nd July, 1956.</td></tr>
</table>

Dear Sirs,

I wish to apply for the post of Clerk in the audit department, advertised in today's issue of the *Comet*.

My age is 21. I was educated at Wooltown Grammar School from 1945–1952, and sat for the General Certificate Examination of the Joint Matriculation Board at Ordinary Level in June, 1952, passing in English, Mathematics, Physics, History, and French. I was a Senior Prefect during my last two years at school, and was also a member of the 1st XI for Cricket and Association Football.

On leaving school in July, 1952, I obtained a post as junior clerk in the audit department of Addum and Checkum, Chartered Accountants, New Street, Wooltown.

I was called up for military service in September, 1953, and served for two years in the Royal Air Force, attaining the rank of Flight-Sergeant.

On completing my service, I returned to my post with

Messrs. Addum and Checkum. I have been attending evening courses in Accountancy at Wooltown Technical College, with a view to taking the examinations of the Society of Incorporated Accountants.

My present salary is £8 per week, and I am naturally anxious to secure a post which will offer me an opportunity of improving both my salary and prospects.

I enclose copies of testimonials from:

A. B. Cox, Esq., M.A., Headmaster, Wooltown Grammar School.

D. E. Wise, Esq., B.Com., Head of the Commerce Department, Wooltown Technical College.

The Rev. C. Stott, St. Stephen's Vicarage, Wooltown.

My present employers have kindly consented to answer any inquiries you may wish to make.

Yours faithfully,
J. Mills.

(iv) **Letter to an individual, making a formal request:**

"Crossways",
Shortlands,
Staffs.
21st September, 1958.

Dear Colonel Jameson,

As honorary secretary of the Shortlands Youth Club, I am arranging a series of talks by voluntary lecturers for our winter evening programme, and I have been requested by our Committee to ask you if you would very kindly consent to give one of these talks.

We have a large and enthusiastic membership of over 400 young people and have our own Club Centre in Stanley Avenue, which contains, in addition to games-rooms and a library, an excellent hall that can be used for lectures, plays, or dances.

Several members of our Committee have had the pleasure of hearing you lecture in Birmingham on your experiences during your expedition to the Upper Amazon, and we should be most grateful if you could spare the time to come here to give us a talk on this subject, which we feel sure our members would find of the greatest interest. I am arranging lectures for the first Friday of each month for the next six months, commencing in October, and can offer you any one of these dates at present, as your name is first on the list of lecturers we are inviting.

If you find it possible to accept this invitation on one of the suggested dates, I can assure you that you will have a large and appreciative audience.

Our lectures usually start at 8 p.m., and I may add that we have both a film-projector and a slide-projector.

Yours truly,
A. R. Price
(Hon. Sec.).

(v) Letters to the Press (Informative, Protesting, or Suggesting)

The opening paragraph should indicate the subject under discussion and the subsequent paragraph or paragraphs should convey the writer's views on the subject.

Example: Letter in connection with a report of a concert given in a prison, one item of which was an exhibition by a visiting artiste of bending bars and breaking chains.

"Fourways",
Stoke,
Hants.
3rd December, 1955.

The Editor,
Daily Scene,
Fleet Street,
London, E.C.4.

Sir,

I am aware that "iron bars do not a prison make", but I should imagine the warders present at the concert for prisoners at G . . . Prison, a report of which appeared in your paper yesterday, must have viewed the exhibition of bar-bending and chain-breaking by a famous escapologist with unmixed feelings of alarm.

I sincerely hope that the prison authorities will not now follow up this idea by inviting experts to demonstrate knife-throwing or jujitsu. Surely those who supervise our over-crowded and understaffed prisons have already sufficient problems of discipline.

Yours etc.,
A. B. Carton
(Colonel, retd.).

(vi) **Formal Invitations and Acceptances**

For these the third person is usually employed. An invitation should be answered in the same form (i.e. 1st or 3rd person) in which it is received.

Invitation

The President and Fellows
of the National Rose Society
request the pleasure of the company of

Mr. and Mrs. C. D. Brown

at
the Annual Dinner
at the Horticultural Hall, Westminster
on Thursday, 6*th January*, 1958,
at 7.30 *p.m.*

R.S.V.P. to
The Secretary,
Horticultural Hall,
*Westminster, S.W.*1.

Notice that the address to which an acceptance or refusal is to be sent is placed after the invitation, in the left-hand bottom corner.

The letters R.S.V.P. (French: *Répondez, s'il vous plaît* = "Reply, if you please") have become a recognised abbreviation, and essential borrowing from another language, on account of its brevity.

Acceptance:

Mr. and Mrs. C. D. Brown have much pleasure in accepting the invitation of the President and Fellows for Thursday, January 6th.
"The Old House",
Littletown.
28th December, 1954.

Refusal or Inability to Accept:

Mr. and Mrs. C. D. Brown much regret that they are unable to accept the kind invitation of the President and Fellows for Thursday, January 6th.

"The Old House",
Littletown.
28th December, 1954.

Note: Avoid the mistake of writing "will have much pleasure in accepting", as your pleasure, whether genuine or not, is supposed to start from the moment you receive the invitation, so that the present tense, not the future, is required.

II. INFORMAL OR PRIVATE CORRESPONDENCE

There will naturally be considerable difference between letters to relatives and friends written in an examination and those written outside the examination room. As we are concerned with the former type, we must avoid slang and slackness in sentence construction.

There is no reason why informal letters should be dull —they are often mere lists of events and greetings—but attempts at humour should be included only if they are natural and not artificial.

We must avoid beginning every sentence with "I", or overworking some word like "nice" or "marvellous". The main reason so many people dislike writing letters is probably that they have little method or plan, and also a bad memory for news. There is no reason why one should not have a general plan for informal letter-writing provided that it is not allowed to make all letters too stereotyped; the problem of a bad memory can be solved by the excellent habit of keeping a diary.

(In a diary, to avoid monotony and to save time, the subject "I", the definite and indefinite articles, and other words are often omitted as understood, e.g. Tuesday, May 2nd. Woke early, and after quick breakfast, as weather fine, went for cycle run through Lower Woods.)

Most informal letters fall into two types:

(i) Those written in answer to some inquiry, request, or invitation or to acknowledge a gift.
(ii) Those written solely to convey personal news and views to relatives or friends.

The excellent principle of dividing a letter into three parts: (1) Reason for writing, (2) Details, (3) Any action required, is a guide in informal letters as well as in formal letters. In dealing with news, a division into present, past, and future events will be found helpful.

In type (i), for example, the plan can be:

(1) Reference to request, invitation, or gift.
(2) Detailed answer to inquiry, request, or invitation; or appreciation of gift, and details of events connected with gift.
(3) Any personal messages, and greetings to or inquiries about relatives or mutual friends.

In type (ii):

(1) Greetings and reference to any queries in addressee's last letter.
(2) News and views, then future plans.
(3) Personal messages and inquiries.

Type	*Salutation*	*Conclusion*
Friends		
(i) Casual	Dear Mary,	Yours sincerely,
(ii) Intimate	My dear Mary,	Yours very sincerely,
Relations		
(i) Distant	Dear Cousin Jean,	Yours affectionately,
(ii) Close	My dear Aunt Mary,	Your affectionate nephew/niece.

These salutations and conclusions are given only as a guide for foreigners and for examinations; there will obviously be much more variation in informal correspondence not written for an examiner's eye (and heart).

Notes: (i) Note the small "d" in "My dear X".

(ii) Avoid ending with a present participle construction, without a finite verb, e.g. "Hoping you are quite well".

(iii) In addresses on envelopes "c/o" (care of) is often written if the addressee is staying with friends. e.g.

Mrs. A. Brown,
c/o J. Smith,
etc.

Example:

Hôtel Blanc,
9, Rue Cartier,
Paris, XIVᵉ.
24th September, 1955.

My dear Aunt Mary,

I have now been in Paris exactly a week, and am employing this first wet day in dealing with neglected correspondence. As your most generous birthday cheque has helped to make this holiday possible, and as you have always encouraged me in my French studies, here is a brief account of my activities which I hope will be of interest to you.

The journey here seems to take an incredibly short

time—the most tedious part being the coach trip from the London terminus to Heath Row Airport. This cannot be said of the run from Le Bourget to the centre of Paris, as all French drivers, and especially ours, seem anxious to prove that a car is as fast as a jet-plane if pedestrians are not allowed to interfere with the experiment. It was my friend Jane's first experience of air travel, and she says she prefers it to the dangers of the road.

Our hotel is a very modest one, but central, being only a few minutes' walk from the Opéra. By occupying a humble top-floor bedroom, and subsisting mainly on bread, cheese, and fruit, we are managing to keep our spending within our allowance.

We travel mostly by Métro, as we always seem to get lost on the buses, which are still the queer-looking single-deck Renaults that are as typical of the Parisian scene as its tree-lined boulevards.

This first week has been spent in taking Jane to all the places and scenes I feel she ought to see in Central Paris before we venture farther afield next week. We have therefore duly ascended the Eiffel Tower and the Arc de Triomphe, strolled along the Champs-Elysées and the Grands Boulevards, and visited Notre-Dame and Napoleon's tomb. Yesterday, the hottest day of a week of cloudless weather, we made our way up to Montmartre and gazed down on this beautiful city from the Sacré-Cœur.

We spend our evenings sitting on café terraces, watching tourists from every country in the world pass by; semi-tropical conditions and finance have limited our theatre-going to a visit to the Théâtre Français to see Molière's *L'Avare* superbly produced and acted.

Jane is proving a most amusing and congenial companion, but she resolutely refuses to try to speak any French; she says any Frenchman wishing to converse with her must do so in English or forgo the pleasure of her company.

This coming week our plans are more ambitious, and we hope to visit Versailles (by the excellent stream-lined train from Montparnasse), Fontainebleau (in a fellow-guest's car), and Chartres Cathedral (by coach), where Jane is very anxious to try out her new camera.

I will write again later with some account of these excursions. I do hope you and Uncle are having equally good weather for your holiday in Scotland, and that the scenery is not being obscured by Scotch mists. I am looking forward to seeing you on my return early in October. Jane sends her kind regards, and I send you both my love.

Your affectionate niece,
Margaret.

EXERCISES

I. **Formal**

(a) *Commercial.*

    (i) Inquiries or Complaints.

        Write a letter:

1. To a firm of Furniture Removers, asking for their terms, and giving details of the move you contemplate.
2. To a Travel Agency, asking for their terms for arranging a trip to Paris for a party you are organising.
3. To a Motorists' Association, complaining about conditions in a hotel they recommended, or about unsatisfactory repairs to your car, or excessive charges by a garage.
4. To your landlord, pointing out repairs to your house that are urgently needed.
5. To British Railways, inquiring about a parcel or trunk lost in transit.
6. Tactfully pointing out to a customer of your firm that the time has come to settle an account owing for over a year.
7. Write suitable answers to the above letters.

    (ii) Applications.

        Write letters of application for the following vacancies:

1. Junior Assistant (male or female) required by Chemical Manufacturing Co. for laboratory work. Chemistry to G.C.E. standard essential. Write, giving details of education, and experience, if any, to Personnel Manager, Chemanco Ltd., St. Helens, Lancs.

2. Vacancy for young man of good education, smart appearance, as sales representative. Free training. Previous experience unnecessary, but initiative essential. Apply Universal Advertisements, Ltd., Poster Place, Glasgow, C.3.

3. Shorthand-typist for Shipping Office. Give details of education, experience, if any, and speeds. Box 44, *The Clarion*, Fleet Street, E.C.4.

4. Smart young lady wanted to train as buyer in hat department of large store. Some business experience desirable. Apply Dresswells, King Street, Manchester.

5. Young man or woman wanted as cook in yacht for Mediterranean cruise, July and August. State age, qualifications, experience.

6. Well-educated young lady required as assistant receptionist at London Hotel. Knowledge of languages an advantage. Apply Manager, Hotel Splendide, Piccadilly, W.1.

(iii) Circulars.

Write a circular letter (beginning "Dear Sir (or Madam)") drawing attention:

1. To the opening of a new shop, department, or restaurant, outlining amenities offered.

2. To a special sale or display.

3. To the opening of a new business, outlining services offered.

4. To the advantages of joining some club or society (e.g. A Dramatic, Debating, Literary, Photographic, or Philatelic Society; a Sports Club, Walking or Cycling Club, Sketch Club, Model Club, etc.).

(b) *Formal Requests or Inquiries.*

Write a formal letter:

1. To a distinguished author, asking him to give a talk to the Literary Society of which you are secretary.

2. To a neighbour whose dogs make so much noise at night that you can neither work nor sleep. You do not wish to call personally, as he is notoriously rude.

3. To a farmer, asking if you may camp on his land during

part of the summer holidays, and offering your help in harvesting.

4. To the secretary of a club or society you wish to join, asking for particulars, and giving reasons for your desire to become a member.

5. To the leader of an expedition to Central Africa, asking if you may join the expedition as general handyman.

(c) *Letters to Press.*

Write a letter to the editor of a national or local newspaper:

1. Complaining about the low standard of television or wireless programmes.

2. Complaining about noise from aeroplanes in your district, or neighbours' unnecessarily noisy wireless sets.

3. Complaining about the litter in your local streets and parks, and suggesting some remedies.

4. Complaining about some social injustice, or the inefficiency of some public service.

(d) *Formal Invitations and Acceptances.*

1. Write out a formal invitation from your parents, inviting friends to your twenty-first birthday party, to be held at an assembly hall or at an hotel.

2. Write a formal acceptance of the above invitation as if you were one of the invited guests.

3. Write to express your regret at being unable to attend the party.

II. **Personal Letters**

Write a letter:

1. To a friend with whom you have been staying, thanking him or her, and describing your return journey.

2. To your parents, describing the house at which you are staying on a holiday, and the family who live there.

3. Tactfully declining some invitation, or some offer of employment you do not wish to accept.

4. To a friend abroad, inviting him or her to visit you, and giving instructions for the journey.

5. To a friend, giving your first impressions of a college or university you have just entered.

6. To a friend, suggesting a hiking or cycling holiday, and outlining your plans.

7. To a relative, thanking him or her for a birthday cheque, and outlining how you plan to spend the money.

8. To a friend who is ill, or who has failed an examination, expressing sympathy.

CHAPTER XXVI

ESSAYS

The previous chapters in this section have dealt with the description of definite objects, persons, places, and actions; and subsequent chapters will deal with the writing of reports and reviews, and also with speeches and arguments.

This chapter will be devoted to a form of composition that requires more than a statement of facts, and that is called an essay—a word derived from the French "essayer" (= to try or attempt) that indicates a composition in which the writer essays to present his views and to discourse on a variety of topics in a manner that attracts the reader's interest.

Practice is of more value than precept, but a study of leading articles in newspapers such as *The Times*, the *Manchester Guardian* or the *Daily Telegraph*, or in reviews such as *The Listener* and *The Spectator*, and of the collected essays of experts such as Hilaire Belloc, G. K. Chesterton, E. V. Lucas, J. B. Priestley, Robert Lynd, and Harold Nicolson, will prove of great value.

It is difficult to enumerate or classify fully the types of subject which come under the heading of essays—as they may vary from topics that call for reflective essays to scientific, historical, literary, and sociological* topics, that call for analytical essays, or topics that can be classified under the heading of imaginative essays, which require the writer to exercise his imagination about the

* Sociological = dealing with the nature or conditions of human society.

unknown future or to project himself into some imaginary conditions in the past or present.

Here is an example of a suggested general classification:

Reflective:

> On Keeping Pets.
> Christmas Presents.
> Gambling.
> Holidays at Home.

Analytical:

> Atomic Power (Scientific).
> The French Revolution (Historical).
> Detective Novels (Literary).
> The Value of Youth Clubs (Sociological).

Imaginative:

> If I won £1,000.
> Planning a Perfect Holiday.
> The Future of Air Transport.
> Life in A.D. 2000.

As subjects which come under the heading of Arguments require a different treatment from the above, these are discussed in a separate chapter.

It must be clearly understood that the above classification is merely intended to be a helpful suggestion. There are many subjects that will require analytical, reflective, and imaginative treatment.

When we have selected or been given a subject on which to express our views—and the whole point of an essay should be that in it the writer expresses his own views and so gives it a personal quality instead of producing a series of stereotyped statements or platitudes—the first problem is to collect ideas.

It is obviously a great mistake to start writing the first paragraph of an essay immediately the subject has been selected. Several minutes at least should be given to putting down relevant ideas briefly in the order in which they occur to the writer. It is too late for the writer to add to the middle of an essay some brilliant idea when that idea suddenly occurs to him just as he is completing the concluding paragraph.

When we have made a list of all the ideas which the subject suggests, the next stage is to arrange these in the required order, bearing in mind that not all the ideas which have been jotted down may fit suitably into the essay as it is finally planned.

First, an introductory paragraph will be required, to outline the aim of the essay and/or to attract the reader's attention. Then comes the development, in which the numbers of paragraphs will depend on the number of ideas selected for inclusion, and finally a concluding paragraph which must "round off" the essay satisfactorily.

Before giving an example of a complete essay, here are examples of the planning of essays of the three types indicated: (1) reflective, (2) analytical, and (3) imaginative, in which each idea noted will represent a paragraph.

Type 1. *Reflective:* "Christmas Presents".

(*a*) *Introduction.* Origin of Christmas Presents.

(*b*) *Development.*

1. The writer's earliest memories of presents and of Father Christmas.
2. Presents that have made a deep impression on the writer.
3. The pleasure of giving presents and the value of surprise.
4. The problem of choosing suitable presents.

(*c*) *Conclusion.*

Except in the case of children, the giving of Christmas presents is becoming a farcical and tiresome exchange of articles of equal value, with the true idea of Christmas forgotten.

Type 2. *Analytical:* "Coal".

(*a*) *Introduction.* Large-scale mining of coal in the nineteenth century inaugurated the industrial age, and revolution.

(*b*) *Development.*

1. Origin, general location of deposits.
2. Methods of mining coal.
3. Transporting coal: rail, ship, barge.
4. Main uses: railways, ships, factories, gas, and electricity plants.
5. By-products: tar, petrol, etc., numerous chemicals for various purposes.
6. Advantages England has with its rich deposits. Many countries handicapped by lack of coal.

(*c*) *Conclusion.* Will the importance of coal rapidly diminish as oil, hydro-electric, and eventually atomic power supersede?

In essays on scientific or sociological subjects, some forecast of future developments forms an excellent concluding paragraph. In essays on historical or literary subjects, a final appreciation of the value and influence of the events or persons discussed in historical essays, or of the works or writers under discussion in literary essays, will form an obvious and necessary conclusion.

Type 3. *Imaginative:* "If I won £1,000".

(*a*) *Introduction.* Not really a large sum—equally foolish to spend it on sudden whim, or to save it in these uncertain times.

(*b*) *Development* (Examining possibilities).

1. Purchase of a car; or car and caravan.
2. Start a business of one's own.
3. Other suggestions.

(Decision).

4. A year's trip round the world.
5. Method of travel and other detailed plans.

(*c*) *Conclusion.* Material possessions are usually of only temporary interest. Travel has a permanent value in its broadening effect on the mind, and in its memories.

EXAMPLE OF AN ESSAY

The following is a student's effort which, though it lays no claim to be a work of genius, provides a good example of a well-planned essay, correctly punctuated and paragraphed, with interesting and clearly expressed ideas.

Subject: "New Towns"

Plan:

(a) *Introduction.* Necessity for new towns due to increase in population and to need to transfer many industries from overcrowded cities.

(b) *Development.*

1. Great opportunity for planners and architects. General lay-out: wide streets, spacious squares; station and factories on outskirts. Parks and playing-fields.
2. Main buildings to be grouped in centre. Scope for originality, but some uniformity in design essential; central gardens.
3. Shops—covered arcades? Car parks.
4. Schools and churches. Types of private dwelling-houses and flats.
5. Planning for future. Aerodrome. Green belt. Limiting eventual development.

(c) *Conclusion.* Essential to inculcate in citizens of new towns where there are no traditions, civic pride, and a community spirit, as success of new towns will depend finally not on planners but on the spirit and efforts of new citizens.

NEW TOWNS

The considerable increase in population in England since the war, particularly in urban areas, has made it essential to plan the rapid development of completely new towns, particularly around London, which has already reached a stage where its further development would be undesirable, if not impossible. To relieve this congestion, and to make the new towns self-supporting, and not mere dormitory towns, many light industries are being removed from overcrowded areas

319

to these new centres, and new industries are also being established there.

It is obvious that these new towns offer a great opportunity to planners and architects to show efficiency and originality, which is rarely possible in the confines of older cities. "A new broom sweeps clean", and the scope for sweeping changes in town-planning is considerable. There have actually been successful new towns built before the war, such as Welwyn Garden City and Letchworth, both of which can contribute valuable lessons.

In considering the general lay-out of a new town—and we have a right to presume it will be sited sufficiently far from London to prevent its becoming a mere suburb or satellite of the metropolis, with no individuality of its own—it is clear that the planner's first aim must be spaciousness. There must be wide streets, with an extensive central park or garden. Railway stations, power stations, waterworks, and factories must be relegated to their own area on the outskirts, and parks and playing-fields should be suitably placed around the rest of the perimeter.

The main administrative buildings—the town hall, the general post office, and police and fire headquarters—the principal shops, and such cultural or recreational centres as the assembly hall, art gallery, theatres, and cinemas, should form a central block of buildings surrounding a square or garden. The main hospitals, and space for any other hospitals or clinics, should be sited on the more peaceful and rural outskirts of the town. In such a central block there will be scope for originality of design, but there must be some degree of uniformity in the design of each main building, or the effect will be incongruous.

The shopping-centre of a new town should be something better than the haphazard jumble of styles of architecture and grouping found in older towns. Coventry is planning a central block of shops forming four sides of a square into which cars are not permitted to penetrate—a short flight of steps at each entrance to the square prevents such an invasion—and the show windows will be protected from the weather by a covered walk. This would be an excellent example to copy.

To deal with the problem of cars, it is essential that adequate car-parks should be planned, preferably underground, and it might be advisable to mark off a central area into which no motor traffic is allowed to penetrate.

To build a large central church and school would obviously be a mistake. Both churches and schools should be sited to serve the residential areas that will surround the centre and be placed either at the centre of the northern and southern halves of the perimeter, or at four major points of the compass on the perimeter, each school having playing-fields adjacent to it. A technical college and a grammar school to serve the whole town must also be allotted special space on the perimeter.

The residential area will form an outer circle, connected to the centre by broad tree-lined avenues. It would be wiser to divide these up into four or more areas, each with its own churches and schools and with intervening green spaces, rather than to allow them to form a single unit. Houses—both detached and semi-detached—and flats should be erected, and styles can be varied in different well-defined areas, but bungalows should be reserved for the outer-perimeter areas.

Some definite limit should be set on the height of all buildings, the administrative and cultural block alone being permitted to form an impressive and dominating central point.

The planners will fail, too, if they do not fix limitations on the development of the town, or "the last state will be worse than the first". A broad green belt should be the line of demarcation separating the town from a rural area which must not be allowed to be despoiled by the builder.

Finally, they must not forget to provide space for an aerodrome somewhere on this green belt; whether they should provide a more central landing area for future helicopters is a debatable point.

But whatever foresight and skill the planners and architects show, the success of these new towns will depend finally on the spirit and efforts of their new citizens. It is essential in these towns without traditions that wise leaders should inculcate the virtues of civic pride and a community spirit.

EXERCISES

A

Reflective.

1. Spring.
2. Summer.
3. Autumn.
4. Winter.
5. Hiking.
6. Keeping a Diary.
7. Litter.
8. Posters.
9. Modern Art.
10. Modern Architecture.
11. Collecting as a Hobby.
12. Keeping Pets.
13. Mountaineering.
14. Superstitions.
15. Examinations.
16. The Choice of a Career.
17. Museums.
18. Maps.
19. Camping Holidays.
20. Ghosts.
21. Postage Stamps.
22. Waiting-rooms.
23. Wild Flowers.
24. Country Cottages.

25. The English Climate.

B

Analytical. Informative.

(a) *Scientific :*

1. Atomic Power.
2. Television.
3. Coal.
4. Oil.
5. Photography.
6. The Control of Pests.
7. Electricity.
8. Improvements you would like to see in Cars or on Railways.
9. The Three most important Scientific Discoveries.
10. The Three future Inventions that are most required.
11. Canals.
12. A Great Scientist.
13. Printing.
14. Developments in Building.
15. Inter-Planetary Travel.
16. Tunnels.
17. Problems of Modern Traffic.
18. Ants.
19. Butterflies.
20. Bees.

(b) *Historical:*

1. The Development of Roads.
2. The Three most important Events in History.
3. The Elizabethan Age.
4. A Great Explorer.
5. A Great General or Admiral.
6. Famous Women in History.
7. A Great Prime Minister.
8. The historical event you would most like to have witnessed.
9. Life in England in the Middle Ages.
10. The Greatest Century in our History.
11. Famous Ships.
12. Vanished Empires.
13. Great Historians.
14. The Victorian Age.
15. Cathedrals.

(c) *Literary:*

1. Detective Novels.
2. Five Books for a Desert Island.
3. Your Favourite Novelist.
4. Your Favourite Poet.
5. Books that have influenced the World.
6. Women Novelists.
7. Planning a Library.
8. Modern Films.
9. Humorous Writers.
10. Diarists in Literature.

(d) *Sociological, etc.:*

1. The Value of Youth Clubs.
2. Films as an Aid to Education.
3. The Ideal School.
4. Sunday Entertainments.
5. The Influence of Newspapers.
6. National Service.
7. The Influence of Television.
8. Holiday Camps.
9. The Impact of Advertising.
10. Gambling.
11. The Decay of Good Manners.

12. Boredom.
13. Noise in Modern Life.
14. The Influence of Radio Broadcasting.
15. Automation.

C

Imaginative.

1. If I won £1,000.
2. Plans for a Perfect Holiday.
3. The Future of Air Transport.
4. Life in England in the year A.D. 2000.
5. A Day in the Life of a Caveman.
6. The House I should like to Build.
7. How I should live alone on a Small Island.
8. Plans for a World Tour.
9. A Visit to another Planet.
10. The Car I should like to Design.

CHAPTER XXVII

I. ARGUMENTS OR DEBATES
II. SPEECHES OF THANKS, ETC.

The following points should be noted before attempting essays (or speeches) on controversial subjects.

1. It is essential to decide what your point of view is going to be (i.e. which side you are going to take) before you start an essay.

If your concluding paragraph—naturally the most important in a controversy—fails to uphold the opinions you have expressed earlier, you have obviously failed to convince even yourself.

2. Do not start to write your final version until you have made notes on every aspect of the subject under discussion.

It is not sufficient or fair to put forward one side of the question only, and you will strengthen your argument by discussing (and refuting) points that may be made against your views.

3. A short, clear opening paragraph is essential, and it is best to devote this to defining briefly the subject to be discussed, and to indicating its importance.

4. Avoid in written composition the use of "I think", "In my opinion", etc. The personal touch is often an asset in the work of experienced authors and journalists, and essential in the arguments of a speaker, but a snare leading to monotony in an essay of this type. The reader knows that the essay expresses your opinion, and "It is obvious that . . ." or "There is no harm in . . ." need not be turned

into "I think it is obvious that . . ." or "I feel there is no harm in . . ."

5. You need not necessarily be an expert on the subject under discussion, though a general knowledge of the subject is obviously necessary. Write on the subject from your point of view.

6. Avoid platitudes—pompous statements of the obvious—such as "If everyone unites there will be fewer separate parties", for such pronouncements are a waste of time. Some politicians consider platitudes to be brilliantly original and penetrating remarks, but examiners do not share this opinion.

7. Finally, the method of arrangement of the "pros" and "cons" (the points for and against) is of the utmost importance, in order to avoid confusion.

I. ARGUMENTS OR DEBATES

It will be found that controversial subjects fall into two types:

A. A single topic or idea, where only one set of arguments for and against is required.

   e.g. Is co-education advisable?
      Is gambling an amusement or an evil?

B. A comparison of two topics or ideas, where the arguments for and against each must be set out.

   e.g. Which is preferable, to live in a town or in the country?
      Which are of more value, hedges or walls?

In both types it is essential to arrange points for and against in an orderly and logical way, and to avoid an unmethodical, confusing presentation of arguments. Points in favour should be set out first, followed by points against.

For example, in Type A, taking "Is co-education advisable?" as a topic for discussion, your preliminary plan could be:

1. *Introductory paragraph.* Growth of co-education in 20th Century—but still a subject for controversy.

2. *Advantages of Co-Education.* Eliminates mutual shyness and awkwardness. Improves manners. Prepares for adult social life.

3. *Disadvantages of Co-Education.* Distracts pupils from their studies at impressionable age. Impossible to share or compete in most games. Intellectual development of boys and girls takes place at different ages.

4. *Concluding paragraph.* Final opinion.

In Type B, with two conflicting ideas, it is all the more essential to arrange arguments in a logical sequence to avoid switching rapidly from one subject to the other. Taking the subject "Which are of more value, hedges or walls?", your plan could be:

1. *Introductory paragraph.* Both hedges and walls a feature of the landscape in many lands, and both serve a useful purpose.

2. Hedges:
   (i) *Advantages.* Soft outlines and variety of colours. Wealth of flowers, and also fruit (nuts, blackberries).
   (ii) *Disadvantages.* Offer less protection than walls in winter. Require frequent trimming. Often obscure the view and offer no resting-place.

3. Walls:
   (i) *Advantages.* Better protection than hedges, especially in winter. More durable and need less attention. Offer a firm resting-place and viewpoint.
   (ii) *Disadvantages.* Bare and less colourful than hedges. Harsh outlines.

4. *Concluding paragraph.* Both have their uses and their attractions. Each acts as a foil to the other in the English landscape. The wall, less attractive in the valleys, is superior on the hills, where hedges could not survive.

In many cases the discussion could well take the form of a dialogue between the two contestants, who can state their views in turn (e.g. a dialogue between a postman and a policeman, discussing which has the harder life).

Debating Procedure

The normal arrangement of a debate whose subject is announced beforehand to allow for preparation is to have a Chairman or President, and two Proposers and two Opposers of the motion, who are selected beforehand.

In an impromptu debate the Chairman draws both the topic for debate and the names of the opening Proposer and Opposer from a hat, and the debate opens at once, without further preparation.

The Chairman's duties are to introduce the debate, to keep order, and to see that no speaker transgresses the rules of libel or the bounds of time, and to select speakers when the debate is thrown open to the "house".

The Proposer of the motion speaks first, followed by the Opposer; then the Proposer's Seconder followed by the second Opposer. The debate is then thrown open to general debate, those desiring to speak indicating their wish by raising a hand or rising to attract the Chairman's attention.

It is the practice in formal debates to allow the Opposer and the Proposer, in that order, to sum up finally, but time does not usually permit this in informal debating.

The method of presenting ideas will differ in a debate from the method employed in an essay, for although the opening speaker—the proposer of the motion—will obviously first indicate all the advantages of his side's point of view, and then refer to the main errors on the opposite side, and will be followed by the first speaker for the opposition, who will employ similar methods (though he may prefer to reverse the procedure and to criticise his opponent's claims first, before building up his own case), subsequent speakers must obviously avoid repetition. They must concentrate on two things: (i) making any advantageous point that has not previously been made, and (ii) criticising, and if possible refuting or undermining points made by opponents (particularly the immediately preceding opposing speaker) that have not been previously criticised.

It is important, and in fact essential, that intending speakers should make notes of all relevant points raised during the course of the debate.

At the conclusion of the debate, on which it is advisable to set a time limit (which can also be applied to individual speeches), the decision of the audience is ascertained by the Chairman, who calls for a show of hands, and can be aided in the task of counting votes by appointed "tellers".

A Secretary, whose duties are to deal with notices, minutes of debates (a summary of each speech of any importance, and a note as to the result of each debate), and any necessary correspondence, is often appointed. A Treasurer may also be appointed if any financial accounts are necessary (i.e. in cases where there is a fixed subscription for a meeting or a series of meetings).

Specimen of an Agenda drawn up by the Secretary of a Debating or other Society.

Order of Business:

1. Minutes of last meeting.
2. Matters arising from minutes.
3. Any official announcements.
4. Question time.
5. Committee's report, if any.
6. Nominations for vacant official post, if any.
7. Any motions for discussion.
8. Any other business.

II. SPEECHES OF THANKS, ETC.

There are other types of speeches we may be called upon to make, in which there is no question of putting forward any arguments.

We may have to compose speeches of introduction or

speeches of thanks, and these will also require some preliminary thought and a plan.

In the case of a speech introducing a speaker who has come to address a meeting, a summary of the speaker's career and qualifications will be necessary, and an appreciation of his or her personality.

If the speech is to be made at the opening of some new society or building, the origin and aims of the new undertaking must be discussed first, followed by a reference to its main features and amenities, and some ideas on future developments. The speech should close with a vote of thanks to all those who have made the undertaking possible.

A speech of thanks by the recipient of some commemorative gift will obviously begin with an appreciation of the gift (even if it is unsuitable—though, as the recipient will probably have chosen it in advance, this is an unlikely occurrence). Next the recipient can give some impressions of his work and the friends he has made in connection with it, mentioning any outstanding experiences or changes he has seen. He can then conclude with a brief outline of his future plans.

Finally, if a student is called upon to compose a speech to be given in any imaginary circumstances he cares to select, he is more than likely to visualise himself as presenting the prizes at his old school on Speech Day, and the views he can then express on his past experiences at the school and on education in general offer such wide scope that it will be unnecessary to offer him any suggestions on how to deal with such a topic.

EXERCISES

Arguments.

1. Is co-education preferable to educating boys and girls separately?

2. Are television and radio a menace to education?

3. Are pet animals becoming a nuisance in the home?

4. Should men and women have equal pay for similar work?

5. Are railways now an obsolete means of transport?

6. Is the teaching of a "dead" language, such as Latin or Greek, a waste of time?

7. Is it advisable to make all betting illegal?

8. Do people today devote too much time to watching sport?

9. Should conscription into the armed forces be abolished?

10. Is it preferable to live in a town or in the country?

11. Should wild animals be kept in captivity?

12. Should a universal language be compulsorily taught in lla countries?

13. Who has the strongest claim to be the greatest man who has yet lived?

14. Should boarding-schools be abolished?

15. Do you consider the present century the most satisfactory for its social conditions?

16. What invention do you consider the most important?

17. What invention do we now most require?

18. Do newspapers do more harm than good?

19. What country is the best to live in?

20. What do you consider the ideal way of spending a holiday?

21. Do international athletic contests promote mutual understanding?

22. Is it possible to do away with all international frontiers?

23. Are flats preferable to houses?

24. Is television preferable to radio?

Speeches.

1. Write a speech of welcome (*a*) to a distinguished explorer who has come to address your club or society, or (*b*) to a distinguished Frenchman who is giving a talk on France to your society.

2. Write a speech to be made (*a*) when presenting the prizes at your old school, or (*b*) when opening a fête in aid of some charity.

3. Write a speech of thanks to be made (*a*) when you receive a gift from your colleagues on leaving to take up a new appointment, or (*b*) to those who have subscribed to give you a farewell presentation on your retirement.

CHAPTER XXVIII

DIALOGUES AND THE SHORT STORY

DIALOGUES

The writing of dialogue ("dialogue" = a conversation between two or more persons; "monologue" = one person speaking uninterruptedly; "duologue" = a conversation between two persons) is not only excellent practice for the future playwright, but also a valuable exercise for the short-story writer or novelist, as dialogue plays a vital part in lightening the effect of continuous narrative prose, and makes every form of story more vivid and interesting.

Most playwrights find that if the dialogue of a play is to flow naturally it must be written not a little at a time, with long intervals between each session, but rapidly in a few consecutive hours, while the characters are clearly in focus and the writer's vision of them leads to fluent and "live" dialogue.

The art of writing dialogue is a difficult one to master; some dialogues appear artificial and stilted, others perfectly natural—and this is largely due to careful observation or the lack of it.

To write successful dialogue we must first have a clear picture of the character of each person to be portrayed, and the type of vocabulary each would naturally employ. It follows that characters we really know and have studied carefully, memorising their peculiarities, will "live" more than those that exist only in our imagination.

Notice that conversations in everyday life have interruptions or sudden changes of theme. Sometimes it will be necessary to indicate stuttering, or at least hesitation. A taciturn person will speak in short sentences, or even monosyllables, while a talkative character will make more frequent and longer speeches than a reserved one. A bully will shout at times or interrupt; a pompous person will use long words; some characters will drawl, and others lisp. Every variation can be conveyed by a skilled writer.

Abbreviations such as "won't", "can't", "I'm", "it's", will be often used, and colloquialisms and slang will be permissible—and indeed necessary—to convey the speech of certain characters.

The reproduction of some particular dialect, such as West Country or North Country dialect, presents difficulties for the beginner, and is best avoided unless he is really familiar with the correct idioms of such dialogue. As to the spelling of dialects, the principle of this is to spell the dialect words or phrases phonetically—i.e. approximate the spelling as nearly as possible to the actual sound or sounds of the words.

When a dialogue is set as a form of composition—a duologue is the usual form chosen—a definite plan is as necessary as it is in other forms of composition.

For example, in the case of a discussion or argument between two persons, each speaker will state his case or point of view in turn, though there may be brief interruptions for agreement or disagreement on the part of the other person.

In some dialogues, of course, one character is the expert and the other is seeking information, so that the latter's rôle will be principally that of asking questions. In others, some topic of conversation crops up simply as a result of the meeting of the characters or of a certain incident.

Here is a plan that will cover most cases:

1. Greeting.
2. Matter arising for discussion.
3. Points of view.
4. Conclusion—and parting.

Notice that stage directions are always given in the present tense, and that the scene and characters are described briefly before the conversation opens. It will sometimes be necessary to indicate the period of time in which the scene is set, and also the actual time of day, e.g.

Dialogue between a Cat and a Canary.

Scene: A suburban dining-room with the usual table, chairs, and sideboard.

A birdcage containing a canary is suspended from a hook fixed in the ceiling near the french window.

Characters: Timothy, a cat.

Topsy, a canary.

(When the scene opens, Topsy, the sole occupant of the room, is alone in his cage.)

> *Topsy* (talking to himself): Well, this is my first day in my new home, and I think I'm going to like it here. A roomy cage, plenty of food, and an interesting view. (He sees cat entering by open french window.) Ah! Who's this? I don't like the look of him.
>
> *Timothy* (looking up at cage and speaking in an undertone): What's this? A new pet? A rival, possibly. I must look into this. (He addresses the canary.) Good morning. I hope it *will* be a good morning. My name is Timothy. May I ask yours? I'm sure we shall be friends. (He smiles ingratiatingly.)
>
> ... etc., etc.

THE SHORT STORY

There is no space in composing a short story for the lengthy description of appearance, character, or scenery in which a full-length novel can indulge. It has often been claimed, and with reason, that it is far harder to be a successful short-story writer than a successful novelist. Wells, Kipling, G. K. Chesterton, W. W. Jacobs, Somerset Maugham, Katherine Mansfield, and H. E. Bates are outstanding short-story writers; in American literature

O'Henry, Edgar Allen Poe, and Ambrose Bierce have excelled in this difficult art; and the French writer, Guy de Maupassant is probably the greatest exponent of all, and the ideal model to follow, with his clear style, economy of words, vivid characterisation, gift for description and dialogue, and his flair for a plot and an effective ending.

It is inadvisable to lay down definite rules for the method of telling a short story, for such rules would cramp all originality and lead to a stereotyped style; but the following points may prove helpful:

The scene, time, and characters must be presented by selecting only those details which are essential and most striking.

The short story must have unity of theme and must not wander from one idea or plot to another. There must be a single idea with a definite beginning, development, and conclusion—and the most essential but difficult thing is to delay the issue or climax of the story until the final paragraph.

As to the problem of finding plots, there is really an infinite variety of comedies and tragedies going on all around us in our ordinary daily life if we develop the gift of observation. It is not the sensational events but, as Maupassant says, it is "certain chance encounters, certain inexplicable combinations of circumstances, without appearing exceptional, that contain life's secret essence".

Generally speaking, the first paragraphs will set the scene, and indicate if necessary the period of time in which it is set, though dialogue or action may be skilfully used as an opening.

The method of development of the plot depends on the nature of each individual story, but the conclusion is an art which cannot really be taught. Much can be learnt, however, by studying the endings of stories by such masters of the art as Maupassant, Somerset Maugham, and O'Henry.

In Maupassant's famous story *The Necklace* it is not

until the last line that we realise the lost diamond necklace the young couple had ruined themselves to replace was merely of imitation stones—but how difficult it is to stage the climax, and to achieve it successfully, in the very last sentence, every writer will discover for himself.

The introduction of dialogue obtains two valuable results: firstly, the introduction of direct speech helps to add interest and variety to the story and often makes it more vivid; secondly, dialogue skilfully handled can convey in a few words an impression of the speaker's character and personality.

From the following example the reader quickly gathers that Mr. Dennis is a man of few words and also not inclined to over-exertion; his wife, on the other hand, appears to be much more talkative, and to be highly-strung and inclined to worry.

"Really, Henry, you seem to have no sense of urgency, or even responsibility. You sit there in your deck chair sunning yourself and dozing, as if you hadn't a care in the world, while the garden is becoming a wilderness," snapped Mrs. Dennis in her querulous voice from the french window, flicking her duster in his direction.

"Do you think so, my dear?" replied her husband, in a voice surprisingly quiet and reedy for one of his vast bulk and rather forbidding Prussian appearance.

"Yes, I do. The least you can do is to cut the lawn. Just look at it! And this door needs mending—and then there are the bills to attend to."

"Yes, I might do that later, perhaps," he suggested mildly, settling farther back in his chair, without having made it clear to which task he referred.

Remember, as has been pointed out in the first part of this chapter, the limitations of vocabulary in the case of uneducated characters; visualise the habits of each character so that the dialogue may be natural; and avoid introducing any special dialect unless you are really familiar with it.

Remember, too, that when introducing dialogue into

a story, *each* speaker's remarks must be placed on a fresh line, and form a new paragraph.

It is very important to avoid monotony by varying interpolations—i.e. "He said", "He replied", "He suggested", "He remarked", "He interrupted", etc.—and to vary the position of such interpolations, placing some before and some after the actual words spoken (e.g. "He called: 'Come in'"—or "'Come in,' he called"). Varying interpolations is an important part of style in story-telling, and increases effectiveness.

Study any story by one of the short-story writers that have been previously mentioned, and see how they handle dialogue and interpolation. Notice, incidentally, that when it is quite clear which person is speaking in a conversation between two people, the interpolations "he said", etc., can be, and often are, omitted.

> e.g. For a moment neither the Manager nor Johnson spoke; then the latter suddenly said: "You mean that I am dismissed from the firm?"
>
> "Are you surprised, after what has happened?"
>
> "No, I suppose not—but I should like to ask you one favour."
>
> "What is that?"
>
> "Will you give me a testimonial?"
>
> "How can I? Do you really expect one?"
>
> "Hardly. But how can I get other employment without one?"
>
> "You should have thought of that before."

Colour can be added to descriptions by the use of comparisons and contrasts (as long as these are not too obvious and trite).

> e.g. *Comparison*. The little engine puffed along like a fat man out of breath.
>
> *Contrast*. Mr. Jones was tall, pale-faced, and cadaverous: his wife short and fat, with full red cheeks.

Finally, notice that the use of a series of short sentences often speeds up the action in a story, just as longer sentences slow the action down, and give contrast by doing so. Longer sentences are suited to descriptions of people and scenes—short sentences to sudden actions.

Here, as an example, is a short story submitted by a student in response to a request for a story of not more than 500 words about an animal. In a longer story there would naturally be more scope for detail, and for the use of comparisons to add colour and emphasis.

THE PET RABBIT

Mrs. Brown finished her shopping in the market, then suddenly remembered Christopher's eighth birthday, and the promised rabbit.

"You can have one this year, but on one condition," Mr. Brown had warned. "You must look after it yourself. I know what kids are with pets—can't do too much for them for a week—then they're forgotten."

Mrs. Brown made her way to the pet stall, and found to her joy a hutch full of young rabbits. A grey one in a corner looked up at her with appealing eyes. "Five bob, mum," said the man, extracting it deftly. "Don't give him too much green stuff. Bran at night. Thank you."

"Looks like a wild one to me," remarked Mr. Brown on viewing it, but Christopher was enraptured. His father unwillingly spent the evening making a hutch from packing-cases, and the boy got up at dawn the next morning to scour suburban grass verges for dandelions.

At week-ends Monty, as he was christened, on account of his bright eyes, was liberated in the garden, but his sole idea seemed to be not to make friends, but to escape under the fence, and he grew daily wilder rather than tamer.

As the weeks passed, Monty spent his entire time gnawing the woodwork of his cage, and when given the run of the garden he was harder to catch than ever. Placed in a pen on the lawn, he tunnelled the sacred turf in his search for freedom.

"No good as a pet," sighed Mr. Brown, exasperated. "Wants setting free somewhere."

"Comes of wild stock, if you ask me," suggested Mr. Smith over the fence. "But you can't set him loose now. Cruel. Couldn't fend for himself."

Mr. Brown, however, had other ideas. Indifferent to public opinion and advice, but deeply concerned about his lawn, he rose early one Sunday morning, crept downstairs, and placing Monty in a box which he tied securely to the carrier, he mounted his bicycle and made for the nearest common.

On arrival, Mr. Brown surveyed the bushes and flourishing bracken with satisfaction, and placed the rabbit on the grass. An ecstatic kick or two of his back legs, a trial hop, and Monty vanished at speed in the undergrowth.

Mr. Brown, greatly relieved, lit his pipe and settled with his back against a tree to enjoy it. He must have dozed off under the genial influence of the sunshine. When he woke with a start it was midday. He felt hungry. Putting his hand down to feel for his pipe in the grass, his fingers encountered something warm and soft snuggled against his side. It was Monty.

EXERCISES

Dialogues.

Write an imaginary conversation between:

1. A parrot and a cat trying to attack it.

2. A television enthusiast and a television-hater.

3. A sailor and a soldier, comparing their modes of life.

4. A pet-lover and a person who dislikes animals.

5. A bee and a wasp, comparing their usefulness.

6. A seagull and a crow, comparing life in the country and life by the sea.

7. A cart-horse and a cow, comparing their lives.

8. A walking-enthusiast and a motorist, comparing their enjoyment of the scenery.

9. A farmer and a shopkeeper, comparing their work.

10. A film-actor and a bank-clerk, comparing their working conditions.

Short Stories and Anecdotes.

A

The following lines are extracts from stories that have not yet been completed. Write a short story to suit each extract, the exact words of which must be included at some point.

The stories may be serious or humorous.

1. The tramp picked up the wallet, and examined its contents.

2. A flash of lightning lit up his face. It was the wanted man.

3. "Surely we've met somewhere before," said my fellow-passenger, lowering his newspaper.

4. I pushed my way through the crowd to see what was happening.

5. I rang, and knocked. There was no answer. I tried the door, and to my surprise, it opened.

6. "You're not going yet," he said, covering me with his revolver.

7. "I never want to see a lion again," Mr. Brown assured them, as he relit his pipe.

8. "It's all a mistake," replied the terrified old man. "I can explain everything."

9. Someone was moving about in the room. I switched on the light.

10. "Could it be a coincidence?" the detective wondered as he examined the handwriting.

B

Write out an anecdote (a) recounting some amusing incident, (b) some clever or unexpected retort, (c) illustrating some moral, (d) concerning some animal or bird, (e) concerning a child or children, (f) describing a practical joke, or an embarrassing moment.

C

Expand the following summaries into short stories, including some dialogue in each:

1. Sailor, who is ventriloquist, enters inn, carrying parrot in a cage—makes parrot talk fluently. Innkeeper impressed—does not realise voice is sailor's—offers large sum for bird. Sailor goes away—innkeeper finds parrot cannot talk—parrot dies later, is stuffed, and left in cage. Sailor returns from voyage—enters inn and makes parrot talk—angry innkeeper explains—demands money back.

2. Old lady with pet dog enters railway-carriage—she objects to pipe smoked by other passenger—snatches it and throws it out of window—passenger retaliates, throws dog out of window. Next station dog waiting on platform, pipe in mouth.

3. Absent-minded professor, fond of walking, visits on foot friends in country cottage—heavy storm breaks out—professor invited to stay night—accepts gratefully—hosts unable to find him later in evening—still raining—knock at door at midnight—professor on doorstep—explains he went back to town to get his pyjamas.

D

Write a short summary of characters, scenes, and plot for a film idea you wish to submit.

E

Write a short scene for acting about (*a*) an historical event, (*b*) your home, office, or school.

F

Write a short story based on some unusual personal experience.

G

Write a short story to suit each of the following titles: "A Narrow Escape"; "The Biter Bit"; "His Last Chance"; "An Unusual Ghost"; "The Gipsy's Warning"; "Beginner's Luck"; "The Secret Drawer"; "Never Too Late"; "An Unexpected Guest"; "A Cottage in the Country".

CHAPTER XXIX

REVIEWS, REPORTS, AND STATISTICS

REVIEWS

We are often called upon to give a review of some book we have read or of some play or film we have seen.

This does not mean that it is necessary to give a detailed description of every incident of the scenic background or of every character.

Books. In reviewing a book we must first indicate the type of book it is—i.e. a story of adventure, war, exploration, a romance, an historical novel, a psychological study, a detective story, a study of social conditions at some given period, etc.—and the scene or scenes which form its setting. Next, a very brief summary of the plot should be given, and then some criticism, favourable or unfavourable, of the way in which the plot is developed, the way in which the main characters are drawn, and the background described, with some remarks about the author's style.

The review can conclude with a personal opinion of the value of the book as literature.

Here, as an example, is a student's review of Dickens's *A Tale of Two Cities.*

A Tale of Two Cities

It is surely a remarkable fact that it is an Englishman who has written by far the finest novel on the greatest event in French history, the French Revolution.

If I were condemned to spend a year on a desert island with only one book to read during my stay there, I would unhesitatingly choose this remarkable work of fiction, set in London and Paris at the time of the French Revolution: the tale of the sacrifice made by an English barrister, a failure in his chosen profession, to save the life of a French aristocrat who, having escaped to London and married there, returned from a sense of duty to France, only to be seized and sentenced to death by the Revolutionary tribunal.

The plot holds the reader's interest from the beginning, and its increasingly dramatic situations reach a thrilling climax. There is in the background a remarkable reconstruction of the historical and social conditions at the time of the Revolution, with many brilliant word-pictures.

The main characters, unlike those in many of Dickens's novels, are not caricatures, but are vividly portrayed—the cynical but strangely attractive unsuccessful barrister, Sidney Carton; the pathetic figure of Dr. Manette, so long a prisoner in the Bastille; Jarvis Lorry, the dignified, reliable representative of Tellson's Bank. Charles Darnay and Lucie, the young couple round whom the plot is woven, are necessarily less colourful, but are accurately observed.

The minor characters, too, are rich in variety and excellently drawn: Miss Pross, the staid, devoted English governess; Madame Defarge, the merciless leader of the female rabble of St. Antoine, are memorable character studies, while Jerry Cruncher, odd-job man of Tellson's Bank, adds welcome humour to a grim portrait gallery.

This must surely be, both in its striking word-pictures and in its brilliant characterisation, one of the outstanding historical novels in our literature.

Plays and Films. Reviewing a play or film will call for the additional consideration of the dialogue (its naturalness, wit, etc., or lack of these qualities), of the scenic background and effects (including the use of colour, and of original settings and effects in some cases), and in the case of films, of sound effects and incidental music in many instances.

To write a successful play calls for far greater skill in the handling of the plot than is required in a novel, for we may read a novel with little or no plot merely because of some fine descriptive writing it contains, or because of the interest the background or some special character evokes, but a play, if it is to be successful, must never allow our attention to wander or our interest to lapse. We cannot "skip" an act in the same way as we can glance rapidly at some dull page or chapter that does not appeal to us in a book, or close our eyes when bored by some parts of a film.

In addition, unless we are reviewing a play we have merely read and not seen performed, we can comment on the skill or lack of skill of the actors who portrayed the various characters.

As an example, here is a review, by a student, of the film of Shakespeare's *Julius Caesar*.

Julius Caesar

The fact that the scenic limitations of a stage prevent the theatre from showing "the glory that was Rome" gives the cinema an advantage which it does not fail to take.

This film, the dialogue of which faithfully follows Shakespeare's play, deals with the assassination of Caesar at the height of his power by Brutus, and with the subsequent defeat of the rebel forces under Brutus, by the army, led by Mark Antony.

That two of the leading parts, those of Caesar and Mark Antony, are played by American actors may shock those who feel that Shakespeare's lines should be spoken only by English actors, but it must be admitted that Marlon Brando as Mark Antony gave a brilliant and forceful performance, and Caesar was played with dignity, though the interpretation of his character seemed to lack those dynamic qualities he must have possessed, and at times suggested a rather tired though successful business man.

It must equally be admitted, however, that the way in which James Mason as Brutus and Gielgud as Cassius spoke their lines was an object lesson to all Shakespearean actors.

This is essentially a man's play, and the female characters, with the exception of Caesar's wife, adequately played by Deborah Kerr, are of little importance.

What is almost as important in this play as the characters is the magnificent scenic background of Rome at the height of its architectural glory and military triumphs, and this receives full justice from the film cameras. Hollywood rarely fails when given the task of producing vast scenes and crowds. The fact that some of the small children lining the route of the triumphal procession to the Senate acclaimed the leaders with a marked American accent can be forgiven when there is so much to praise in this production, but it is difficult to understand how a general of Brutus's ability can plunge his army, apparently without scouts, into a narrow gorge which simply invites ambush and massacre. This surely is pure Hollywood scenario and based on no historical facts or military principles.

The incidental music does not intrude unduly, as it does in some modern films; and the absence of colour—this is a "black-and-white" film—far from detracting from its effectiveness, adds dignity to epic scenes which might have seemed tawdry if too highly coloured.

REPORTS

We are all only too familiar with school reports, in which —after details of our successes or weaknesses in individual subjects have been tabulated and some facts about our athletic prowess, punctuality, and attendances added— the headmaster or headmistress gives a summary of our potentialities or shortcomings, so as to provide our parents with guidance for any necessary further action.

Later in life, particularly in industry or commerce, we may be called upon to give similar reports to a board of directors or governors, to the head of some department on such subjects as the efficiency of some factory or shop, the possibilities of some projected scheme or site or the activities of some company, group or society or of some accident on land or sea such as a fire or a wreck.

In making such reports, our first task will obviously be

to collect all the necessary facts and figures. Next, these must be carefully arranged in logical order, and finally reports usually conclude with a summary of satisfactory and/or unsatisfactory features that have emerged, with some recommendation for action where there is room for improvement.

Reports are usually written in the form of a letter, and are addressed to the person or group at whose request the investigation has been undertaken. The person asked to report is usually selected because he is an expert on a particular subject, but a company secretary is often asked to undertake reports on a variety of subjects with which he must make himself conversant by inquiry and research.

Here is an example of a report on one of a chain of restaurants owned by The Eatwell Catering Company.

REPORT ON EATWELL RESTAURANT
52, MAIN STREET, LONDON, W.1.

Eatwell Catering Co.,
15, Smith Street,
London, E.C.5.
1st June, 1955.

The Managing Director.

Sir,

In accordance with your instructions, I have carried out a careful inspection of our branch at 52, Main Street, and beg to submit the following report.

The premises are excellently situated and have an attractive exterior, but the interior is less satisfactory.

The restaurant is sufficiently spacious and its furniture modern and adequate, but the rooms require redecorating in a lighter and brighter colour scheme. An improved cooling system is also necessary for the summer.

The kitchen equipment is now definitely inadequate to deal efficiently with the recent marked increase in the number of clients. More electric cookers and grilles are needed at once; there is also now insufficient space on the

346

premises for food storage, especially refrigerated storage, and this must be rectified by adding an additional storage room with suitable refrigeration.

The manager is an efficient organiser, and gets the best out of his staff, who appear to be quite satisfied with their working conditions, but there is room for improvement in the design of the waitresses' uniforms, which are rather drab and old-fashioned.

Yours faithfully,
I. N. Spector.

Notice the order of presentation of the facts, and the recommendations under each heading for improvements where necessary.

STATISTICS

Having seen how to deal with a request to visit and report on some factory, company, or undertaking, we must now examine the information that can be extracted from statistics.

We may often be required, especially in business or in the Civil Service, to draw conclusions from statistical tables or tabulated facts.

Here is a typical example, and from these data, if we interpret them correctly, we should be able to deduce sufficient facts to make a helpful report.

BIRTHS AND DEATHS
(England and Wales)

Year	Birth-rate (per 1,000)	Death-rate (per 1,000)	Survival-rate (per 1,000)	Infant Mortality (per 1,000)
1900	29·9	18·2	11·7	145
1910	25·8	16·2	9·6	110
1920	18·9	12·5	6·4	80
1930	14·7	11·7	3·0	64
1940	14·3	12·9	1·4	57
1950	15·8	11·6	4·1	33

347

Make notes on the conclusions you draw from the study of each column, remembering that these may be obtained by studying the columns not only vertically but also horizontally.

The first paragraph of your report will indicate the subject with which you are dealing. Next, put down in what you feel to be the correct order the facts you have deduced from the list. Finally, sum up the lessons of the data you have examined and make, if necessary, some recommendations for improvement in cases where facts are revealed which are disturbing and call for such suggestions.

Give your report a heading, e.g.

REPORT ON THE SURVIVAL-RATE FOR ENGLAND AND WALES (1900–1950)

A survey of the statistics covering this period reveals the following interesting facts:

(a) The birth-rate, as high as 29·9 per 1,000 in 1900, fell alarmingly by 1940 to 14·3, and this latter figure cannot be attributed to war conditions, as the fall was most rapid from 1910 to 1920.

(b) Fears of a further fall, with serious results for the future of this country, have been dispelled by the survival-rate figures for 1950, which show an increase of 2·7 on the low figure of 1·4 for 1940.

(c) The most reassuring figures are those of the Infant Mortality rate, which have fallen from the regrettable figure of 145 deaths per 1,000 in 1900 to 33 in 1950, a remarkable tribute to the progress of medical knowledge and the development of pre-natal and post-natal welfare services.

The fact that the birth-rate, though it has been slowly rising since 1940, is still far below the figure for the period 1900–1920, and is likely to remain so in the future, can be attributed to improvement in social conditions and in general education, so that the intelligent planning of families is now the rule rather than the exception.

EXERCISES

Reviews

1. Write a review of (*a*) a recent film, (*b*) a recent play that you have seen.

2. Write a review of what you consider is (*a*) the best film, (*b*) the best play that you have ever seen.

3. Write a review (*a*) of a recent book you have read, (*b*) of the book you consider the best you have read.

4. Write a review of the work of any novelist, poet, dramatist, artist, composer, or musician you admire.

5. Write a review of any television or wireless programme that has specially appealed to you.

Reports

Write a critical report on:

1. A real or imaginary factory you have visited.

2. An imaginary island you have discovered, and consider worthy of development.

3. The year's trade of an imaginary shop or firm of which you are secretary.

4. An inventor's claim to have solved the secret of perpetual motion.

5. The current year's activities of a social, athletic, literary club, of which you are secretary.

6. The sales possibilities upon your firm's goods in a foreign country you have visited for this purpose.

Statistics

A

Give a summary based on the following statistics of the changes that have taken place in our diet since the 1939–45 war.

	Meat	*Potatoes*	*Greens*	*Fish*	*Game*	*Butter*
1938	110 lb.	180 lb.	52 lb.	21·8 lb.	4 lb.	24·2 lb.
1955	103·8 lb.	221 lb.	40 lb.	18·4 lb.	1 lb.	14·2 lb.

349

	Margarine	*Tea*	*Bread*	*Milk*	*Cereals*
1938	8·7 lb.	9¼ lb.	220 lb.	152 pints	50 lb.
1955	18·4 lb.	9½ lb.	256 lb.	310 pints	100 lb.

(All figures represent the average per person per year.)

B

Give a summary based on the following statistics of the increase in road casualties since 1938.

Road Casualties in Great Britain

(Annual Totals)

	Total casualties		Nature of casualty				Class of road user		
	All ages	Under 15 years	Killed	Seriously injured	Slightly injured	Pedes-trians	Pedal cyclists	Motor cyclists and their passengers	Other drivers and their passengers
1938	233,359	43,160	6,648	50,782	175,929	77,239	67,128	32,771	56,221
1951	216,493	42,676	5,250	52,369	158,874	59,861	48,077	42,680	65,875
1952	208,012	40,927	4,706	50,351	152,955	54,503	47,244	42,644	63,621
1953	226,770	44,246	5,090	56,522	165,158	58,553	49,618	49,438	69,161
1954	238,281	44,133	5,010	57,201	176,070	61,381	49,295	52,531	75,074
1955	267,922	48,710	5,526	62,106	200,290	63,807	52,447	63,602	87,976

CHAPTER XXX

POETIC OR VERSE COMPOSITION

Some text-books use the term "Prosody" instead of "Poetry" or "Verse" as a chapter heading, but prosody is a term now used for the laws which govern verse-making, and does not cover all aspects of poetry.

We must first make a general distinction between poetry and prose, though at times the two mediums are not easily distinguished, as some prose reaches by its rhythm and emotion to poetical levels.

Two principles contribute to make poetry—rhythm and rhyme—though the latter is not an essential feature of every type of verse.

Rhythm can, and often does, occur in prose, and is essential in verse composition. Rhythm is a balance or pattern of stressed words or of stressed syllables, a syllable being either a vowel, or a vowel and one or more consonants, uttered in one breath impulse (e.g. a, to, the), and it is this regular pattern of stresses which gives harmony to verse. Individual words of more than one syllable, as has already been indicated in dealing with spelling and pronunciation, have certain syllables which are stressed.

e.g. súddenly, impénetrable, austére.

When words are arranged so that such stresses fall at regular intervals, the result is rhythm, or a regular beat, as we say in music.

351

e.g. Cánnon to ríght of them,
    Cánnon to léft of them,
    Ćnnon in frónt of them,
    Vólley'd and thúnder'd.

Rhyme, the second (but not essential) feature of verse, is the repetition at the end of a line (though this repetition can also occur elsewhere in a line) of a particular sound.

e.g. On either side the river lie
    Long fields of barley and of rye
    That clothe the wold and meet the sky.

When the last syllables only of lines rhyme, they are called single rhymes, but rhymes may be double or rich rhymes, i.e. rhymes in which the last two syllables rhyme,

e.g. roaming   vigorous.
    gloaming   rigorous.

or even treble, or more.

Both rhythm and rhyme appeal to and depend on the ear. We do not see poetry with the eye, and this is particularly true in English, where many words spelt in similar ways do not rhyme at all.

e.g. "though" does not rhyme with "plough",
    "row" (with oars) does not rhyme with "bow" (to bend).

But "lie", "rye", and "sky"—though spelt differently—all rhyme with one another.

Perfect rhymes should have (a) the same vowel sound and the same following consonant sound (if any), and (b) the same stress on the rhyming syllable (e.g. lament, content)—and should obviously not have the same consonant preceding the vowel sound (e.g. "remote", "denote" are correct, but "appear" and "bear" are imperfect because the vowel sounds are not exactly the same).

Verse, unlike prose, is metrical, i.e. it is written in lines that we measure usually by the number of stresses or feet they contain.

A **Foot** is either a single accented syllable or a combination of two or more syllables of which one must be accented. (Accent is the stress thrown on the pronunciation of one particular syllable.)

e.g. lóst
     upón
     perdítion
     unwórthily

The process of dividing lines of verse up into feet is called Scansion.

Lines may vary in length, and a line may contain any number of feet (within reason!).

There are technical terms to differentiate different types of feet, and also different types of lines and of verses or groups of lines. The combination of certain types of feet, lines, and verses or stanzas gives us what is called metre, which is the measure of lines of verse, the manner in which such lines are regulated.

A Stanza is an Italian word to indicate what we often call a verse, i.e. the groups of lines into which a poem is often divided. Stanzas may vary in length and structure.

The word "verse" was originally used to indicate a single line of poetry, but it is now employed in the sense of a stanza or group of lines.

The following notes on types of feet, lines, and metre are included only for reference, and for those wishing to study further the technique of poetry. Too much importance need not be attached to technical terminology, however, as it may discourage the study of poetry instead of encouraging it.

If poetry has beauty of sound and thought, or even if it is experimental in sound and humorous in theme, as it can equally be, it is to be read and spoken—not subjected to a tedious analysis of the feet and metre employed in it to such an extent that its beauty (or sometimes wit) is forgotten.

It is sometimes argued that a knowledge of craftsmanship is essential to all crafts, and it cannot be denied that professional critics should be conversant with poetic rules and terminology to attain a standard of judgment, but poets are a race apart, and some of our greatest poets have succeeded in writing immortal verse without any study of these classifications and terminologies, and even without any knowledge of rules.

Technical Terms in Verse

1. Kinds of Feet

In English verse a line is measured simply by the number of accented syllables or stresses in a line, but in Latin and Greek verse a line was measured by groups of long and short syllables (i.e. by vowel quantity).

In this latter classical system a short or unstressed syllable was marked ˘ and, a long or stressed syllable marked –. These signs indicated the *quantity* of a syllable, that is the length of time it took to pronounce the syllable in question (e.g. tŏdāy, fārewēll).

In English verse we use these signs to mark stressed or unstressed syllables instead of quantity, and when we mark out or emphasise the accented or stressed syllables in a line we are said to "scan" the line, and this exercise is called "scansion".

In the following examples the stressed syllables only are marked in (1) and the stressed and unstressed in (2).

(1) A mágic wéb with cólours gáy.

(2) Ă māgĭc wēb wĭth cōloŭrs gāy.

Strictly speaking, scansion is not only a question of marking the stresses, but also of indicating the number and type of feet in a line.

There are only four kinds of feet at all frequent in English verse whose technical names we need to learn.

Note that a single consonant between two vowels

354

belongs to the second vowel; groups of two or more consonants between two vowels divide (e.g. pro duce, ar cade, coun try), but prefixes are separate (e.g. re place) and also suffixes (e.g. tempest uous).

(1) *The Iambus* (˘ —).

When Ī | cŏnsī | dĕr hōw | mў līght | ĭs spēnt.

This foot is used more than any other in English poetry.

(2) *The Trochee* (— ˘).

Īn thĕ | stōrmў | ēast-wīnd | strāinĭng.

(3) *The Dactyl* (— ˘ ˘).

Ōftĕn Ĭ | thīnk ŏf thĕ | bēautĭfŭl | tōwn.

(Notice how in this example, there is an accented foot of one syllable at the end of the line.)

Cānnŏn ĭn | frōnt ŏf thĕm

Vōllĕy'd ănd | thūndĕr'd.

(Notice that here a trochee has replaced the dactyl at the end of the second line.)

The dactyls ending lines 2 and 4 are incomplete.

Tāke hĕr ŭp | tēndĕrlў,

Līft hĕr wĭth cāre;

Fāshĭonĕd sŏ | slēndĕrlў,

Yōung ănd sŏ fāir!

This foot is often used to convey solemnity; it has a slowing-down effect in contrast to the anapaest, which follows.

(4) *The Anapaest* (˘ ˘ —).

Thĕ Ăssў | rĭăn cāme dōwn | lĭke thĕ wōlf | ŏn thĕ fōld.

(Notice how "-rian" is "slurred" to make a single syllable.)

This foot is often used to convey the idea of rapid movement, as its lilting rhythm makes verse flow swiftly.

Two other kinds of feet sometimes occur:

(5) *The Amphibrach* (⌣ — ⌣), as in the line "Mŏst frĭendshĭp ĭs fēignĭng".

(6) *The Spondee* (— —), which is used as an occasional variation, to give a slow and impressive effect.

In English verse, where scansion rules are elastic (unlike the rigid rules of Latin and Greek verse), a foot consisting of a single accented syllable is frequently used at the end of a line; sometimes a line has one foot or one syllable too few and sometimes it has one too many; sometimes the type of feet used in a line varies, as for example when a trochee is inserted in a line of dactyls, or when iambuses occur with anapaests.

Kinds of Line

If teachers or critics insist on employing the cumbersome technical terms of Greek origin to indicate types of lines, the following table will be helpful:

Dimeter	= a line of 2 feet.
Trimeter	= a line of 3 feet.
Tetrameter	= a line of 4 feet.
Pentameter	= a line of 5 feet.
Hexameter	= a line of 6 feet.
Heptameter	= a line of 7 feet.

It is simpler to refer to the line

"Beside the lake, beneath the trees"

as a line of four iambic feet than as an iambic tetrameter.

The feet in a line are usually all of the same type, but this similarity is not essential, and variation of the type of feet is sometimes employed to avoid monotony.

Lines, like feet, may vary in length, and need not necessarily be regular in their construction, as long as rhythm is present in the completed effect.

Notes: (1) When a line, instead of having a natural sense-pause at the end, overflows into the next line to complete its sense, it is termed a "run-on" line, as distinct from an "end-stopped" line.

> e.g. 'Tis sweet to know there is an eye will mark
> Our coming, and look brighter when we come.

This device of continuing a phrase or sentence from one line into the next is known as an "enjambement" (French for "stepping over or across").

(2) The reader will notice that in most verse, especially in a long line, a natural pause occurs in each line (usually but not necessarily, in the middle; its position can vary to avoid monotony), and this is called a "caesura" (= a break or cutting).

> e.g. Two principles ‖ in human nature reign:
> Self-love, to urge, ‖ and reason to restrain.

The pause must always be a pause in sense and must never cut a word in half. In the first line of the example the caesura is not in the middle of the line, whereas in the second it is.

Poetic Devices

Notice that, in addition to rhyme, run-on lines, and the pause or "caesura", there are other poetic devices.

(i) *Alliteration*—the employment of a series of words which have the same initial letter (or the same letter occurring in some other position) can be very effective in poetry.

> e.g. "*D*eep in a *d*ungeon was the *c*aptive *c*ast,
> *D*eprived of *d*ay, and held in *f*etters *f*ast" (Dryden).
> "*T*iger, *t*iger, *b*urning *b*right" (Blake).

(ii) *Assonance*. Assonance is a term indicating similarity

357

of *vowel* sounds in two words which do not completely rhyme (e.g. "hearth" and "heart").

(iii) *Inversion*—particularly of nouns and their adjectives (e.g. roses red), and of verbs and their subjects, with the adverb placed first for emphasis (e.g. Softly came they . . .).

(iv) *Transferred Epithet.* The transfer of an adjective or adverb from the word to which it naturally belongs to another closely associated with it.

e.g. "The breezes stir the *gusty* grass."

It is not the grass which is "gusty", but the breezes.

(v) Other figures of speech may be employed, as in prose, especially simile or comparison, and antithesis or contrast; onomatopaeic words may be used for sound effects, and repetition to secure emphasis. (See Chapter XV "Figures of Speech".)

(vi) *Length of Words.* As in prose, the use of short words in verse will increase the speed of movement in a poem or give it lightness, whereas the use of long words will slow down the movement, or give solemnity and a majestic quality.

(vii) *Elision* of vowels (e.g. o'er (over), e'er (ever)), etc., and slurring or fusing together two adjacent vowels (e.g. "tem pest uous" not "tem pest u ous").

Kinds of Stanza and Metre

Stanzas, or verses, are, as we have already seen, the groups in which lines are arranged or into which they are divided.

A Couplet is the simplest group, and consists of two lines which are of equal metre, or measure, and which usually rhyme.

e.g. For sweetest things turn sourest by their deeds;
    Lilies that fester smell far worse than weeds.

The term "Heroic Couplet" is used for two rhyming lines each of five feet, a metre very popular with such poets of the eighteenth century as Pope, Cowper, Gray, and Goldsmith.

e.g. How often have I paused on every charm
The sheltered cot, the cultivated farm.

A Quatrain is a group of four lines of verse. Notice in the example which follows how the rhyme scheme is indicated by labelling the lines that rhyme with each other with the same letter of the alphabet.

e.g. Take her up tenderly, *a*
Lift her with care; *b*
Fashioned so slenderly, *a*
Young and so fair! *b*

The quatrain is the easiest and most popular form of stanza, and is used particularly in ballads (and in many hymns) in a metre which consists of a 1st and 3rd line of 4 iambic feet, and the 2nd and 4th lines of 3 iambic feet, with only the 2nd and 4th lines rhyming usually. This is known as Common or Ballad Metre.

e.g. The bride hath paced into the hall,
Red as a rose is she; *a*
Nodding their heads before her goes
The merry minstrelsy. *a*

A quatrain consisting of two heroic couplets rhyming alternately is called an Elegiac Stanza. The best-known example of this is in Gray's "Elegy".

The curfew tolls the knell of parting day, *a*
The lowing herd winds slowly o'er the lea, *b*
The ploughman homeward plods his weary way, *a*
And leaves the world to darkness and to me. *b*

Another much employed arrangement of a quatrain is sometimes called "In Memoriam" metre, from Tennyson's poem. In these lines of four iambic feet the 1st line rhymes with the 4th and the 2nd and 3rd rhyme.

e.g. Now rings the woodland loud and long, *a*
The distance takes a lovelier hue, *b*
And drowned in yonder living blue *b*
The lark becomes a sightless song. *a*

Stanzas may be of any length, however, but longer stanzas obviously present more difficulties in rhyme and construction.

There are technical terms for stanzas of various lengths, and metres of various types, and these can be studied at a later stage. For example, the Sonnet, such a feature of Elizabethan poetry, is the name given to a fourteen-line stanza divided into two parts of eight lines and six lines.

The most interesting way to study stanzas and metres is to examine the construction of poems which appeal to us in a good anthology, and to see how poets handle the longer stanzas after the quatrain.

Shelley, for instance, in his ode "To a Skylark" employs stanzas of five lines, the first four rhyming alternately and the fifth rhyming with the fourth line, but being a much longer line; Wordsworth in "Daffodils" employs stanzas of six lines, rhyming *a*, *b*, *a*, *b*, *c*, *c*.

Finally we come to two important types of metre which rely on rhythm but not rhyme, Blank Verse and Free Verse.

Blank Verse

This is verse which has rhythm but not rhyme. The lines are of regular length, and rhythm, having usually five or six feet in a line (the classical form copied by Longfellow in "Evangeline"); modern blank verse has been written with fewer feet to a line.

Shakespeare is our most famous exponent of blank verse, but Milton and Tennyson have also employed it in their chief works. Shakespeare usually employed lines of five feet.

e.g. Once more unto the breach, dear friends, once more;
Or close the wall up with our English dead!

Note: Some lines have an additional unaccented syllable and this is called a feminine ending.

e.g. To be or not to be; that is the question.

Free Verse

This consists of lines of blank verse, but the lines vary in length and have usually no definite plan in their arrangement, though they convey an underlying sense of rhythm.

The American poet Walt Whitman (1819-1892) was a great exponent of this type of verse (and sometimes broke into prose with no metre at all), which is now much used in modern English poetry.

Here are two brief examples of his verse:

"At the last, tenderly,
   From the walls of the powerful fortress'd house,
   From the clasp of the knitted locks—from the keep of the
      well-closed doors,
   Let me be wafted."

"I think I could turn and live with animals, they are so
      placid and self-contained.
   I stand and look at them long and long.
   They do not sweat and whine about their condition,
   They do not lie awake in the dark and weep for their sins."

Whitman's considerable output of free verse has undoubtedly influenced its wide use in the present century, but it must not be thought that free verse is a recent development, for some of the finest examples are to be found in the Psalms, in the Authorised English version which dates from the seventeenth century. The metrical version used in the service of the Church of Scotland is, in contrast, mainly in blank verse.

Types of Poetry

Poetry may be employed to do many things that prose does, i.e. it can narrate an event or describe a scene; it can be didactic (teaching something) or satiric (attacking by ridicule); it can deal with humorous subjects as well as serious subjects.

There are certain important types of poem, a definition of which will be helpful.

A Ballad. A poem that narrates some event, usually historical. Ballads were originally handed down orally, hence ballad-singers, and the fact that they often have a refrain repeated at intervals.

> e.g. Macaulay's "Lays of Ancient Rome".
> Coleridge's "The Ancient Mariner".

An Elegy. A short serious poem, usually a lament, often for some person who has died.

> e.g. Gray's "Elegy in a Country Churchyard".
> Tennyson's "In Memoriam".

An Epic. A long narrative poem dealing with some great or heroic theme.

> e.g. Matthew Arnold, "Sohrab and Rustum".
> Milton's "Paradise Lost".

An Idyll. A short poem describing rustic life.

> e.g. Tennyson's "Aylmer's Field".

(Exception: Tennyson's "Idylls of the King", which is not an idyll but a series of narrative poems woven round the legends about King Arthur and his Knights.)

A Lyric. A short poem with a single theme, i.e. expressing one emotion, incident, or situation. Originally meant to be sung to the lyre. (We speak of the music and the lyrics of a musical play, showing the close connection lyrics have always had with music.)

A Madrigal. A poem with an amorous theme, intended to be sung as a part-song. The Elizabethan age was rich in madrigals.

An Ode. A long lyric poem, addressed to some particular person or thing, or dealing with one particular idea.

> e.g. Keats's "Ode to a Nightingale".

A Parody. A poem (though there can be parodies in prose also) copying the style and metre of some serious poem, but with a theme which is usually humorous, a burlesque of the original.

> e.g. Lewis Carroll's "Father William" is a parody of a
> ballad by Southey.
> Cowper's "John Gilpin" is a parody of all serious
> ballads.

Examples of every type of short poem can be studied in Palgrave's *Golden Treasury*, in the *Oxford Book of English Verse*, and in *A New Anthology of Modern Verse* (published by Methuen & Co.), but for examples of longer poems (such as epics, ballads, and other lengthy narrative poems) the collected works of individual poets must be studied.

Incidentally, amidst such a wealth of serious and romantic poetry, humorous verse, in which our literature is so rich, must not be neglected. Lewis Carroll, Calverly, and Edward Lear had an inspired gift for composing "nonsense" verse.

However uninspired we ordinary mortals may feel at first, there is no reason why we should not try our hand at writing verse. It is better to have tried and failed than never to have ventured to write verse at all.

The easiest way of starting to write verse is to attempt a parallel, but not a parody, of some well-known poem, i.e. to copy the metre and style of the original while changing the theme. This exercise can have the defect, however, of leading us to copy slavishly the work of some poet we admire so that there is a lack of originality in all our efforts. Nevertheless, it may be found to have considerable value as a foundation.

The simplest metre for the beginner is the ballad-metre, in which we can attempt the narration of some serious or humorous event.

To write parodies of serious poems is also a useful (and amusing) exercise, but we shall find that considerable skill is required to produce a really successful parody.

Appreciation of Verse

In the appreciation of verse the points to be studied may be summed up as follows:

(a) *General impressions* (Theme).

1. What is the central theme or idea of the poem? Has it a message?
2. What is the predominant emotion the poem expresses? Sorrow or regret? Joy or delight? Sympathy? Dislike?
3. What is the main impression and atmosphere the poem conveys?

(b) *Detailed study* (Technique).

1. What metre or rhythm does the poet employ? And what rhyme scheme, if rhyme is employed? Is the metre selected to convey solemnity, or rapid movement, for example? Does it suit the theme? You can hear the brook chattering in Tennyson's poem "The Brook", and the horses' hoof-beats in the lines of "How they brought the good news from Ghent to Aix".
2. What points strike you about the poet's diction (use of words)? Is there frequent inversion of the order of words? Is alliteration employed? Is repetition employed? Are words chosen to give onomatopoeic effects?
3. What imagery—comparisons employing similes and/or metaphors—does the poet employ? What other figures of speech (such as personification) and effects (such as contrast) does the poet employ? Are these employed effectively?

We must consider both technique and ideas, as a poem may be admirable in technique but lacking in ideas or emotion—or may have exactly the opposite qualities; in neither case can such a poem be considered a good poem.

Example: Wordsworth "Upon Westminster Bridge".

> "Earth has not anything to show more fair;
> Dull would he be of soul who could pass by
> A sight so touching in its majesty:
> This City now doth like a garment wear
>
> The beauty of the morning: silent bare,
> Ships, towers, domes, theatres and temples lie
> Open unto the fields, and to the sky.
> All bright and glittering in the smokeless air.
>
> Never did sun more beautifully steep
> In his first splendour valley, rock or hill;
> Ne'er saw I, never felt, a calm so deep!
>
> The river glideth at his own sweet will:
> Dear God! the very houses seem asleep;
> And all that mighty heart is lying still!

(*a*) *General Impressions.*

1. *Theme.* The theme of the poem is the beauty and splendour of London as seen from Westminster Bridge in the light of the early morning sun.
2. *Emotion.* The poet expresses his admiration of the impressive scene, and the sense of peace which the gently (slow)-flowing river and the still sleeping city convey.
3. *Impression or Atmosphere.* The tone of the poem is noble and meditative; it conveys both dignity and wonderment.

(*b*) *Detailed Study—Technique.*

1. *Metre, rhyme.* The poem is a sonnet, of 14 lines of iambic pentameters (i.e. lines each with 5 stresses or beats, employing iambic feet, with occasional variations, as in the first foot).

Earth hăs | nŏt a | nўthing | tŏ show | mŏre fair.

It is divided into two parts, the first consisting of eight lines rhyming—a b b a, a b b a—the second of six lines rhyming c d, c d, c d. (In a true Italian sonnet, the first eight lines expounded the theme, then came a natural break, and the last six lines expressed the poet's reflections.)

The slow rhythm is in harmony with the peaceful early morning scene.

2. *Diction.* In its diction the poem is dignified but unaffected, and employs no uncommon or lengthy words. Notice the effective enumeration "Ships, towers, domes, theatres and temples lie". The poem contains the fine phrases "a si ht so touching in its majesty" and "all bright and glittering in the smokeless air"; and the striking line "Dear God! the very houses seem asleep" and the line "The river glideth at his own sweet will" convey the idea of the slow-flowing, unhurried river and the still-sleeping inhabitants in a remarkable way.

3. *Imagery.* There is an effective comparison ("This City now doth like a garment wear . . ." and a metaphor ("All that mighty heart is lying still").

Inversion is employed for emphasis ("Never did sun . . ., "Ne'er saw I . . .").

EXERCISES

A

Scan the following lines (i.e. mark the stressed and unstressed syllables, and divide each line into feet by vertical lines, as in examples previously given), and indicate the rhyme-schemes.

(*a*) Good people all, of every sort,
    Give ear unto my song:
And if you find it wondrous short—
    It cannot hold you long.

(*b*) Cannon to right of them,
   Cannon to left of them,
   Cannon in front of them
   Volley'd and thunder'd.

(*c*) "You are old, Father William," the young man said,
   "And your hair has become very white;
   And yet you persistently stand on your head—
   Do you think, at your age, it is right?"

(*d*) Willows whiten, aspens quiver,
   Little breezes dusk and shiver
   Thro' the wave that runs for ever
   By the island in the river
      Flowing down to Camelot.

(*e*) Once more unto the breach, dear friends, once more;
   Or close the wall up with our English dead!
   In peace there's nothing so becomes a man
   As modest stillness and humility:
   But when the blast of war blows in our ears,
   Then imitate the action of the tiger.

(*f*) The Assyrian came down like the wolf on the fold,
   And his cohorts were gleaming in purple and gold;
   And the sheen of their spears was like stars on the sea,
   When the blue wave rolls nightly on deep Galilee.

(*g*) Beneath those rugged elms, that yew-tree's shade
   Where heaves the turf in many a mouldering heap,
   Each in his narrow cell forever laid,
   The rude forefathers of the hamlet sleep.

(*h*) Tiger, tiger, burning bright
   In the forest of the night,
   What immortal hand or eye,
   Could frame thy fearful symmetry?

367

(*i*) Under the wide and starry sky,
Dig the grave and let me lie.
Glad did I live and gladly die,
And I laid me down with a will.

(*j*) "Will you walk a little faster?" said a whiting to a snail,
"There's a porpoise close behind us and he's treading on my
tail."

B

Write a narrative poem, using ballad metre, describing

(*a*) Some personal adventure.
(*b*) Some historical event.
(*c*) Some domestic incident.

C

Write a short ode on some suitable subject, such as a season,
month, bird, insect, or flower.

D

Write an elegy in memory of some person or animal that you
knew.

E

Write in blank verse

(*a*) A scene between two characters discussing a controversial
subject.
(*b*) A description of some incident.
(*c*) A description of some scene.

F

Compose a parody based on the metre and style of a selected
serious poem.

G

Write an appreciation of the following passages of verse, discussing
the points suggested in this chapter.

(a) ### HOME-THOUGHTS FROM ABROAD

Oh, to be in England
Now that April's there,
And whoever wakes in England
Sees, some morning, unaware,
That the lowest boughs and the brushwood sheaf
Round the elm-tree bole are in tiny leaf,
While the chaffinch sings on the orchard bough
In England—now!

And after April, when May follows,
And the whitethroat builds, and all the swallows!
Hark, where my blossomed pear-tree in the hedge
Leans to the field and scatters on the clover
Blossoms and dewdrops—at the bent spray's edge—
That's the wise thrush; he sings each song twice over,
Lest you should think he never could recapture
The first fine careless rapture!
And though the fields look rough with hoary dew,
All will be gay when noontide wakes anew
The buttercups, the little children's dower
—Far brighter than this gaudy melon-flower!

Robert Browning

(b) ### FROM "DAFFODILS"

I wandered lonely as a cloud
That floats on high o'er vales and hills,
When all at once I saw a crowd,
A host, of golden daffodils;
Beside the lake, beneath the trees,
Fluttering and dancing in the breeze.

Continuous as the stars that shine
And twinkle on the milky way,
They stretched in never-ending line
Along the margin of a bay:
Ten thousand saw I at a glance,
Tossing their heads in sprightly dance.

The waves beside them danced, but they
Outdid the sparkling waves in glee ...

Wm. Wordsworth

From "The Ancient Mariner"

(c) Down dropt the breeze, the sails dropt down,
'Twas sad as sad could be;
And we did speak only to break
The silence of the sea!

All in a hot and copper sky,
The bloody Sun, at noon,
Right up above the mast did stand,
No bigger than the Moon.

Day after day, day after day,
We stuck, nor breath nor motion;
As idle as a painted ship
Upon a painted ocean.

Water, water, every where,
And all the boards did shrink;
Water, water, every where,
Nor any drop to drink.

The very deep did rot: O Christ!
That ever this should be!
Yea, slimy things did crawl with legs
Upon the slimy sea.

About, about, in reel and rout
The death-fires danced at night;
The water, like a witch's oils,
Burnt green, and blue and white.

S. T. Coleridge

(d)
In the Train

As we rush, as we rush in the Train,
The trees and the houses go wheeling back,
But the starry heavens above the plain
Come flying on our track.

All the beautiful stars of the sky,
  The silver doves of the forest of Night,
Over the dull earth swarm and fly,
  Companions of our flight.

We will rush ever on without fear;
  Let the goal be far, the flight be fleet!
For we carry the Heavens with us, dear,
  While the Earth slips from our feet!

James Thomson

(e)   FROM "THE CLOUD"

I bring fresh showers for the thirsting flowers,
  From the seas and the streams;
I bear light shade for the leaves when laid
  In their noonday dreams.
From my wings are shaken the dews that waken
  The sweet buds every one,
When rocked to rest on their mother's breast,
  As she dances about the sun.
I wield the flail of the lashing hail,
  And whiten the green plains under;
And then again I dissolve it in rain,
  And laugh as I pass in thunder.

I sift the snow on the mountains below,
  And their great pines groan aghast;
And all the night 'tis my pillow white,
  While I sleep in the arms of the blast.
Sublime on the towers of my skiey bowers,
  Lightning my pilot sits;
In a cavern under is fettered the thunder,
  It struggles and howls at fits.

P. B. Shelley

From "The Cataract of Lodore"

How does the water
Come down at Lodore?
Retreating and beating and meeting and sheeting,
Delaying and straying and playing and spraying,
Advancing and prancing and glancing and dancing,
Recoiling, turmoiling and toiling and boiling . . .
And thumping and plumping and bumping and jumping
And dashing and flashing and splashing and clashing;
And so never ending, but always descending,
Sounds and motions for ever and ever are blending,
All at once and all o'er, with a mighty uproar,
And this way the water comes down at Lodore.

Robert Southey

SOME G.C.E. EXAMINATION QUESTIONS

The following questions from recent G.C.E. "O" Level papers in English Language are reprinted by kind permission of the University of London.

1. Write a composition on one of the following subjects.
(*You should spend about forty-five minutes on this question.*)

- (*a*) Changes in entertainment during the present century.
- (*b*) Sources of power in the past, the present and the future.
- (*c*) Recollections of the fears of childhood.
- (*d*) The value of learning a foreign language.
- (*e*) The essentials of a good magazine.
- (*f*) "Science performs miracles, but not always miracles that we want or need."

2. Summarise, *in your own words as far as possible*, the following passage (which contains about 450 words), reducing it to about 150 words. State at the end the *exact* number of words that you have used.

(*You should spend about forty-five minutes on this question.*)

Last year nearly 12,500 people were killed on German roads in more than half a million accidents. This figure of fatal casualties is one of the highest in the world, two-and-a-half times as high as Britain's total, although the number of cars is much the same in both countries and the density of traffic in Germany is less.

Some visitors to Germany, especially those who come from Britain, tend to blame the autobahns, the great systems of double-carriage highways which curve and undulate across the German countryside. They were built after Hitler came to power in 1933. In those days they were designed with a strategic intention—so that troops could be moved swiftly from one part of the country to the other. Ironically enough, it was the Allies that made the best use of them, because when the war finally reached the frontiers of Germany itself Hitler's armies were too short of petrol for much movement by road.

The autobahn from Austria through Bavaria is a world on its own. There are no horse-carts, no cyclists, no pedestrians: they are not allowed. There are no intersections, no traffic lights: you are just part of an unending, restless stream of cars, all in a desperate hurry to reach some distant destination, and you feel quite remote from the land you are driving through. Dawdling along at sixty miles an hour all day, you are being constantly overtaken by drivers whose impatience matches the speed of their cars. The giant trucks with trailers, with an all-out weight of some forty tons, are only a little slower.

The main enemies on these journeys are boredom and fatigue, and the slackness they lead to. Add to them the prevalent high speeds and you have one of the main causes of the serious accidents, sometimes involving several vehicles, which happen on the autobahns every day. Perhaps the character of the German driver has something to do with the high road casualties as well: he is determined, somewhat inflexible, always in a hurry, and he has a marked propensity for not giving way, especially when he feels he is in the right; and most German drivers do feel that.

The German authorities are concerned at this mounting toll of road casualties, and their remedy is wider and better roads—more autobahns, in fact. Although accidents on these great highways are often serious because of the high speed, the statistics show that for each accident on an autobahn there are three on an ordinary road carrying the same amount of traffic. Between now and 1965 Germany plans to add four hundred miles to the present autobahn system.

3. (a) Analyse into clauses the sentence given below, *writing out each clause in full.* Give the grammatical descrip-

tion of each clause, and state its grammatical function in the sentence:—

As John had not seen *his* brother since the day he left for *America*, it is not surprising that he found it *difficult* to recognise him *when* they met again twenty years *later*.

(*b*) State the part of speech and give the grammatical function of the following words as used in the passage in (*a*): his, America, difficult, when, later.

4. (*a*) Give, for each of the following sentences, a single word which could exactly replace the italicised phrase:—

   (i) Lord Nuffield is famous as a *man who is generous to his fellow-men*.
  (ii) The secretary's proposal was adopted *with the full agreement of all of the members*.
 (iii) We asked for an explanation, as some of his remarks were *capable of bearing more than one meaning*.
 (iv) I am afraid he must be regarded as *pretending to be better than he is*.
  (v) It was a *practice bound up with the life* of the school that every new boy shook hands with the headmaster.
 (vi) Old English poetry was remarkable for *the recurrence of the same initial sound in words in close succession*.
 (vii) The equipment used by mountaineers must be *easily carried from place to place*.
(viii) The two authors decided to *work in association with each other* in the production of a book on Shakespeare.
 (ix) The committee *suspended proceedings and dispersed* until the following Thursday.

(*b*) Use *three* of the following expressions figuratively in separate sentences so as to bring out clearly the meaning of each:—

(i) a dog in the manger; (ii) a fly in the ointment; (iii) a pig in a poke; (iv) a wolf in sheep's clothing; (v) a bull in a china-shop; (vi) a snake in the grass.

(Questions 1–4 are reproduced from London G.C.E., "O" Level, Autumn, 1957.)

5. Read the following passage carefully, and then answer the questions below, using your own words as far as possible:—

To town and country Winter comes alike, but to each he comes in different fashion. To the villager, he stretches a bold, frosty hand; to the townsman, a clammy one. To the villager, he comes wrapt in cold clear air; to the townsman, in yellow fogs, through which the street-lamps blear at noon. To the villager, he brings snow on the bare trees, frosty spangles on the roadways, exquisite silver chasings and adornments to the ivies on the walls, tumults of voices and noises of skates, smouldering orange sunsets that disdain the snows, make brazen the window-panes, and fire even the icicles at the cottage eaves. To the townsman, he brings influenza, the hazard of treacherous slides on unlighted pavements, showers of snow-balls from irreverent urchins, damp feet, avalanches from the roofs of houses six stories high, taxi-fares woefully begrudged, universal slush. Winter is like a Red Indian, noble in his forests and solitudes, deteriorated by cities and civilization.

The signs of his approach are different in the town and in the village. To a certain northern city, whose spires fret my sky-line of a morning, his proximity is made known by the departure of the last tourist and the arrival of the first student, by the re-assembling of schools, and by advertisements in newspapers relative to the opening of the University. By these signs, rather than by the cawing of uneasy rooks, or the whirling away of the last red leaf, the inhabitants know that the stern season is at hand; the re-opening of evening classes announces that he is in their midst, and the re-appearance of the lawyers in the long-deserted halls of Parliament House is regarded as a prophecy of snow.

(a) Give, each in a single word or *short* phrase, the exact meaning of *four* of the following words as they are used in the passage: clammy (1. 3); exquisite (1. 7); disdain (1. 9); begrudged (1. 14); deteriorated (1. 16); fret (1. 18); proximity (1. 19).

(b) Explain clearly (i) how the window-panes were made brazen (1. 10), (ii) why the urchins are said to be irreverent (1. 13), and (iii) why the rooks should be uneasy (1. 23).

(c) In what sense is Winter like a Red Indian (1. 15)?

(d) Give *three* reasons why the writer calls winter "the stern season" (1. 24).

(e) Show, by close reference to the passage, how Winter is presented as a living person throughout the passage.

6. (a) Choose *three* of the following words, and use each one, in a separate sentence, in a figurative sense, and explain clearly the figurative usage:—

heart, tower, sea, harvest, veil, spirit.

(b) Write sentences, one for each word, to show the difference in meaning between the words in *three* of the following pairs:—

complement, compliment; official, officious; industrious, industrial; imminent, eminent; intolerant, intolerable.

(Questions 5 and 6 are reproduced from London G.C.E., "O" Level, Summer, 1957.)

INDEX

379

INDEX